WOMEN IN DARK AGE AND EARLY MEDIEVAL EUROPE c.500–1200

European Culture and Society
General Editor: Jeremy Black

Published

Lesley Hall *Sex, Gender & Social Change in Britain since 1880*
Helen M. Jewell *Women in Dark Age and Early Medieval
Europe c.500–1200*
Helen M. Jewell *Women in Late Medieval and Reformation
Europe 1200–1550*
Keith D. Lilley *Urban Life in the Middle Ages: 1000–1450*
Jerzy Lukowski *The European Nobility in the Eighteenth Century*
Neil MacMaster *Racism in Europe, 1870–2000*
Noël O'Sullivan *European Political Thought since 1945*
W. M. Spellman *European Political Thought 1600–1700*
Gary K. Waite *Heresy, Magic and Witchcraft in Early Modern Europe*
Diana Webb *Medieval European Pilgrimage, c.700–c.1500*

European Culture and Society Series
Series Standing Order
ISBN 978-0-333-74440-6
(outside North America only)

You can receive future titles in this series as they are published by placing a standing order. Please contact your bookseller or, in case of difficulty, write to us at the address below with your name and address, the title of the series and the ISBN quoted above.

Customer Services Department, Macmillan Distribution Ltd
Houndmills, Basingstoke, Hampshire RG21 6XS, England

WOMEN IN DARK AGE AND EARLY MEDIEVAL EUROPE c.500–1200

Helen M. Jewell

First published 2007 by
PALGRAVE MACMILLAN
Houndmills, Basingstoke, Hampshire RG21 6XS and
175 Fifth Avenue, New York, N.Y. 10010
Companies and representatives throughout the world

PALGRAVE MACMILLAN is the global academic imprint of the Palgrave
Macmillan division of St. Martin's Press, LLC and of Palgrave Macmillan Ltd.
Macmillan® is a registered trademark in the United States, United
Kingdom and other countries. Palgrave is a registered trademark in the
European Union and other countries.

ISBN 978-0-333-91259-1   ISBN 978-0-230-21379-1 (eBook)
DOI 10.1007/978-0-230-21379-1

A catalogue record for this book is available from the British Library.

Library of Congress Cataloging-in-Publication Data

Jewell, Helen M.
    Women in Dark Age and early Medieval Europe, c. 500–1200/Helen
M. Jewell
        p. cm. — (European culture and society series)
    Includes bibliographical references and index.

    1. Women—Europe—History—Middle Ages, 500–1500. I. Title.

HQ1147.E85J(Jewell)
305.4094'09021—dc22   2006048584

10 9 8 7 6 5 4 3 2 1
16 15 14 13 12 11 10 09 08 07

CONTENTS

PREFACE

Over 40 years ago, in my enlightened single-sex school, the historians entering the Lower Sixth were required to prepare a short talk on a subject of their own devising, and I decided to work on women in medieval France. I remember the most helpful book in the school library was Joan Evans's illustrated *Life in Medieval France* and I leaned heavily on the illustrations! At that stage in my development I was just growing out of amassing facts for the fun of it and beginning to be aware of gaps in my knowledge and wondering why it was so difficult to find ways of filling them. The opening up of women's studies since then has exposed a lot of gaps, but more significantly for historians has drawn attention to a vast range of usable source material and developed a variety of interpretative approaches particularly suitable for the subject. Over the past dozen years I have attended many women's history sessions at the International Medieval Congresses at the University of Leeds, and examined the latest outpourings at the associated book fairs. I write under multifarious influences for all of which I express a debt of gratitude, but the principal acknowledgement I would like to make is to Lynette Ramsay, who encouraged me to go ahead with that project all those years ago.

My policy with regard to names of both people and places has been to standardize them in their simplest commonly used Anglicized spelling. Where names have not been widely simplified, they are left as per source. Monetary terms are similarly left in the currencies cited, with no attempt to value them consistently against each other or from one period to another. Only the English (pre-decimal) currency with 240 pence (d) to the pound (£) and 12d to the shilling (s) is given in abbreviated form.

Feeling the English Authorized King James Bible inappropriate for a work on Catholic Europe I was directed by Catholic friends to The New Jerusalem Bible, which I have found a most informative edition.

Helen M. Jewell

1

INTRODUCTION

The Timescale and Geographical Range of the Book

The whole European land mass north of the Mediterranean, Black and Caspian seas, separated from Asia by the Urals, is too vast an area of climatic, cultural, ethnic, linguistic, racial and religious differences to be a feasible area for study. Within it, however, certain swathes have stronger cultural and historical bondings. First chronologically was membership of the Roman empire, which embraced, to the north of the Mediterranean, the land from the straits of Gibraltar to the Rhine (taking in England and Wales beyond the English Channel), and the area to the south of the Danube. When the western Roman empire disintegrated, it left behind three major legacies: the Latin language, the root of the Romance languages of western Europe; a civil law system, operative piecemeal in successor states and revitalized in law schools spreading from twelfth-century Bologna; and the Christian religion, as presided over by the Pope in Rome. The terms Latin west, or Catholic Europe, give us a good entity for focus, eventually extending to areas beyond the old Roman empire, including the wider German territories and Poland and Scandinavia, and lasting as a religious monopoly until the Reformation of the sixteenth century.

German territories, only borderland zones in and alongside the Roman empire, became much more significant as the centralized European block from the ninth and tenth centuries, as the Franks rose to dominance. This period led to the emergence of the Holy Roman Empire, which survived our period, outlasting the Viking Age (c.800–1200) when the Danes, Norwegians and Swedes spread across the North Sea and Atlantic and pushed east inland into the Russian territories. The principal legacies of this period are the Germanic languages of northern Europe.

1

Faced with a political kaleidoscope on the surface of a geographical entity, the major obstacle of multifarious languages, both for original material and modern studies, and huge variations in source availability, it would be totally impossible to cover the lives of all the women who ever lived in Europe at its widest geographical definition, with equal attention to all areas at all times. This book will therefore be limited to a more realistic project: a survey of the place of women in western Europe, the area now covered by Italy, Germany, Switzerland, France, the Netherlands and Belgium, Spain and Portugal, Britain and Ireland, and Scandinavia (including Iceland).

The centuries covered in this volume extend from the sixth to the twelfth, inclusive. With the fifth-century collapse of the western Roman empire any superimposed standardization of government, laws, and religion in its once subject lands faltered. However, the degree of standardization in the late empire seems to have been rather exaggerated, likewise any immediately noticeable difference between its society and the successor societies in the western provinces. The later Roman empire was itself much influenced by the 'barbarian' peoples and they by it. The uneven and haphazard withdrawal of central Roman control (a control often exercised through men of non-Roman origin) did not mean that Roman characteristics everywhere yielded to a myriad of localized customs and life styles. The indigenous inhabitants of the provincial territories within the imperial boundaries had been Romanized to different extents and were then taken over in varying degrees by different, by no means ethnically exclusive, invaders. In this migratory period things were rather less settled than in Roman times, and disruption made for only patchy source survival. It is indeed a Dark Age before around 800, and migration and instability continued to be the keynote of the next four centuries. In general terms such a society cannot be expected to record much about its women, who were neither kings nor military leaders, though certainly a few individuals were credited with holding together alliances with other rulers by marriage. Around 1200 events become more stable and evidence more copious. The later middle ages are the subject of a companion volume.[1]

The Variety of Social Groupings and Communities within Europe

The women who inhabited Europe during this period lived through times of migrations and warfare, and have been almost totally disregarded by political historians concentrating on power. Inevitably, the later identities of states such as Italy, Spain, France and Germany draw historians to place emphasis on these countries' separate past histories, which does not actually fit well for times when peoples straddled later boundaries or were forced into different allegiances at different periods. The western empire had formally ended in 476 and by the early sixth century the Ostrogothic kingdom covered Italy and extended north and east towards the Danube. The Visigothic kingdom covered most of the Spanish peninsula and extended across Mediterranean France to march with the Ostrogoths. North of this lay the Frankish kingdom, from the Pyrenees to the Weser, excluding the independent kingdom of Burgundy. Angles and Saxons had begun penetrating England from a homeland on the North Sea west of the Elbe. Generalization about mass movements of whole peoples should be cautious since there was much ethnic mixing; furthermore identified power bases fragmented and regrouped. The Ostrogothic kingdom in Italy disappeared in the mid-sixth century and the Lombards became dominant there, though parts of southern Italy such as Calabria retained connection with the eastern empire until the Normans took Bari in 1071. In the early eighth century the Visigoths lost out in Spain to the Arabs, with Christians in the Asturias holding out, and eventually Castile-Leon, Aragon and Navarre began reversing the Arab hold in the peninsula in the eleventh and twelfth centuries. The Frankish empire, extending from the Pyrenees to Frisia to Carinthia under Charlemagne (whose dominance in Europe was reflected in his penetration of Italy and imperial coronation by the Pope in Rome in 800) was several times partitioned and reunited, until by the mid-ninth century the division of west Francia (later France) and east Francia (later Germany) became established, with the middle territories, including Burgundy, uncomfortably squeezed and claimed between the two greater powers. During the twelfth century Provence, Burgundy and Lorraine were within the boundaries of the Holy Roman Empire, making places in modern France, such as Marseilles, Grenoble, Besançon and Verdun part of the empire.

The Germanic peoples had poured into the late Roman provincial territories driven west and south by the Huns and Scandinavians, and from c.800 the Scandinavians (Danes, Swedes and Norwegians) followed them southwestwards, becoming a serious menace on the continental mainland and in the British Isles, and colonized Iceland. Defence against the Vikings proved the main factor unifying England under the West Saxon dynasty, and led to the emergence of Count Odo of Paris, the first Capetian king, in western Francia, while defence against the Magyars led to the acquisition of power in eastern Francia by the line of Duke Otto of Saxony. A succession of successful and outward-reaching king-emperors came of this descent through the tenth and eleventh centuries, expanding into Italy as far south as Rome. France in this period was less powerful, especially while the Angevin empire, based on Normandy, England and (by marriage) Aquitaine, was at its height, c.1180.

This rough outline is sufficient to make obvious the hazards of applying the broad adjectival terms Italian, French or German, derived from today's political boundaries, to women over this period, or at any one moment of time in it. A woman in Calabria was under a different regime from her contemporary in the Po valley, a woman in Rouen in a different society from her contemporary in Provence and so on. Furthermore, some legal codifications, for example Visigothic and Burgundian, separated practices for those of Roman descent so that people living among others could be following different rules.

The migratory developments described above in their chronological order show that ethnic cultures might be sought to explain certain characteristics of social behaviour with regard to women in various places at different times. It is claimed, for example, that Germanic women were held in high respect, witness the high fines and wergilds for killing, abducting or violating women, but essentially the women are cast as the daughters, wives and sisters of *men*. However, the Germanic respect for women did feed down into recognition of women's legal rights to land in the Carolingian period and even earlier in Anglo-Saxon England, and Visigothic inheritance traditions left a favourable position for women in parts of the Spanish peninsula. On the other hand, insufficient unification can be found binding the legal position in the German empire for any systematic discussion of an overriding legal situation for medieval women there to be mounted. In the early Frankish realms, there was a north/south divide between the northern territories, which operated by custom, influenced by Germanic law, and the southern, which retained Roman written law and administration. Within localities in Italy whether Roman or Lombard law prevailed made a difference: the Roman was more favourable to women. Everywhere urban practices could be contrasted with rural society, tending to be particular to each town, yet overall classifiable as distinctly urban. Rural societies too had their differences: arable communities differed from pastoral, the former requiring co-operation to till crop-growing fields, the latter offering a nomadic element where flocks were moved to summer pastures on higher ground (the practice is termed transhumance). Generally speaking, pastoral economies offered more economic opportunities to women, through dairying and spinning and textile work. Crops of course varied with climate, from olives and vines in the south to wheat and barley further north and rye and oats in harsher climes.

Thus there were differences born of ethnicity and differences born of economic environment, customs of a people, such as the Franks or Lombards, practices of an urban setting, such as Bruges or Venice, traditions of rural communities, say the Pyrenees and Île de France. On top of this were shared influences of civil law and, after the conversion period, of Christianity and canon law. Effect must also be allowed for evolution, such as the tightening grip of feudalism. Class differences made clear demarcations between what queens and noblewomen and urban women and rural free women and servile peasant women could do, even in the same area and time. Finally, as the period advanced, there were changes due to the settling down following the main migration period, disrupted by the arrival of the Vikings, and changes due to the expansion of population, particularly from the tenth century, and the emergence of greater commercial and trading activities.

The Effects on Women of Political, Economic, Demographic and Religious Developments over the Period

The Roman empire had won, and held, provinces by military force and occupation. It drew conquered peoples into its military forces, and it used confederated peoples, especially to hold frontiers. Imperial territories held indigenous inhabitants and both temporarily serving alien soldiers and administrators and settled (retired) ones, not just from Rome but from all corners of the empire. After Rome's withdrawal, its garrisons disappeared but many of the non-indigenous people did not return to their place of origin. Thus mixed groups were taken over by new barbarian conquerors – Romano-Britons by Angles and Saxons, Gallo-Romans by Franks and so on. Obviously, to achieve control the dominant people must have applied military force, which means, in the first instance, they must have been armies, and warlords must have preceded kings. So the first big issue for women's history is, when invaders won themselves a kingdom, did they send back home for wives and children, or commandeer wives from the subjected population? Only if the former was the case was the next generation significantly Frankish, Anglo-Saxon, Danish, Norman. If the latter prevailed, the incomers from the start bred from women of the dominated race, immediately mixing the gene pools. If mass migrations occurred, we might expect evidence of receiving zones being overfull, and exporting zones somewhat depopulated, and if the sex ratio in Scandinavia had been wildly thrown, reflecting the emigration of men only, and that of Normandy or the Danelaw reflecting the immigration of mostly males, we might hope for some indication of sudden imbalance.

Evidence points both ways. The *Anglo-Saxon Chronicle* refers to the Danes' women, but it is not clear whether these were Danish-born women or Anglo-Saxon collaborators. Individual leaders, such as Hasteinn, to whom King Alfred restored his wife and two sons in 894, seem to have brought their wives, but this does not mean every Viking did. Wulfstan's 1014 'Sermon of the Wolf to the English' indicates gang rape of Anglo-Saxon women, in front of their powerless menfolk, by Viking marauders. Women certainly had to be taken to Iceland, because there were no indigenous inhabitants when the Vikings began settling there, but Carol Clover makes a convincing case for a shortage of females there, also in Viking Scandinavia and indeed in early Europe generally.[2] Genetic traits, such as longish skulls and fair hair and particular blood groupings, have long been claimed to be traceable in the Danelaw area of Britain which suggests interracial breeding was only slow to develop, and that there were many Scandinavian genes in the pool, which is now beginning to emerge with greater scientific certainty from DNA testing of the modern population. The finding of male long-headed skulls with female short-headed ones in the cemetery of Muid underlies a claim that Germanic invaders married Gallo-Roman women.[3] After the Norman Conquest of England, marrying an Anglo-Saxon heiress was one of the ways for the several hundred incoming Norman lords to inherit land. In the twelfth century it was said it was impossible to tell who was English and who was French because the races were so intermixed.

If kingdoms originated as conquests, they did not become peaceful quickly. There was infighting within the new territory. Gregory of Tours' Frankish kings march hither and thither against each other, and hapless townsfolk suffer siege as a consequence. There were also renewed invasions, and kingdoms and territories changed hands, for example Burgundy, Provence, and southern Spain. So it is obvious that long after the original barbarian invasions the societies they established remained highly military. This meant command lay with military men, and was used for military motives. It meant that kings were warriors more noticeably than legislators. It made military service the main demand of the state. None of this thrusts women into prominence in events or their record. Even if war, as the means of appropriating territory by might and opportunity, did give way a little to politics, in the sense of argued defence of title and policy, both war and politics were men's work throughout the period. The women who gained renown did so either as (usually youthful) pawns in the marriage bed, or, if surviving this experience and more, as widowed regents for sons. The rare references to individual women in Collins's *Early Medieval Europe*, for example, come mostly in one of these contexts: consider his statement about the diplomatic use of marriage by Theoderic (d 526) – 'alliances, cemented by marriages of one of Theoderic's sisters and one of his daughters to the Thuringian and Burgundian kings respectively, preserved the security of the areas north of the Alps and a similar link with the Vandal ruler Thrasamund (496–523) helped to ensure good relations with Africa'.[4] The use of women for dynastic policy continued everywhere throughout the period. Urraca, daughter of Fernán González, Count of Castile, was married to Ordono III of Leon (951–6), Ordono IV (958–9) and finally Sancho II of Navarre (970–94). Emma, daughter of Duke Richard I of Normandy, surviving her first husband, the incompetent Ethelred II of England, was married by the king's supplanter, the Danish Cnut – and after his death in 1035 commissioned the *Encomium Emmae Reginae* which presents her, idealistically, as a unifier of English and Dane. It may seem a bit much to expect preservation of security in such insecure times from an alliance cemented by marriage, and to demand a lot of the bride. Sometimes she may have seemed to represent an overlord and to have been accepted resentfully by an underling; if she was a stepping stone for a client ambitious to work his way up with his patron she may have been more welcome but must have felt insecure – if her powerful relative ceased to be a good ally her *raison d'être* disappeared. The position of Theodelinda, daughter of Garibald of Bavaria, illustrates that she had some personal weighting as a continuity bearer – as maternal granddaughter of the Lombard king Waco (d 540) she was a suitable wife for the Lombard king Authari. At Authari's death in 590 she married Agilulf of Turin who succeeded to the throne (Paul the Deacon indicates that she chose him), and their son Adaloald was the next successor, but when he died and the male line with him, the throne passed successively to two men who married Theodelinda's daughter Gundipurga, and eventually the succession passed to descendants of Theodelinda's brother Gundoald. This shows the accepted significance of the blood line and the value of a woman in its transmission. Transmission might seem the key to women regents too: it may be less as widows of the late king than as mothers of the next that some women remained entrenched at the centre of power. However, this may prove deceptive. Theodelinda had no son by Authari when she conveyed the throne to Agilulf, and Theoderic's daughter Amalasuntha is represented as regent for her son Athalaric until he died, when she is represented by Jordanes' *History of the Goths* as sending for Theodehad, her cousin, to take the throne, the line also taken in her own letters. Modern historians express distrust towards the decisive roles credited to Theodelinda by Paul the Deacon and Amalasuntha by Jordanes, but it cannot be denied that those writers presented these women in this way, as Emma's Encomiast flattered her role too. Why represent these individual women as exercising such extraordinary power if it was quite contrary to the truth? Where their role is presented to smooth a succession it must have been an acceptable spin on events and not a ludicrous invention.

Nevertheless, the military cast to society and the educational advantages largely monopolized by churchmen, making them the obvious civil servants to kings needing diplomatic and secretarial support, meant that contemporary record of events, that is ecclesiastically composed chronicles or annals, paid most attention to military matters and very little attention to women. The activities of the Vikings form a major interest in the chronicles of the continent, England and Ireland. The activities of women do not. In some circumstances the expeditionary activities of men seem to have produced some greater empowerment of their women. As will be seen below, there are archaeological signs of greater wealth and influence enjoyed by Scandinavian women left managing estates when their men roved a-viking. Later, the absence of the landed aristocracy on Crusades is argued to have left its womenfolk managing its affairs. Lower down society, the effects of wars and conquests may be expected to have been less noticeable. Slaves would be transferred to new owners, and a free peasantry would render services to new landlords. The new lords, however, would have even less sense of personal social community with their servants than the old, bringing new customs, languages and probably more ruthless extortion to the relationship. The womenfolk of the vanquished have always been at risk of sexual exploitation by the victors.

Around 500, when this study commences, there was no homogeneity of religion in western Europe. Although the Roman empire had sponsored Christianity since the fourth century, and outlawed pagan rituals, many pagan traditions survived. The successors of St Peter in Rome, especially Leo the Great (440–60) had shown some vision of responsible leadership, but the last Roman emperor of the west had been driven out by the first barbarian king of Rome in 476. Constantinople, as the seat of the eastern empire, overshadowed the west, especially in the reign of Justinian (527–65). Parts of Italy were under imperial control in the sixth century, but other parts were ruled by barbarian kings who were themselves often Arian

Christians, and Arian Visigoths ruled over Spain. Clovis, the leader of the Franks, married to a Christian wife Clothild, was either pagan or Arian until his Catholic conversion around 500. The Anglo-Saxons in Britain were practising paganism when Gregory the Great (592–604) sent St Augustine's mission in 597. Further north, the Scandinavians remained pagan into the tenth and eleventh centuries. Thus we have to consider women's status and roles in established Christian churches and the effect of Christian conversion on women coming from other religions, as well as the situation of Jewish and Muslim women resident in Europe.

Conversion was more demanding when the gap between the pre-Christian and Christian customs was wider, and time affected this as well as place. For example, the southern philosophers of antiquity and late antiquity had put forward ideas of self-discipline, including sexual restraint, which made Christian morality less startling in the early Christian Mediterranean. By contrast Iceland, uninhabited until the arrival of pagan Scandinavians, had no forces recommending restraint before Christianity came demanding it c.1000 CE. Moreover the Christian code of the eleventh and twelfth centuries was more demanding – for example on clerical celibacy – than in earlier times and made more uncompromising demands on the lax practices of secular and religious leaders, trying to hustle the young Scandinavian churches into the standards the churches of southern Europe had taken several centuries to espouse.

The Evidence

There is a huge range of evidence about women from the period, but it is patchy – variable in quantity and type for different areas at any one time, and far from continuous over periods for any one zone. The ensuing survey is arranged to move from the most concrete evidence (archaeological material) through inscriptions to documentary evidence, separating administrative writing (laws, estate surveys and charter material, written to record rather than reflect upon situations) from constructed narrative (travel accounts and annals, where the original writer's opinions have more obvious input) and more imaginative literary sources (epics, sagas and shorter poetry which are much more reflective of the attitudes of composers and readers, or in this period listeners), with focus finally on literary work by women. It must be stressed that documentary evidence often comes to us through texts written down considerably later than the period of origin, and almost always in texts written for other purposes than impartial record, increasing the problems of interpretation. Buried material might well be considered more 'open' for interpretation than the potentially more deliberately propagandist written word, but interpretation can be manipulative. Archaeological studies have long been androcentric, with researchers starting from their own contemporary preconceptions about gender roles and accordingly interpreting artefacts to suit. With males expected to be stronger, more aggressive, active and dominant, and females weaker, more passive and dependent, finds have been categorized from gender assumptions and then interpreted to strengthen those assumptions. Settlement archaeology does show us 'how things were', enabling us to measure houses and streets, and investigate diets and even the parasites plaguing our forebears. Work on Viking York suggests town dwellers lived in close packed squalor. There is not much gender polarization in settlement archaeology, unless it is possible to ascribe convincingly the use of space by different sexes. Bitel cites the archaeology of early Irish farmsteads to conclude that women in early Ireland moved within a small space and group.[5]

Graves are more clearly polarized. Biologically, skulls and pelvic bones can be measured to determine the sex of skeletons – it has been claimed from work on prehistoric skeletons that well-preserved adult skeletons can be sexed with over 95 per cent accuracy, and even fragmentary remains with 85 per cent or more,[6] but in past practice a much lower rate has been achieved, and only then with the aid of grave goods deemed indicative of gender. Analysis of 320 Viking Age skeletal remains used by Jesch for illustration provides average heights of 172.6 centimetres (5 feet 9 inches) for the 85 men and 158.1 centimetres (5 feet 3 inches) for the 73 women, 162 remaining undetermined. Analysis of the age at death suggests 75 per cent of these women were over 35, apparently this marking a big improvement over the pre-Viking period when many women died between 20 and 35.[7] Children's skeletons cannot be sexed. Such archeological evidence may mislead because a site is not typical or a distribution is skewed, but the information in each instance cannot be gainsaid. As medical knowledge increasingly enters dialogue with archaeology we shall get better at reconstructing typical workloads from evidence of degenerative arthritis, nutritional health from deficiencies in the skeleton, possibly the number of pregnancies from parturition scars on the pelvis, even age at weaning from strontium in a tooth. Besides the 'facts' relating to physique and environment, archaeological distributions can also lead to rather more opinionative conclusions. The good representation of women's burials in Scandinavian graves examined in Russia surely indicates that Scandinavian merchants took their own womenfolk with them there – of 99 late ninth-to eleventh-century graves examined by Anne Stralsberg, cited in Jesch, 60 per cent contained women, 55 per cent men, some both. One young woman in her twenties died and was buried with a newborn child in Westness Orkney in the ninth or tenth century, apparently a colonist of some sort, as were the women buried in Greenland and Iceland. Typically, weaponry was, we believe, buried with men, and jewellery and domestic implements with women, but there are items common to both sexes – pots, wooden vessels, knives, whetstones, and beads. Scandinavian women's most characteristic jewellery was the paired oval brooch, worn on the chest to fasten their dresses, which were strapped over the shoulders. They also had necklaces, arm rings, disc brooches, and trefoil buckles, and their graves contain caskets and spindle whorls, wool combs and weaving battens. Women definitely seem to have been associated with textile working. Some idea of their dresses – linen or wool sleeved underdress and wool over-dress (like the modern pinafore dress) with sometimes an intermediate tunic – can be gauged from burials, especially at Birka, but probably represent a woman's best garments. Grave goods clearly often include objects which reflect the deceased's status and life style, but there is always the possibility that some inclusions were symbolic; weapons, weights and balances might fall into this category. Upper-class Merovingian women's expensive jewellery and layers of clothing reflected their status. Vikings continued burying the dead with grave goods longer than their Christian neighbours, and the practice diminished only in the later tenth century. However, they also cremated – 1100 graves from Viking Birka are about evenly inhumation and cremation graves; 59 per cent of the determinable graves are female. Christianity discouraged burial with goods, and it also discouraged cremation.

Settlement archaeology, hopefully, is giving us the normal, ordinary picture, but some grave archaeology is patently of extraordinary origin. The Oseberg ship burial, containing two female bodies, dating from the first half of the ninth century, is well analysed by Jesch. Despite the fact that this is the richest known Viking burial, suggesting interment of a queen, so little is known about the circumstances in which these two women, one in her fifties and very arthritic and one in her twenties, were buried, in an oak burial chamber on a great 21.6-metre-long ship, that it is not certain which of them was that important figure. Was the older woman buried with a young servant, or the younger with her old nurse/maid? Had they died naturally at the same time, or had the attendant been killed to serve her mistress? (A few other female graves contain mutilated male skeletons suggesting the sacrifice of a slave boy, and a written Arab source observes the killing of a slave girl to accompany her master in Scandinavian Russia.) Due to robbery of the jewellery which one must imagine would have adorned at least one of the Oseberg corpses, we cannot tell which body was wearing the array which might have defined her superiority. But a fine collection of worldly goods for travel, rest and domesticity was buried with the pair – including a cart, sledges, 12 sacrificed horses, beds, oak chests, and domestic implements. Two oxen, bread dough, apples and spices were packed for food, and four looms and other spinning and weaving implements and textiles of fine quality including tapestries. Two pairs of shoes of handstitched calfskin had been made to fit the swollen feet of the arthritic one. The thirteenth-century Icelandic historian Snori Sturkuson mentions two wives of the Vestfold king Guthrothr, Alfhuldr and Asa, who have been favourite candidates for the queen here.

Viking Age Scandinavia is an instance where later and often Christianized sources have been allowed to dominate over abundant archaeological ones. Saga and law, sometimes at odds, place Viking women as kin avengers, respected if of good birth, but not men's equal, and home dwellers. Archaeology unearths the richest and most numerous women's graves on long-established farms and where contact with the British Isles was strong, suggesting these women ran the estates in their men's absences on military expedition or a-viking, or grew prosperous on textile skills (as in Iceland), or possibly won respect through roles in fertility cults. The distribution of the graves can be contextualized, but the explanations remain guesswork.

Latin inscriptions had been widely used in the Roman world and the habit was not lost in southern Europe. Epitaphs cited by Skinner to show the value of epigraphy for documenting women in the Lombard period in Italian history were sometimes astonishingly flowery, reflecting a desirable image of the deceased as a pious wife or mother, or abbess. Madelgrima, the wife of Count Radoald of Naples, was thus commemorated by her husband for her noble birth, decorous life and care for the poor when she died c.732; Countess Bertha of Tuscany was praised as a wise matron when she died in 925, and abbess Theodota (c.705–20) as a virgin mother.[8] Dhuoda composed her own epitaph which she wanted inscribed on her funeral slab. In the north, Germanic and Scandinavian Europe used runic script until conversion to Christianity brought the Latin alphabet and writing with ink on parchment. Incising, especially in runes, was clumsy so the message conveyed was usually short. The distribution of runic inscriptions discussed by Jesch covers Norway, Sweden and Denmark, the British Isles and Ireland. In Denmark 45 memorial stones mention women, in about half the cases as the sole commissioner of the monument. Most date from the tenth century. Eleventh-century Christian stones dominate the evidence from Sweden, where stones erected by one Inga, wife of Ragnfast and later Eirik, and her mother Getlaug, show how Inga had inherited from her son by Ragnfast (who had inherited from his father), from her second husband, and from her own father, and how her mother inherited from her – women could not inherit directly from their husbands if there were surviving children. Some women used their wealth for public good – Sigrid built a bridge for her husband's soul, and her daughter Gunlaug was also a bridge builder. Norwegian runestones (fewer than 40) include commemorations and records of boundary and legal matters, and bridge building. Twenty-six interpretable stones exist on the Isle of Man, mainly tenth-century, eight mentioning women but all as the object and none as commissioners of the memorial.

From administrative record, legal sources are widely used in the study of women's history, being available from many areas and periods in the middle ages, and indicating aspects of both theory and practice. There was much legal variety, embracing surviving Roman civil law, especially in southern Europe, and barbarian custom, itself fragmented between Franks, Visigoths, Lombards, Burgundians and so on. (There was, however, much in common within these codes, for example the Icelandic *mundr* and *heimanfylgja*, the groom's family's brideprice and bride's family's dowry, correspond to the Lombardic *meta* and *faderfio*.) There was no single European legal system, and though canon law became a centralized system by the end of the period, even that was only a development of the last 200 years of it. Historians often make a distinction between public and private spheres of activity, and point to the clear disability of women in the public sphere everywhere; their relative disabilities and abilities in the private sphere were more varied. From laws we can see where and under what conditions women could inherit land, act as executors and guardians, and make wills and contracts. Dower and dowry were areas of law only existing because man and wife were treated differently after the death of the other. Much law was extremely local in application. In early medieval France the Salian Franks in the north denied women the right of succession to real property, but the Visigoths in the south supported equal division between male and female heirs. Laws from early Ireland and Wales show common characteristics derived from the Celtic past. Women in towns were under different laws from rural women, and a woman's social class affected her legal status. Noblewomen were from early times able to inherit fiefs, but only if there was no male heir. In Italy the Roman law inheritance was more favourable to women's activity, allowing them a legal personality and some management of their property, but the Lombards favoured the male protection of women which enhanced patrimonial power.

Canon law, potentially of wider application and by the twelfth century effectively centralized, gradually took increasing control of marriage over this period, and made divorce more difficult to achieve. Approximately a tenth of the body of canon law related to women, in the areas of marriage, dowry, inheritance, bequests and sexual issues. The translation of canon law into practical Christian guidance can be seen in Penitentials, handbooks for priests guiding them in the treatment of penitents – hearing confessions and prescribing appropriate penitential acts. A sixth-century Irish monastic development adapted for use with the laity, they were exported to England and the continent through Irish missionary influence and were modified for each culture. Penitentials had reached Italy by the late eighth century and Spain by the early ninth; the Frankish ones achieved their final shape by the end of the ninth century. Texts varied in the sins and penances included, but they certainly give some insight into behaviour and reflect the difficulties of upholding Christian standards in societies where paganism was far from eradicated. As sources of information relevant to gender differences, they deal more with men's sins than women's, and offer greater protection to women, children and the unborn than the laws of the time. The various laws overlapped, took different stances, and contradicted each other: for example on a woman's rape the offence could be treated as an act of violence against her, or as a crime against property, injuring or damaging a man's wife or daughter or sister.

Estate surveys provide data about the inhabitants of a few church estates from the early ninth century. The surveys of serfs on 128 households belonging to St Victor of Marseilles redacted in 813–14 produce a sex ratio of 102 men to 100 women, whereas the more famous records from the estates of St Germain-des-Prés from c.820 yield one of 135:100. From Italy there is a similar though less full survey from Farfa in the early ninth century, giving a ratio of 122:100.

The final class of source material of an administrative nature comprises grants of land made to individuals and to churches, including wills. Thousands of charters survive from this period, some of which document transactions by women. Of 265 Lombard documents dating from 650 to 774 edited by Schiaparelli, 77 mention women and in 23 they were the active agents. Charter material shows us that some women could possess land and use this possession, with or without male associates. It relates, however, only to fairly prosperous levels of society. The Lorsch cartulary of 3500 deeds from the mid-eighth to the end of the ninth century supports analysis of women's participation in property transactions, which Wemple compares with ninth-century Cluny, St Vincent of Mâcon and Brioude charters, and the Breton cartulary from Redon, while twelfth-century charters from Anjou have been similarly examined by Gold.[9]

Moving on from archival record, one type of source material from this period continues the Roman genre of comment on foreigners, as found in classical times, for example in Tacitus' *Germania*. Unfortunately we do not always know if the supposed visitor really was present and saw what he claims, still less that he understood it, or represented it fairly, nor how many reworkings there may have been between the visit and the version we have. Into this category come the twelfth–thirteenth-century Ibn Dihya's account of the ninth-century embassy of Al-Ghazal to an unidentified Viking court, and the thirteenth-century Al Qazwini's version of the tenth-century Ibrahim b. Yaqib's visit to a coastal town identified as Haithabu/Hedeby (Schleswig), cited in Jesch. At the former, the envoy flirted with the king's wife, who seems the more smitten with him; she told him that in her country women stayed with a husband only while it suited them. The Schleswig visitor, too, noted that women had the right to divorce. Ibn Fadan's eye-witness account of a mission from Baghdad to the Bulgars in 921–2 is better located in historical fact, and describes the Rus he met. This is the source of the description of the ritual sacrifice of a slave girl for a dead man alluded to above.

Annal writing was a Christian practice, tied up with the keeping of church calendars. The annals of the kingdom of the Franks date from the late eighth century and their monastic continuations from St Bertin, Fulda, Xanten and St Vaast, along with the Anglo-Saxon Chronicle, and Irish annals, especially the Annals of Ulster (though like most these are only available in much later manuscripts) are very much taken up with the scourge of the Vikings, as viewed by Christian monks, and offer only small references to women, mainly relating to native women being captured by the invaders and taken off as slaves, invading leaders' wives being baptized with them, or a native royal bride being given by treaty to an invader.

A comparison of Bede's *Chronica Majora* with his *Ecclesiastical History of the English Peoples* clearly shows the difference between the bald chronicle and the fleshed-out history. Histories of this date rarely focus on women, though both Bede (d 735) and Gregory of Tours (c.539–594) indicate the role of queens as converters of pagan kings, and Paul the Deacon's *History of the Lombards*, from the later eighth century, has already been cited with reference to Theodelinda. Ari Thorgilsson's *Íslendingabók*, written in the

1120s, describes the Viking settlement of the then empty Iceland and lists Audr daughter of Ketil Flatnose as one of the four key settlers. Audr, alias Unnr, is also featured in *Landnámabók* and *Laxdœla saga*. Though much associated with her may be legendary, she does represent surely the most a woman might achieve in the Viking Age. History in this period was almost entirely the work of male writers. Hrotsvit of Gandersheim's *Gesta Ottonis* was exceptional. Male-authored too was the vast majority of theological and philosophical writing, homilies, polemical treatises and medical tracts. A good deal of this writing was positively and deliberately misogynistic; where less aggressively derogatory, it was still based on an assumption of female inferiority which is the general perspective of the medical tracts treated in Chapter 2 below.

For a written literature to be produced in this period the Latin alphabet had to be in use, for Latin itself and for vernacular languages. Earlier scripts, such as runes and ogam, were not suitable for recording lengthy communication. A flourishing oral tradition, however, produced a literature of epics, sagas and shorter elegiac poems and riddles, which were eventually written down, in times well past the original Christian conversion, and they were inevitably written refracted through the newer religious prism. Thus the pursuit of women through the early literature of this period is a task requiring a large amount of interpretation. Epics and sagas set in patently pagan times are not presented to us in the unadulterated words of those who knew no other religion, but with a conscious sense of the difference between the times of the setting and the Christian epoch of the writers, who were putting down text anything between the tenth/eleventh century turn (*Beowulf*) and the thirteenth century (the Icelandic sagas). They are thus a mixture of the societies they describe, the societies which penned them, and the latter societies' imagination about their past. A matter such as the place of women, where the conversion to Christianity proved quite significant, emerges uneasily in sources engendered in one society, handed down in traditions and finally frozen in writing long afterwards. In the last century under review, literary sources are more plentiful and more sophisticated, bringing us the early manifestations of the Arthurian canon.

Much medieval writing was anonymous, nevertheless it is believed the vast majority of it came from men. The imbalance of educational facilities for the sexes would contribute to such a state of affairs. We do, however, find a very wide range of literary genres in the works attributed to individual women. Women wrote letters, biographies, saints' lives and visionary literature, histories and travel accounts and instruction manuals; they wrote lyric poetry, short stories, epics and drama, also allegories and treatises on a wide range of subjects. A few outstanding communicators in our period included Radegund of Poitiers (520–87), Dhuoda (writing in 841–3), Hrotsvit of Gandersheim (c.930–c.975), Heloise (1100–1163/4), Hildegard of Bingen (1098–1179), Elisabeth of Schönau (1129–1165), the late twelfth-century Marie de France and the controversial Trota of Salerno. Though each female-authored text is specifically testimony to that one writer's urge to communicate, and to her skill (and to the preservation of the attribution of the authorship as texts were copied and spread), the products are also testimony to the writer's educational achievements and background. Wilson and McLeod point out that Radegund's 'Fall of Thuringia' embraces classical traditions and Germanic themes, with autobiographical input, and that Dhuoda's manual typifies Carolingian learning in its use of far-fetched etymologies, mnemonic verses and semi-magical numerology, combining learning from late Antiquity with a Germanic view of society.[10] Hrotsvit's dramas take and invert the pattern of Terence's plays, which surely she could not have achieved without getting under the skin of the genre. The encyclopaedic collection the *Garden of Delights* of Herrad of Hohenburg incorporates some of the Arabic knowledge filtering into the west. Marie de France wrote lays (short narrative poems) which could be enjoyed in themselves, but which can also be seen as challenging traditional values. Is it not reasonable to suppose that these women writers, though few as writers, represent a somewhat larger group of women educated to a similar standard? To write in Latin, like Hrotsvit, requires mastery of that language, but more women surely had a similar degree of language training without leaving behind written compositions in it. To parody Terence, or to invert values in Arthurian traditions, requires first an understanding of the existing literature. Perhaps this was a little more widespread than might at first be imagined. This is not to argue that literacy, in Latin or the vernacular, was other than unusual (in fact in either sex) in the early middle ages, but it is to suggest that rarities such as Hrotsvit and Hildegard may be the visible tips of icebergs.

The Historiography of the Subject

An attractively crafted essay by Eileen Power on the position of women was published as early as 1926 in *The Legacy of the Middle Ages*, edited by C. G. Crump and E .F. Jacob. Wide ranging in time and geographical scope, with citations from writers from the second to sixteenth centuries, it was hardly improved upon 50 years later when Power's widower, M. M. Postan, published a small book of what he called her 'popular lectures' on the subject under the title *Medieval Women* (1975). Little advance in women's studies had been made in the interim, particularly when compared with the thirty years since.

While women were not attracting much dedicated research, it is not surprising that they were also receiving little attention in general history books. F. Heer's *The Medieval World, Europe 1100–1350* (1962) translated by J. Sondheimer from his 1961 *Mittelalter*, did give women half a chapter, pairing them with Jews, as two disadvantaged groups of people who made positive contributions to medieval society. However, women also crept into his study in places other than their shared chapter, for example in the chapter on courtly love and courtly literature. This serves to illustrate the point that both in contemporary sources and later interpretation women can be found to be visible even where they have not been made a central focus.

Women's studies in the context of the Middle Ages began to quicken in the 1970s, with conference activity and multiauthor publications drawing attention. A conference in New York in 1972 resulted in the publication of six papers edited by R. T. Morewedge under the title *The Role of Women in the Middle Ages* (1975). These included Herlihy's valuable study of life expectancies for women in medieval society in part relating to the early middle ages. *Women in Medieval Society* (1976), edited by S. M. Stuard, brought together some extremely useful studies, with a sound introduction putting the sociological approach to historical study of women into perspective. This volume includes Herlihy's 'Land, Family and Women in Continental Europe 701–1200', Coleman's 'Infanticide in the early Middle Ages', Dillard's 'Women in Reconquest Castile', and McNamara and Wemple on 'Marriage and Divorce in the Frankish Kingdom'. With practically the whole field of sociological interpretation lying untouched, these early essay collections were free to combine varied topics with no need to defend the selection, and this genre continued with *Women of the Medieval World* (1985), edited by J. Kirshner and S. F. Wemple in honour of J. H. Mundy, a collection of 14 multithemed essays with those relating to the period before 1200 all on religious themes. Multiauthor collections continued to emerge, for example *Women in the Middle Ages and Renaissance* (1986), edited by M. B. Rose, is more about the later period but does have a contribution from Schulenburg on 'The Heroics of Virginity: Brides of Christ and Sacrificial Mutilation'. R. Bridenthal, C. Koonz and S. Stuard, *Becoming Visible: Women in European History* (2nd edition 1987) starts in pre-history and works its way through the ancient world and the Roman empire, sparing two chapters for the middle ages, Wemple's 'Sanctity and

Power: the Dual Pursuit of Early Medieval Women' and Stuard's 'The Dominion of Gender: Women's Fortunes in the High Middle Ages', before moving on through renaissance and reformation to early modern and later times. M. Erler and M. Kowalcski, *Women and Power in the Middle Ages* (1988), is mainly post-1200 but includes McNamara and Wemple on 'The Power of Women through the Family in Medieval Europe 500–1100', and Schulenburg on 'Female Sanctity, Public and Private Roles c.500–1100'; it also contains an article by Rezak on 'Women, Seals and Power in Medieval France 1150–1350'. The same editors' *Gendering the Master Narrative*, subtitled *Women and Power in the Middle Ages* (2003), advances their earlier volume in the light of subsequent research.

From the late 1970s specialist essay collections began appearing, for example the *festschrift* for Rosalind Hill, *Medieval Women* (1978), edited by D. Baker for the Ecclesiastical History Society, which has, as one would expect from its origin, a strong religious thread. More than half the book relates to the period before 1200, embracing Margaret of Scotland, Christina of Markyate (whose *Life* had been edited by C. H. Talbot in 1959) and the 'Jezebels' Brunhild and Balthild. Religious men's treatment of women threads through from Bede to Robert of Arbrissel to Aelred of Rievaulx. Three volumes of somewhat mixed historical quality on *Medieval Religious Women* were edited by J. A. Nichols and L. T. Shank between 1984 and 1995: *Distant Echoes, Peaceweavers* and *Cistercian Women* (itself in two volumes).

Significant single-authored books, on general and particular themes, emerged from the early 1980s. S. Shahar's *The Fourth Estate: a History of Women in the Middle Ages* (1983), translated by C. Galai, had a big impact. It centres on the period from the early twelfth century to the second quarter of the fifteenth, and covers western Europe excluding Scandinavia and Scotland and Ireland. The book is arranged by theme rather than chronology or country, as has become common to general books on women, though the chosen themes vary. From consideration of public and legal rights, Shahar moves on to nuns, and then married women, then offers three chapters divided by class, noblewomen, townswomen and peasant women, and a final chapter is on witches and heretical movements. As always, writers on broad topics have to make divisions, and sections devised to make more sense of one aspect also tear rifts in the whole, for the noblewoman may be also a town dweller, may be married, or may eventually enter a convent, married women may be noble, or townswomen or peasants, pious or heretical. The desire to classify constantly wrenches individuals from one context to another. M. W. Labarge's *Women in Medieval Life* (1986) covers France, England, the Low Countries and Germany c.1100–1500.

Labarge adopted within the book an effective classification by function – women who ruled (separating queens and noblewomen), women who prayed (separating nuns and beguines from recluses and mystics) and women who worked (townswomen and peasants), and women as healers and nurses. However, most of the work concerns the period after 1200. E. Ennen's *The Medieval Woman* (1989) translated by E. Jephcott, offers more on the early period, two of her three sections being the early middle ages defined as 500–1050 and the high middle ages defined as 1050–1250 (the final section goes to 1500). The book places heavy emphasis on marriage and position, consistent with its conclusion that the great constant was the woman as rich heiress, bearer of successors and guardian of the dynasty. On more restricted areas, S. F. Wemple's *Women in Frankish Society: Marriage and the Cloister 500–900* (1981) covers a key period in cultural assimilation and argues the role of women well. C. Fell's *Women in Anglo-Saxon England* (1984) is a highly reliable book, with plenty of illustrations, mostly from manuscripts but also of material items, jewellery, coins and ivories; it treats women in thematic chapters. P. S. Gold's *The Lady and the Virgin: Image, Attitude and Experience in Twelfth-Century France* (1985) concentrates on the secular image in chansons, romance and charters and the religious image in Marian iconography and monastic developments. Of the geographically defined studies three of the best are H. Dillard's *Daughters of the Reconquest: Women in Castilian Society 1100–1300* (1984), J. Jesch's *Women of the Viking Age* (1991), and J. Jochens's *Women in Old Norse Society* (1995). Dillard's study, of women in frontier/settlement societies, largely based on municipal laws, shows women in the context of marriage and conjugal life and domestic tasks and widowhood, enlivened by consideration of abductions, mistresses and prostitutes – a mine of information presented with verve. Jesch's chapters are somewhat arbitrary focal points, but the topics are firmly handled, well illustrated and clearly sectionalized, where necessary, between Norway, Sweden and Denmark. Jochens, a historian deeply into Icelandic literature, offers a more logical framework, with an introductory discussion of Nordic-Germanic continuity and then chapters on marriage, reproduction, leisure and work, before delving more deeply into one sort of work, the economics of homespun. The two books combine to leave the reader very well informed about Scandinavian women and feeling familiar with their mind-set as well as their domestic tasks. By contrast P. Skinner's *Women in Medieval Italian Society 500–1200* (2001) seems more traditional in its chronological, heavily political treatment. Within time-scaled chapters recurrent themes come up in orderly fashion, angled appropriately to the prevalent conditions: women's land, property, work and power, and a lot of the detail is about women at the top, the wives of emperors, kings, dukes and counts. Few such women are identified in Jesch and Jochens. The two approaches vary so much partly because of the different raw material and societies portrayed. Whereas Italy and its invaders are comparatively sophisticatedly recorded, producing placeable persons and datable campaigns and institutional foundations and legislation, hardly any such particulars are known about Iceland, but the laws and sagas from Iceland, and the archaeological work at Birka and Hedeby permit us to feel more familiar with the actual homes and domestic practices of the women in the north. L. Bitel's *Land of Women: Tales of Sex and Gender from Early Ireland* (1996) is different again, more fancifully focused than the three just discussed, and her *Women in Early Medieval Europe 400–1100* (2002) is disappointing: idiosyncratically constructed and inclined to draw on later evidence (even from fourteenth- and fifteenth-century England) to make some of its points.

Women and religion have continued to form a fruitful area of research. *Sainted Women of the Dark Ages*, edited and translated by J. A. McNamara and J. E. Halborg with E. G. Whatley (1992), selects 18 Frankish female saints of the sixth and seventh centuries biographed by contemporaries or near contemporaries, but is of much broader significance than this suggests. S. K. Elkins's *Holy Women of Twelfth-Century England* (1988) shows how much more crisply analytical the subject of women religious has become, outdating E. Power's *Medieval English Nunneries* (1922), and S. Thompson's *Women Religious* (1991), dealing with England after the Norman Conquest, is something of a partner to it. P. Ranft, *Women and the Religious Life in Premodern Europe* (1996) is an admirably compact survey, from the origins to Mary Ward. B. L. Venarde's *Women's Monasticism* (1997) is confined to England and France 890–1215, and J. T. Schulenburg's *Forgetful of their Sex* (1998), subtitled *Female Sanctity and Society ca500–1100* is stimulating. The huge modern popularity of Hildegard of Bingen has resulted in many publications, including B. Newman's *Sister of Wisdom* (1987) and S. Flanagan's *Hildegard of Bingen* (1989). Nine years later followed the collection of multiauthored essays *Voice of the Living Light: Hildegard of Bingen and her World* (1998) edited by Newman, and the following year selections from her *Cause et Cure* were edited by M. Berger as *Hildegard of Bingen On Natural Philosophy and Medicine* (1999) in the Brewer Library of Medieval Women, a series testifying to the demands of readers for medieval women's own writings. Three volumes of Hildegard's *Letters* have been published in translation, the last in 2004 (edited by J. L. Baird and R. K. Ehrman). Numerous recordings of her music have been issued, mostly since 1990.

The Library of Medieval Women also gives us K. Wilson on *Hrotsvit of Gandersheim: a Florilegium of her Works* (1998); her plays have been staged in recent years. Heloise remains a perpetual favourite: there are many editions of her correspondence with Abelard, of which B. Radice's is probably the most accessible. For recent interpretation see B. Wheeler, *Listening to Heloise: the Voice of a Twelfth-Century Woman* (2000), C. Mews' article therein, and his *Abelard and Heloise* (2005).

Medieval queens and queenship flourished in 1990s publications so vigorously that the phenomenon seems to need particular comment. Standard textbooks often provided genealogies of the royal dynasties of the main kingdoms, on which wives appeared, named by place of origin/dynastic affiliation but not by precise parentage. Nobody was seriously analysing what a queen could do, within the early customs or later emerging constitutions of the realms, what influence she might have, and what personal motivation she might have for exercising it. A fairly uncritical, admiring, glance was cast towards the nonpareil Eleanor of Aquitaine, credited with beauty, intelligence and attractiveness (could the heiress to Aquitaine have seemed other than attractive?). The picture of Eleanor from Andreas Capellanus's satirical *De Amore*, dispensing rulings from a court of love in Poitiers, was better known than her political role in England at the start of Richard's reign, which is only just emerging at the probing of J. Martindale, though the contemporary Roger of Howden put down markers indicating her remarkable wielding of authority in writing of her touring the realm with a 'queenly court'.

Feminism brought an unwillingness to leave queens in their gilded cages. Submitting to being draped with the victor's spoils to parade the mead cup among her husband's riotous retainers seemed an unsatisfactory life purpose. As career women rose into boardrooms, the judiciary and national committees, it began to seem inconceivable that anyone, of either sex, given half the chance, would not be interested in the pursuit of power, and if 'women' and 'power' seemed to have few points of contact, then it showed the need to redefine power more appropriately to the circumstances. From power traditionally identified with politics (decision making in important areas with many repercussions for many people) or economics (policy making to take advantage of monopolized resources and to control or regulate other people's access to wealth) attention turned to a newer identification of power with less ambitious definition, the ability to have and pursue a strategy, even if not wholly successfully.

Some of the recent claims for queens may seem far-fetched and anachronistic but the great contribution of feminism to this subject has been the broader search for sources, making these available to a wider readership and subjecting them to refreshingly new lines of questioning. The traditional setting of the queen in castle and palace made a fairly inert backcloth, but a more dynamic environment is there to be dug out from treatises on royal courts and laws concerning royal households. The artistic aspect of women's seals, with flower motifs and idealized slender female figures, was far less interesting than the analysis of the documents to which they were attached, and the probing of what possession of her own seal meant for a woman, and for what purposes it was used. Contemporary descriptions of queens in chronicles and literary fiction have been probed below the surface, considering the author's attitudes and intentions.

Among the books produced in the course of the above developments one of the most vigorous was also one of the earliest, P. Stafford's *Queens, Concubines and Dowagers* (1983). Restricted to England, Frankia and Italy from the sixth to the mid-eleventh centuries, it is wide-ranging and lively and arranged largely to throw into focus the life cycle of women who are redefined in the subtitle as 'the king's wife in the early middle ages'. Stafford also contributed an article on Emma of Normandy to A. Duggan's *Queens and Queenship in Medieval Europe* (1997), in which she applied the definition of power as strategy pursuit to Emma's position. Emma forms half the story in Stafford's *Queen Emma and Queen Edith*, subtitled *Queenship and Women's Power in Eleventh-Century England* (1997), an interesting book (the two subjects do benefit from being considered together) but set on the smaller stage of England over only some 70 years. A royal biography from later in the period is M. Chibnall's *The Empress Matilda, Queen Consort, Queen Mother and Lady of the English* (1991). There are two good collections of studies about Eleanor of Aquitaine, W. W. Kibler's *Eleanor of Aquitaine: Patron and Politician* (1976) and *Eleanor of Aquitaine: Lord and Lady* (2002), edited by B. Wheeler and J. C. Parsons. Collections of papers and essays on medieval queens often advance further into the middle ages than the present volume, but Parsons's *Medieval Queenship* (1994) has a good deal of early material in it, and Duggan's previously cited *Queens and Queenship* (1997) likewise, with an interesting section here embracing the eastern empire and the kingdom of Jerusalem.

A most timely book, appearing just when much research was proving fruitful and many newcomers to the subject needed introduction to the sources, is J. T. Rosenthal's *Medieval Women and the Sources of Medieval History* (1990), which deserves attention for its method and purpose but is heavily balanced towards the later middle ages. A useful product of the recent flowering of women's studies has been the publication of sourcebooks – compilations of edited and where necessary translated contemporary extracts about women and sometimes even specifically by them. E. Amt's *Women's Lives in Medieval Europe: a Sourcebook* (1993) published primary source material to illustrate the Christian, Roman and Germanic heritage, law, marriage, health and society as conditions of life, the noble life and the agricultural, domestic and commercial life, the Christian religious life and sources on 'outsiders' – Jewish, Muslim and heretic women. The texts come from the Old Testament to the fifteenth century, with just under half originating before 1200. One of the most valuable thus made easily accessible is Caesarius of Arles' rule for nuns from c.512–34. The later extracts are disproportionately English in origin, but this is less of a criticism for the earlier ones. Another collection of sources, on a particular set of related themes, is J. Murray's *Love, Marriage and Family in the Middle Ages: a Reader* (2001), where approximately half the extracts are pre-1200 in origin. They are grouped under the headings of foundations and influences, love and its dangers, marriage and the church, marriage ceremonies, rituals and customs, husbands and wives, marriage and family, childbirth, parents and children and 'beyond Christendom'. (It is almost a standard to put 'outsiders', 'others', into this final slot, be they aliens by race and religion, such as the Jews and Muslims, or the wilfully unorthodox, witches and heretics.) Many readers might feel that Murray's book would have been more satisfactory out of the classroom if the comprehension questions at the end of each document had been removed and the space used to supply notes about the persons or events in the text which are sometimes unnecessarily obscure. Still, it makes available in English some extracts from key texts such as Jerome against Jovinian (393), sample St Germain-des-Prés polyptych entries, and Pope Nicholas I's letter to a Bulgarian king (866), commented on by M. Sheehan in *Marriage, Family and Law in Medieval Europe* (1996), edited by J. K. Farge. C. Larrington's *Women and Writing in Medieval Europe: a Sourcebook* (1995) is a mixture of writing by, for and about women, from Iceland to Byzantium, set out under the headings 'Marriage', 'Love, Sex and Friendship', 'Motherhood and Work', 'Women and Christianity', 'Women and Power', 'Education and Knowledge', 'Women and the Arts'. This is a more scholarly piece of editing with excellent forewords to each extract. M. Thiébaux compiled an anthology entirely of *The Writings of Medieval Women* (2nd edition, 1994), where the texts follow short essays about them, and have notes and further reading. Most of the writers come from before 1200. At the least these anthologies and sourcebooks give the flavour of writings or legal pronouncements often cited in secondary works, and supply nuggets in the vignettes of life or philosophical comments on customs and practices, but at the best they are presented with good editorial interpretation accompanying the source material.

Prolific women writers, most notably in this period Hildegard and Hrotsvit, have had their works made available to a popular readership by the Library of Medieval Women extracts, and for those wishing to read works of theirs in full in translation there are several editions of Hrotsvit's plays, and of numerous works of Hildegard. M. H. Green's *The Trotula* (2001) translates women's medical texts and offers an up-to-date appraisal of their authorship, asserting that one piece really was by the elusive and much questioned Dame Trota. Two editions of Dhuoda's Handbook have been published, as *Handbook for William* by C. Neel (1991) *and Liber Manualis: Handbook for her Warrior Son* by Thiébaux (1998). Studies of principal women writers are to be found in P. Dronke, *Women Writers of the Middle Ages: a Critical Study of Texts from Perpetua († 203) to Marguerite Porete († 1310)* (1984) and *Medieval Women Writers*, edited by K. M. Wilson (1984).

Sex was seized upon boldly for investigation in the 1990s, for example with J. Cadden's fairly clinical *Meanings of Sex Difference in the Middle Ages* (1993) while the *Handbook of Medieval Sexuality* (1996), edited by V. L. Bullough and J. A. Brundage, ventured openly into homosexuality, lesbianism, and cross-dressing as well as 'straight' sex issues such as prostitution and contraception. Riddle's contribution on medieval contraceptive/abortifacient knowledge starting from the Lorsch manuscript (from a Benedictine monastery c.800) is brilliantly set out. Meanwhile the more subtle nuances of gender also came to light, anthropologically and in literature. K. Hays-Gilpin and D. S. Whitley, *Reader in Gender Archaeology* (1998) relates mainly to pre-history but the techniques set out deserve attention, and one contribution is on the Viking period. Using written material, we have C. M. Mooney's *Gendered Voices: Medieval Saints and their Interpreters* (1999), probing the significance of male control of what Mooney terms 'the textualization of women's utterances', which considers Hildegard and Elisabeth of Schönau from the pre-1200 period; E. van Houts, *Memory and Gender in Medieval Europe 900–1200* (1999), a refreshingly original perspective on medieval remembrance of the past; Stafford and A. B. Mulder-Bakker, *Gendering the Middle Ages* (2001) a special issue of *Gender and History* containing nine essays and four thematic reviews, the balance relating to pre-1200; T. S. Fenster and C. A. Lees, *Gender in Debate from the early Middle Ages to the Renaissance* (2002), which has, despite the title, disappointingly little before 1200; and S. Farmer and C. B. Pasternack, *Gender and Difference in the Middle Ages* (2003) which is a challenging collection of essays ranging over different cultures and categories of difference. *Gendering the Crusades*, edited by S. Edgington and S. Lambert (2001), is a particularly effective application of the perspective to a topic.

History and literature studies are companionable bedmates and there are whole books on aspects of women in relation to literary sources for the purposes of socio-historical research. J. C. Frakes's *Brides and Doom: Gender, Property and Power in Medieval German Women's Epic* (1994) looks into the *Nibelungenlied* and *Kudrun*, while P. McCracken's *The Romance of Adultery: Queenship and Sexual Transgression in Old French Literature* (1998) trawls through the Arthurian literature which emerged in the twelfth century, and carries the subject through to the 1320s and the nonfictional accusations of adultery against two of the French king's daughters-in-law. *New Readings on Women in Old English Literature* (1990), edited by H. Damico and A. H. Olsen, is broader based than its title implies, and has for example the interesting study by Clover on the sex ratio in early Scandinavia which was cited above.

While new topics such as sex and gender have come into the picture a focus on women from the legal perspective has continued throughout, from D. Jenkins and M. E. Owen, *The Welsh Law of Women* (1980) to *Medieval Women and the Law* (2000) edited by N. J. Menuge, which contains Smith's 'Unfamiliar Territory: Women Land and Law in Occitania 1130–1250'. Jaski's 'Marriage Laws in Ireland and on the Continent in the Early Middle Ages' is a useful contribution to C. E. Meek and M. K. Simms, *The Fragility of her Sex? Medieval Irishwomen in their European Context* (1996). There is a section on law in the excellent collection of essays edited by L. Mitchell, *Women in Medieval Western European Culture* (1999), where Reyerson and Kuehn's article on 'Women and Law in France and Italy', and Mitchell's own on 'Women and Medieval Canon Law' are particularly useful. With regard to canon law, however, it is salutary to remember that a couple of the experts in this field, J. A. Brundage and the late M. Sheehan, have many useful things to tell about women to be found in journals and collections which do not particularly draw attention to themselves as feminist studies. Fortunately, however, demand has led to the republication of essays on selected themes by these and other authors, bringing together scattered writings for ease of access, for example Sheehan's *Marriage, Family and Law in Medieval Europe* cited above, and D. Herlihy's *Medieval Households* (1985) and *Women, Family and Society in Medieval Europe* (1995). Similarly there are many studies of marriage, for example G. Duby's *Medieval Marriage: Two Models from Twelfth-Century France*, translated by E. Forster (1978), *The Knight, the Lady and the Priest: the Making of Modern*

Marriage (1983) translated by B. Bray, and C. N. L. Brooke, *The Medieval Idea of Marriage* (1989). K. M. Wilson and N. Margolis have recently edited the useful *Women in the Middle Ages* two-volume encyclopaedia (2004).

Medieval women have been pulled from the shadows of history in the last 30 years, and will remain in the sun. The input from religious seminaries seems likely to keep aspects of women and religion in the spotlight. The ever-changing fashions in literary criticism will keep the interplay of literary sources for historical research active. The increased mobility in the enlarged European Community seems likely to foster an increased interest in the effects of migration on the generations which move. There is a fascinating subject for women's history here, but it is not one which will be easily dredged from the sources, particularly if the study of Latin to any real depth becomes any more extenuated. One source of material and two technical developments may take us much further quantitatively in the future. The source is organic matter, where new techniques of biological/medical analysis will tell us much more about vegetational history (and thereby climate and diet), animal life (from the age at which meat was butchered to the parasites in the environment) and human health and disease – even throwing in the odd scandal where DNA may prove a lineage did not descend from its supposed ancestor – and, by study of gene pools in groups of population, also tell us more about migration. Interpretation and imagination have limitations in historical study if source material is lacking or inappropriate for the questions we want to ask. A quantitative input from science would be hugely valuable at this point. The other technical advance helps us cope with quantitative data on large scales: the computer is an easier tool to become competent with than the Latin language is a communication medium to master.

2

Contemporary Gender Theory and Society's Expectations of Women

During the period covered in this book, western European society emerges from the obscurity of the Dark Ages and the place of women becomes more realistically generalizable. Male-authored literature from classical times and late antiquity shows the gender theories which underpinned social activity then, and no like literature replaced it at the start of our period. Time had passed since Romans had commented on the behaviour of barbarians beyond their borders, leaving us with pictures frozen in context. Was Tacitus' portrayal of Germanic society ever accurate, and if and where it was so, had those traits survived? It is necessary to be aware of the classical legacy because classical writers were models for and influences on later writers. Thus the attempt to focus on contemporary gender theory and society's expectations of women must begin by looking at the Mediterranean Judeo-Christian inheritance, and the secular legacy of late antiquity.

The Judeo-Christian Inheritance

The Judeo-Christian inheritance can be traced from the Bible itself and from comments of the Church Fathers. This inheritance was important in the tradition of the Latin West because the Bible was the central text of Christianity, and though only a tiny proportion of the population had access to the written word, many more imbibed knowledge of it from hearing preachers tell biblical stories and comment on them, from seeing carvings and paintings on biblical themes in ecclesiastical art, and from watching religious drama. In *The Study of the Bible in the Middle Ages*, Beryl Smalley credited even medieval peasants with some idea of the content of both

28

Old and New Testaments gained from visual aids and oral teaching. Biblical texts treat women, and their rights and duties, in respect of three phases of life: the young unmarried (in need of protection), wives and mothers (due respect chiefly as wives of their husbands), and widows (treated as poor and deserving), or occasionally according to occupation (for example, whores) or condition (such as pregnant or menstruating). Sporadically, individual women were named, such as Martha or Jezebel, giving rise to their citation in later Christian works as reference points to particular behaviour. A huge weight of interpretation built up over the centuries, and not without controversies.

Virginity before marriage was the Old Testament ideal and it was assumed the girl and her family would defend it and avenge dishonour. This Old Testament virginity was valued largely as a prerequisite for marriage. Its loss damaged a girl's standing and shamed her family. In the New Testament and for Church Fathers, however, celibacy became an aspect of a higher level of religious life, and virginity became the aim of some women, not to keep themselves marriageable, but to keep themselves chaste. Virgins or widows dedicating themselves to asexual asceticism were an inheritance from the early centuries of Christianity, where they had lived privately in their original homes, or joined others in holy households, and by the fourth and fifth centuries, in enclosed convents. Often, in writings from the Church Fathers, the merits of virginity were emphasized in physical terms as an avoidance of the negative aspects of marriage and procreation: St Gregory of Nyssa (c.330–c.395) and St John of Chrysostom (c.347–407) described married women's anxieties – fear of being childless, or over-fecund, dread of miscarriage or having a malformed baby, terror of labour pains, and all the worry over an infant's health or sudden death. Tracts took similar viewpoints to the end of our period and beyond, as in *Hali Meidhad* of around 1200. But virginity was a positive inspiration for the spiritually ambitious, and preferable to marriage, which was seen as a device primarily to avoid fornication, the perspective of St Paul in 1 Corinthians.

Once married, the biblical woman was expected to remain chastely for the husband. The ideal wife and mother emerges from Proverbs 31:10–31, a passage worth reading in full. (The salient points are her trustworthiness, domestic industry, generosity to the poor and needy, wise speech and praiseworthiness.) This virtuous woman is defined in a household context, with children to call her blessed, and marriage was expected to be for procreation. The Old Testament is full of women whose noted role was childbearing: virile patriarchs wanted sons, from wives, and if necessary from their maids and concubines. In Genesis 29–35, Jacob fathered twelve sons, six from his less preferred wife Leah, two from his favourite wife Rachel (her sister), and two each from Rachel's maid Bilhah and Leah's maid Zilpah. These women's role in the story was to produce children, and the temporarily barren wife met the obligation by providing a maid as a proxy womb; Jacob's maids, however, remained servants, concubines, or second-class wives. Biblical writers were interested in the consequences of copulation – desirably conception and preferably the birth of a son – not the psychology of sexual relations, so the sex act is reported straightfor-wardly, with little concern for wooing.

The childbearing wife entrenched herself in her husband's respect, and in due time basked in the honour and respect of her children. The Apocryphal Book of Tobit 4:3–4 goes beyond the fifth commandment with a flash of insight, telling his son to honour his mother and please her, and to remember that she saw many dangers for him when he was in her womb. Jerome goes into more detail, reminding a difficult daughter of her mother's care – 'she washed your soiled napkins and often dirtied her hands with their nastiness. She sat by your bed when you were ill and was patient with your sickness, even as she had endured before the sickness of maternity you caused.'[1] The single-minded pursuit of procreation was con-tinually stressed, so Jerome and Augustine held that a husband sinned if he had intercourse with his wife without the deliberate intention of procre-ation. The procreative need, however, presented controversies. Deuteron-omy 25:5–6 required the childless widow to be married by her husband's brother, their first son to take the dead brother's name, but Leviticus 20:21 condemned to childlessness the man marrying his brother's wife, leaving a conundrum which complicated the marriage of Henry VIII of England and Catherine of Aragon.

Marriage in the Old Testament was not lifelong monogamy. Aside from the early generations' multiple wives, divorce was comparatively easy: see Deuteronomy 24:1–4. By contrast in the New Testament Matthew, Mark and Luke in similar passages indicate that Christ was tough on divorce: for-bidding human beings to divide what God had united and considering it adultery for a man or wife to divorce and remarry. This set an uncomprom-ising line for the Christian church, and Paul upheld it in 1 Corinthians 7:10–11: 'the Lord commands a wife must not be separated from the hus-band, or if she has already left him she must remain unmarried, or else be reconciled to her husband: a husband must not divorce his wife.' Writing in early Christian times when guidance was needed concerning marriages between believers and nonbelievers, he went on in verses 12–14 to ban Christians from divorcing nonbelieving spouses who wished to remain with them, because the unbelieving could be sanctified by the believing spouse and the children made holy. This situation regained relevance in the barbarian conversion period. Pope Boniface V quoted 1 Corinthians 7:14 to Ethelburga of Kent, Christian wife of the then still pagan Edwin of Northumbria, working over her to bring her husband to the faith. The corollary that believers could be separated from nonbelievers choosing to leave (verse 17) was taken up in Penitentials.

Paul's influence on the standing of women in Christian society was immense and uncompromisingly insistent on their inequality in both public and private life. Chapter 11 of 1 Corinthians lays down that the head of every man is Christ, the head of woman is man, and the head of Christ is God. Unlike a man, a woman praying or prophesying should have her head covered, because the man is the image of God and reflects God's glory, but the woman is the reflection of man's glory. The man did not come from the woman, rather woman from man; nor was man created for the sake of woman, but vice versa. Already, in 4:34 Paul had written that women should keep quiet in churches, having no permission to speak. In the first epistle to Timothy 2:12–13 he wrote 'During instruction, a woman should be quiet and respectful. I give no permission to a woman to teach or have authority over a man.' Old and New Testament prophetesses, however, presented an awkward alternative perspective, which Blamires shows Origen (c.185–254) tried to turn, defensively, with the argument that such women as Deborah and Anna had not spoken publicly in an assembly, and that the teaching mentioned in the Epistle to Titus was merely of good behaviour, to younger women (which was true).[2]

Bridled in church, the wife was supposed to seek enlightenment privately from her husband. Paul wrote in 1 Corinthians 14:35: 'If there is anything they want to know, they should ask their husbands at home, for it is shameful for a woman to speak in the assembly.' Furthermore, Paul did not restrict his comments to a married couple's public decorum, but tackled their private sexual relationship. In 7:2 he wrote: 'To avoid immorality, every man should have his own wife, and every woman her own husband. The husband must give to his wife what she has a right to expect, so too the wife to her husband. The wife does not have authority over of her own body, but the husband does' (and vice versa). These relationships may look fairly equal, but in Paul's letter to the Ephesians 5:22–5, 28 and 33, the inferiority of the woman creeps in. 'Wives should be subject to their husbands as to the Lord, since as Christ is head of the church and saves the whole body, so is the husband the head of his wife.' Reiterated to the Colossians in 3:18–19 was the message that wives should be subject to husbands, and Peter had a similar message of wifely obedience in his first letter 3:1 and verse 7 refers to the wife as the weaker partner. St Augustine (354–430), who did much to formulate Christian marriage doctrine, after living himself with a concubine for 13 years before his own conversion, upheld a wife's obedience to her 'head', but rallied women against the traditional lenience towards men in sexual matters, urging them to show no tolerance of husbands' infidelities. Paul's mistrust of the marital state was echoed in Gregory the Great's doubts about carnal pleasure in lawful conjugal union.

Much less is said in the Bible about widows, but their lot was agreed to be pitiable: Deuteronomy 24:19–21 reserved overlooked sheaves and olives and grapes for the foreigner, orphan and widow. Christ's parable of the widow's mite in Mark 12:41–4 and Luke 21:1–4 assumes a common lowly and impoverished condition. In treatises Ambrose and Jerome recommended certain widow models, such as Anna, Naomi, Judith and Deborah.

Individually identified women appeared in both Testaments, and could be used as role models or subjects for moral teaching in later generations. In the Old Testament Deborah was boldness itself in saving the Israelites, and not modest about her role; Ruth was the ideal daughter-in-law, Abigail intelligent and resourceful in dealing with her first husband; Jezebel became proverbially awful. In the New Testament, Mary and Martha came to symbolize the mystic and active options of faith, while Mary Magdalen had a vast cult in the Middle Ages. Both named and anonymous women were visible in the Bible performing normal tasks such as baking, fetching water, tending sheep, spinning and making clothes. These tasks were common to successor societies and continued to fall to women.

Potentially more controversy adhered to Eve, and indeed to the Virgin Mary. Although Eve was created later than Adam, in Genesis 2, and as a helpmeet for man, both factors indicating her secondary position, it could also be argued she was made of qualitatively superior material (organic bone as distinct from clay), and inside the Garden of Eden, unlike Adam, who preceded the Garden. Genesis 3 shows Eve being tempted by the serpent and putting up feeble resistance before succumbing and tempting Adam. This circumstance led to the personification of woman as the cause of mankind's misfortunes, blamed on her fatal curiosity and lack of resistance to temptation, her error of judgement and her harmful tempting of her husband. Gislebert's twelfth-century relief of Eve at Autun shows a most seductive siren, apple in hand. Blaming Eve for everything, however, seemed too sweeping for some. St Augustine argued that the serpent dared not speak to man, but used the woman to get at him, thus 'framing' the weaker, intellectually inferior and more credulous party. Chrysostom went further and criticized Adam for yielding to Eve's temptation rather than correcting her.

Mary the mother of Jesus, as the blessed vessel of God's purpose, had to be elevated above the day-to-day imperfections of her sex. To fulfil Isaiah's prophecy 'a virgin shall conceive and bear a son', Mary, 'espoused' to Joseph, had to become pregnant 'before they came together', and the church consistently upheld the virgin birth. The Gospels were not as interested in Mary as her central role seemed later to require, and later generations created a whole personal history for her, including an Assumption and heavenly Coronation. Her role was taken up in the second century, and Ambrose, Jerome and Augustine all helped determine the character of her later significance. Feasts associated with her multiplied – Purification, Annunciation, Assumption and Nativity, and later Conception and Presentation in the Temple. Mary was already in high respect in Carolingian times, and the tenth-century English manuscript the Benedictional of Ethelwold contains the earliest surviving depiction of her death in a western manuscript, and the earliest of her coronation. After the Norman Conquest Eadmer of Canterbury was the first to formulate the concept of her Immaculate Conception, and St Anselm's nephew Anselm further promoted regard for her. Mary was too untouchable to be a model for normal women, but her prominence in a male-dominated religion cannot be denied.

It is therefore clear that the Bible contained a dynamic gendering of society, containing internal contradictions which were food for thought for the Church Fathers, and remained influential through the church's teachings throughout and beyond our period. Interpretation was the key to development in this sphere, but prescription, via canon law, was even more effective in influencing behaviour.

Canon Law

Canon law, the Christian church's rules or laws concerning faith, morality and discipline, developed throughout this period, embracing Christ's own pronouncements, Pauline recommendations, patristic texts, the decrees of church councils and episcopal and papal pronouncements. From the tenth century there is evidence of experts wrestling with this disorderly body to codify it, the great achievement of Gratian of Bologna, whose *Decretum*, or *Concordantia Discordantium Canonum* of c.1140 arranged contradictory texts together. This work became the basis of the full *Corpus Iuris Canonici* created by the addition of successive pronouncements over the rest of the middle ages.

Canon law touches women mainly in its prescription of norms for marital and celibate lifestyles. Christian marriage became characterized as consensual, monogamous, exclusive and permanent, but this took time. There was a lot of unease about widows' remarriage, and Paul, for once, emerged on the liberal side in 1 Corinthians 7:39 – 'a wife is tied as long as her husband is alive. But if the husband dies she is free to marry anybody she likes, only it must be in the Lord', a clear assertion not only of the widow's freedom to marry again, but also to choose her spouse, a position not always respected by feudal law. (However Paul added she would be happier if she stayed as she was, to his way of thinking.)

Choice, for first and subsequent marriages, was increasingly hedged about with limitations. Leviticus 18 had set out prohibitions on sexual relationships with specified close relatives including in-laws. (Consanguinity is relationship by blood, affinity relationship by marriage.) Limitations to the marriage of over-close kin were in place by the start of our period, and much at issue in councils and papal rulings in the sixth to eighth centuries. By Gratian's day marriage was generally forbidden within the seventh degree. This was relaxed to the fourth by the Fourth Lateran Council, but could be suspended by papal dispensation.

Jacob's fecund ménage of many females was no longer acceptable but Charlemagne's may be compared – he had five successive marriages and at least six concubines condoned by the church. Hincmar Archbishop of Reims (d 882) stoutly opposed divorce but powerful dynastic interests tended to prevail; with the compliance of locally involved bishops and sometimes popes, kings rid themselves of unwanted wives on grounds of incest or nonconsummation and/or adultery by the wife. The potentially limiting effect of monogamy on the production of heirs was lessened a little by transforming concubines into wives, by the reluctant recognition of clandestine marriages, and by the legitimation of offspring by the subsequent marriage of the parents.

Besides defining who was free to marry whom, the church increasingly influenced the actual rituals of marriage. It stressed continuously that couples must be willing to marry, as well as being free to do so. Elevating the necessary consent of bride and groom eventually undercut the power of consent, or of withholding consent, once held by parents and/or lords. Canon law supported the custom of dowry (Roman *dos*), the gift from the bride's family to the groom, alias *maritagium*, and that of dower (Roman *donatio propter nuptias*, German *dos*), the husband's endowment of the wife, and it extended its concern to the redistribution of these resources if marriages were dissolved. In 866 Pope Nicholas I described western marriage procedure to the Bulgarian king Boris as beginning with an engagement (*sponsalia*), a promise of future marriage made by the couple, followed by the giving of a ring from the man to the woman, and the endowment of the woman, performed with witnesses for both parties and put in writing. (No mention is made of the dowry from her side.) Next, in church, a priest blessed the couple and covered them with a veil, unless one party was marrying for the second time. The couple left church wearing crowns which the church owned.[3] However, though such public ceremony was desirable, it was not necessary: consent was the crucial factor.

Privately expressed consent established a valid marriage (provided the parties were free to marry each other) whether it was expressed in the present tense or the future, in which latter case it was made operative by subsequent consummation. The church, though disapproving, consistently supported the validity of clandestine marriage until 1563 (1753 in England), giving the benefit of the doubt to such unions, despite their slackness making them difficult to prove either way if, afterwards, either party wished to disengage from a relationship. A good deal of marriage litigation in church courts was centred on whether a disputed marriage had ever taken place.

By around 700 family structure followed the basic conjugal model across Romano-barbarian Europe, in France, Germany, Italy and England, and the monogamous indissoluble marriage promoted by the Christian church in the following two centuries entrenched it further, though polygamy had run rampant through earlier Merovingian kings and concubinage was common in the Frankish upper classes. The church was entering a period when it was a genuine unifying influence on Christendom, imposing conditions affecting women's property rights and marriage, sexuality and contraceptive and abortifacient practices. Obviously we know more about the workings of canon law in the later centuries, but it was being refined and applied over our period, reaching a state of full development by the late eleventh and twelfth centuries. Most of our evidence of marital cases comes from royal families and the upper classes, but the church did see marriage as equally valid a relationship right down to the unfree, and eighth- and ninth-century Frankish councils clarified the marital capacity of slaves.

The emergence of more or less accepted rules relating to matrimony by the end of the period marked the resolution of several conflicts of interest. Landed families, noble and peasant alike in this respect, tended to favour a defensive endogamy, that is finding a wife from within the kin, to prevent property being lost to the kindred group. On the other hand, exogamy, the taking of a wife from outside the kin, could be an offensive ploy, to bring new property in. The church, desiring to secure endowments, had an interest in supporting the claims of individuals, over their families, as total owners of land, and thus, potentially, fully powered donors of it. Goody has argued that women's freedom as testators and controllers of their own property was to the church's interest, as was their remaining widows and spinsters.[4] Men wanted legitimate sons and heirs, so there was another conflict of interest where a properly married wife proved barren. To be meaningful and offer any security marriage had to be indissoluble, yet it might have to be broken in dynastic interest. The wife had to be chaste (to ensure the sons of the marriage were her husband's) and fertile and the husband had to be potent.

Marriage was the conduit for licit sex, which should be for procreation rather than enjoyment. Churchmen recognized full well that controlling the sexual drive in this way could never be exclusive. With merely lusting after a woman in the mind being condemned by Christ as adultery, in the Sermon on the Mount, many human beings were destined to fail to live purely. Restraint was due from both sexes, but both in the world and in the church there was clearly a double standard – male lapses being treated more leniently than female ones. The legal situation regarding rape was complex, with some attempt to distinguish abduction and sexual assault, and to grade offences from violating a virgin to forcing sex on a married woman, or a prostitute, and to probe the woman's consent or resistance.

The Secular Legacy of late Antiquity

Greece and Rome were the ancient European civilizations, whose cultures were transmitted in part into later European practices. But the process was neither continuous nor integral, and acceptance of Christianity filtered what could be retained from pagan cultures. When common features of classical and medieval womanhood can be found, they may be coincidences rather than derivations, or newly introduced conscious adoptions (following the various renaissances identified in the period) rather than survivals from a very different context. There are, however, two areas where the classical imprint does need bearing in mind: medical science, largely derived from the Greeks, treated separately below, and law, largely derived from the Romans.

Women appear in Greek and Roman laws in the context of their families more than as individuals. Both societies were class-ridden, which affected such matters as dowry size and fines for rape. Both societies arranged marriages, and recognized a particular position as concubine. Both were tough on adultery, especially by the woman. Roman law proved the more influential because it was continually recodified and extended within the wider empire, and especially south of the Loire the successor states retained a good deal of Roman law after the collapse of the empire. In the sixth century the Roman legal inheritance was overhauled by Justinian to form the *Corpus Iuris Civilis*, which provided the basis of law in the parts of Italy still connected to Byzantium, and the foundation of the Roman law renaissance in the twelfth century. Under Justinian abduction and seduction and rape were penalized according to the woman's social status. The dowry from the bride's family to the husband was a feature of Roman marriage law, where it came to be balanced by the husband's counter-dowry or reverse dowry. Justinian required equality in these gifts but when the system was revived in southern Europe in the twelfth century the groom's gift rapidly sank to about a quarter of the bride's family's. Roman law's allowance of women's inheritance rights resulted in women holding more of the landed wealth in Roman law areas than elsewhere.

Barbarian Germanic/Baltic/Celtic Traditions

In barbarian Europe other traditions existed, Germanic, Baltic and Celtic. Wergild rates suggest women were valued here primarily for breeding potential: Aleman and Bavarian codes allocated a woman double the wergild of a man of the same status, while Salic and Ripuarian law tripled the basic wergild for women of childbearing age (12–40). Anglo-Saxon law codes distinguished lying with and forcibly carrying off a woman, imposing graded penalties according to her birth or the status of her husband, employer or owner, sometimes further qualified by her previous sexual experience. The husband's gift to the bride in Germanic tradition began as bride-price balanced by dowry. Another early payment was the *morgengabe*, the gift to the bride the morning after consummation of the marriage, an exchange for her virginity and an acknowledgement of her husband's acceptance of her. The Welsh *cowyll* was similar. More substantial was the groom's long-term dowering of his wife, the Germanic *dos* and Roman *donatio propter nuptias*. Not only do we have great problems defining the varied terminology across times and places, but it is not uncommon to find different translators of the same text disagreeing: the Domesday Book *dos* is translated 'dowry' in the Phillimore edition and 'dower' in the Allecto edition in the same Bedfordshire entry. Germanic clans practised spouse exchange and balanced dowry and dower as agreed by a wider circle than just by the couple. The wife's dower thereafter remained in her family's possession, while the husband managed her dowry, but under her clan's supervision.[5]

In respect of landed property rights, women were inferior, though customs varied between peoples. The Lombards, whose law is considered the most Germanic of the barbarian codes, and the most restrictive on women, preserved the perpetual minority of the woman, who had to be under the control of some man, her *mundoald*, usually father, then husband, and perhaps eventually son, with the king as the last resort if she had no male relatives. Although a woman needed her *mundoald*'s permission to manage property, the Lombard law did recognize her ownership of land and goods. Visigothic law gave women freedom to dispose of their property until this was curtailed in the seventh century: nevertheless later women's inheritance rights were generally more favourable in areas which had been Visigothic. Salic (Frankish) restrictions on female inheritance seem also to be clamping down on earlier freedom. But women generally enjoyed dower and dowry and in some places shares in acquests (property acquired by the husband after the marriage).

Germanic marriage by purchase (*Kaufehe*) was more civilized than marriage by capture (*Raubehe*), common from the fifth to ninth centuries, but neither had much room for the woman's consent. Consequently Christianization, with the growing emphasis on the woman's consent as one of the two consenting parties, brought greater change to Germanic society than to Roman, where consent had been a principle of Roman law. Christianity was, however, slow to reach the Baltic/Scandinavian states – Harald Bluetooth of Denmark was converted only about 950, and the conversion of Norway and Sweden were still to follow, so pagan marriage customs lasted longer in these parts of Europe and are described in Jochens's *Women in Old Norse Society*. Bigamy (especially among kings) and the sexual resort to concubines and slaves also lasted openly longer in the Viking north. Norwegian and Icelandic laws set out a process of two-stage engagement and wedding, apparently of ancient German origin. The suitor, or his father or other relative, opened negotiations with the girl's father or guardian, or, for an older bride, with her legitimate son, if over 16, son-in-law, father or brother – approached in their order of precedence as her 'heirs'. The groom's family had to pay a brideprice, the bride's family a dowry, and when these were agreed, the men from each side repeated the conditions and shook hands before witnesses. Men used marriage to create alliances and cement peaces. The women had no say, and found themselves having to start new lives among strange people, often ones they had considered enemies. The wedding usually followed within a year of the engagement but could be after three years in Iceland, due to the men's journeying to Norway.

Jochens's study stresses the commercial aspect of the engagement, and highlights the sexual and reproductive emphasis of the wedding. The groom was brought to the bride, who awaited him in bed, and he had to be seen to enter it by six witnesses. A banquet preceded the bedding and the guests were given gifts before leaving. A marriage thus constituted secured legitimacy for the offspring, but was not itself much security for the woman as divorce was easy and the men freely utilized concubines, mistresses and slaves. However, women quite often initiated their divorces, at any rate in Iceland, where a wife, if her husband wanted to take her property out of the country against her will, could simply declare herself divorced before witnesses. Violence, by either sex, was grounds for divorce if injurious enough. The sexual purity of wives and daughters in Old Norse society, respectively to keep them for their husbands and future husbands, was valued as family not personal honour. In that society wretched women such as beggars were under no protection and intercourse with them was not punished; slave girls bought for sex fetched higher prices and both slaves and servant girls were clearly used for sexual gratification by their masters or employers and these men's guests.

Medical Beliefs about the Female Body and Psyche

The foundation of western medicine lay in the works ascribed to Hippocrates, from the fifth and fourth centuries BCE, Galen (c.133–200) and Soranus (d c.130), whose *Gynaecology* is of particular relevance, and was still used as a textbook in the eighteenth century. Hippocratic writings, and those of Soranus and Galen, were originally in Greek, as were the scientific philosophies of the natural philosophers Aristotle and Plato who had much influence on later opinions. Joan Cadden, in *Meanings of Sex Difference in the Middle Ages*, explains how the teachings came to be preserved, despite incompatibilities, in Latin translation, in texts which reflected the late Antique and early medieval fondness for practical, collected extracts in encyclopaedic format, or as question-and-answer compendia. Towards the end of our period, this question-and-answer format became better arranged, and expanded to allow follow-up arguments creating a commentary on the matter under review. The diluted legacy of Galen and Aristotle was invigorated by new translations from Greek and Arabic. This in turn influenced the output of medical commentaries especially associated with Salerno. Parts of Europe obviously remained untouched by ancient theories longer than others. Little is known about the medical practices of pagan Scandinavia and Iceland because of the late coming of Christianity and written text there.

Ancient science favoured a balanced interpretation for health, based on a system of four elements, air, fire, earth and water, and four qualities, moisture, heat, dryness and cold, and in the body four humours, sanguine, choleric, melancholic and phlegmatic. Where value judgements were attached, the hot and dry was thought superior to the cold and wet. Woman was generally seen as colder and moister than man, and thus inferior and passive. She was herself a sort of less than perfect male, with an inferior reproductive system. This is essentially Aristotle's perspective. The degree of her contribution to the embryo was disputed, from both partners contributing seed (Hippocrates and Galen), to the father producing active semen, the mother only nourishing menstrual blood (Aristotle). Consistent with the idea of female inferiority was the allocation of space within the womb, the left side for girls and the right side for boys. Babies on the right, warmer side of the uterus would be more fully perfected (and so male).

Soranus, however, considered tension and laxity more important than the humours, and played down the difference between the sexes, thus allowing some conditions common to the sexes to be seen as the same in causation and therefore in cure. All these ideas penetrated the medieval west, some directly, others after translation from Avicenna's *Canon of Medicine*, and different ones prevailed at different times. Soranus did not believe that the uterus could wander about a woman's body in search of moisture if it became too dry, attaching itself to other organs and becoming a hazard to health, but the earlier Hippocratic concept of the wandering womb survived and reappeared. Galen thought celibacy a health risk due to retention of seed, in either sex, but Soranus observed that women untroubled by intercourse and pregnancy were healthier. Menstruation was seen as the disposal of surplus blood when the woman was neither pregnant nor breastfeeding. Its cessation without pregnancy as a cause was therefore a serious matter. Writers generally placed the onset of menstruation (menarche) at 12 or 13, but its cessation (menopause) was more variedly attributed to ages from 35 to 60. It was considered rare for women to bear children after 40. Infertility was disastrous for a married woman; overfertility was recognized, but late Antiquity showed strong pressures against contraception and abortion, and disapproved abandonment and exposure, though these were not legally forbidden in Roman law until infanticide was criminalized in 374. The Christian church was also hostile to abortion (Council of Ancyra, 314). Braga (572) was the first church council to condemn contraception.

Both the pagan medical legacy and the Christian adaptations remained throughout the period predominantly in the hands of men. Monastic scholars, especially those of Monte Cassino, passed the torch to the medical centre developing at Salerno from the later tenth century, and medical study spread from monasteries to cathedral schools, and later to the universities. Female convents were not in this league. As a woman, Hildegard of Bingen, treated below in Chapter 7, was in all respects remarkable for attempting to write medical works in the mid-twelfth century.

The theoretical medicine of this period, the abstract, learned and male-dominated medicine passed down institutionally, has not much to commend it to modern patients or practitioners, though some observation was feeding into it and some causes and effects were being worked out. The practical, remedial side of medicine was more widely understood and practised. Certain herbs, and herbal mixtures, and certain therapies, from hot and cold baths to massages, were practical remedies discovered by trial and error and publicized by tradition, orally as well as in writing. Recent analysis of the eighth-century Lorsch manuscript has revealed a prescription which would have terminated an early pregnancy.[6] Some of the more academic authorities did have a practical bent – Soranus recommended gentle techniques for necessary abortions – medicine, pessaries, massage and warm baths – rather than surgical interference which might well, then, be more dangerous than letting the pregnancy run full term.[7] However, where sensible, that is still approvable, remedies are found in a text, the same source is likely within a short space to recommend equally fervently some totally magic remedy which could only ever have worked by the placebo effect. Reading *The Trotula* (see below, Chapter 7) the texts seem a better guide to what women were suffering from and trying to cure than to treatments of any value.

It is clear that the physiology of the human body was only a little understood, both in general across the sexes and with regard to specific genital differences. Only men could have the institutional training, and gain the qualifications, to make them physicians or surgeons. Women, however, made up the bulk of the natural caring or nursing force, in their own homes and institutionally. Some of them became expert and famous (or to authority's eye, notorious). This situation meant that from the patient's point of view anything curable by amateur attention was likely to be nursed by women in the family, anything needing unqualified but effective experience could be coped with by women known as specialists in their communities, such as midwives, and anything needing expert consultation would need a medical man. Only the wealthy elite could afford expert attention, unless charity offered it more widely. In addition to all these obstacles, a woman's conditioned modesty may have made her disinclined to take her symptoms to a man. The outcome was surely that comparatively few of Europe's women, even fewer than of Europe's men, had expert medical attention, and that for even fewer would it be much good. No wonder miracle healing by Christian saints of both sexes was so popular.

Misogynistic Theories Formulated within the Period

At the start of the period the forces of misogyny were already strong. The Greeks' legacy left the female as body or matter as against the male soul or form. The Judaic tradition, taken up by the Christian church, cast woman as the credulous Eve, easily misled, and in need of purification. Significantly, Leviticus 12:2–5 says after childbirth the mother of a son was considered unclean for 7 days and not purified for another 33, but the mother of a daughter remained unclean for 2 weeks and was not purified for another 66 days. Bede's *History* shows us that the uncleanness of the menstruating woman (in Leviticus 15) bothered the Italian-born St Augustine of Canterbury, faced with teaching the 'rude English' around 600, though Gregory the Great took a more tolerant view of her presence in church, while valuing it if she was sensitive enough to abstain from attending. In Roman literature, satire was often at women's expense, and the courage of the 'manly' woman was admired, not as the phenomenon of a brave woman but as a sort of honorary man, an attitude of mind which lasted right through the middle ages. Christian thinkers were not on the whole much better disposed to women. Clark cites Chrysostom *On Virginity*: 'suppose a husband is moderate, but his wife is wicked, critical, garrulous, extravagant – the usual fault of women.'[8]

   This multiple legacy continued to prevail because of the dominance of the written sources in the Latin-educated west. Men read Ovid and Juvenal, if only in selected collections of abstracted extracts. Christian scholars obviously read the Bible, where Proverbs furnished warnings about the pitfalls women presented to men to set against the favourable picture cited earlier. Ecclesiastical writers saw woman as a dangerous temptress, blaming her for tempting them to stray from high standards. Tertullian (c.160–225), viewing women in this light, felt they should suppress their attractiveness to minimize the danger to men; thus he berated such enhancements as cosmetics and hair dye. Jerome (c.342–420), though he had some sympathies for women, realized a wife was a hindrance to the study of philosophy, as later writers saw the concubine and her children as a distraction to the priest. By the twelfth century there was a veritable outpouring of misogynistic writing, of which the most famous is probably the third part of the *De Amore* (c.1185) of Andreas Capellanus, condemning love. Andreas blamed women for a variety of sins of varying degrees of seriousness – avarice, greed and guzzling, envy and slander, fickleness and disloyalty, disobedience, pride and vainglory, lying, drunkenness, lustfulness and evil disposition, mixed with merely being talkative and telling secrets.

Jokes against women were popular in medieval Latin writing (which women rarely read so rarely responded to) and among readers and writers who were, increasingly from the mid-eleventh century and intermittently before, supposed to be celibate and unfamiliar with women. Some, therefore, traded women jokes like adolescent boys in single-sex schools, and others, seeking refuge from women as the fearsome temptresses they had been taught to believe them to be, wore out their fear of the unknown by joking about it. Much is conveyed in a jesting tone which makes it difficult to interpret. From the contemporary woman's viewpoint the prevalent laws and customs that constrained her freedom of movement were more serious than the misogynistic literature that cast her down, but both, of course, illustrate the predominant attitude of mind which put women in an inferior place. It was not wholly deliberate misogyny. Women were not downtrodden, despised, belittled and constrained out of conscious contempt or cruelty. It was just not generally imagined that they could play any other role. It was not so much a case of keeping them out of particular professions or positions, but of never considering inviting them in. From this was born fairly naturally a suspicion of any who tried to batter their way in, and then an excluding tendency did follow.

The Literary Treatment of Women

Examining the literary treatment of women is always an enjoyable exercise, but it is inevitably somewhat indecisive since we never know how much the representation is descriptive, nostalgic, forward looking, wishful think-ing, poking fun, or deliberately exaggerating the worst scenario. Literature was not set down to be a historical source, and we must be wary of treating it as one. Nevertheless, it should not be ignored. The literature of Europe before 1200 includes Latin works widely disseminated and eventually trans-lated into the vernacular, of which Boethius' *Consolation of Philosophy* was a major influence, and vernacular material often of much earlier compos-ition than the earliest written forms. The vernacular literature represents what was enjoyed by most people, either as illiterate hearers of it, or as lit-erate readers (always, in this period, a minority). Most of this literature is of anonymous composition and undoubtedly passed through many tellings before reaching the comparatively fixed form of written text. There are some works from known authors, a few of whom are known to have been women, but the vast majority must be assumed male creations, education being more widespread among men. The material for consideration includes sagas from Norway and Iceland, written down in the thirteenth century but clearly from earlier traditions, the great German *Nibelungenlied*, dating from c.1195–1205 but embracing long-enjoyed episodes and char-acters, the Old English poem *Beowulf* and elegiac and gnomic poems such as that now entitled 'The Wife's Lament', the Welsh wooing of the Giant's Daughter *Culhwch and Olwen* (c.1100), Irish sagas, especially from the Ulster cycle where Cú Chulainn falls in and out of love with many women, Spain's twelfth-century *Poema del Cid*, and the French romances of the twelfth century, including the works of Chrétien de Troyes from c.1170–90. Ireland boasts several women poets, including the queen Gormflaith (c.870–947) and Ullach 'Arrogant' (d 934), and southern France pro-duced a score of named but obscure trobairitz c.1150–1250, but the highest stature poetess of the period must be Marie de France (fl. 1160–90) whose twelve *Lais* tell Celtic stories in Anglo-Norman (see below, Chapter 7).

Much of this early literature was composed for a male audience. The hall companions feasting in Heorot in *Beowulf* line 1067 may be equated with the kind of audience the epic itself was performed to entertain. This was storytelling strung together to be heard at an assembly, not writing to be read privately by individuals. The assembly was likelier to be all male – the followers of a warrior chief, or courtiers of an aristocrat, even, to Alcuin's disapproval, monks – than all female or mixed. However, Cú Chulainn's charioteer Loeg sings that he saw musicians in the house playing for the women, so it is likely they listened to minstrels' words sometimes. Given the predominant milieu, it is not surprising that much of the vernacular oral entertainment consists of adventurous, roving, fighting material.

Perhaps it is surprising how much women enter this literature at all. Sometimes their role is fairly passive, as with Waltheow, Hrothgar's queen, in *Beowulf*, hosting her husband's court banquets and bearing children to forward the dynasty. Sometimes the wives are more fractious, like the wives of Loegure, Conall and Cú Chulainn, striving for primacy in the 'Feast of Bricriu'. Some women are represented as dangerous to individual men, diverting them from their intentions with long-term consequences. In *Njal's Saga*, Hrutr, engaged to Unnr, fell into dalliance with queen Gunnhildr of Norway, who put a curse on him when he returned to Iceland to marry Unnr. A frequent motif is the woman as inciter of vengeance, the obvious example here being Kriemhild in *Nibelungenlied*. Kriemhild is also an illustration of the common origins of varied versions of tales in different literatures. In *Nibelungenlied* she is sister of Gunther of Burgundy, and marries Siegfried, and after his death Etzel or Attila, the king of the Huns. In Icelandic saga, the sister of Gundaharius of Burgundy, wife successively to Siegfried, Attila and Eormenric the Ostrogoth, is called Gudrun. (Attila is chronicled as dying at his marriage to a Germanic wife Ildico in 453.) This heroine's story may have begun in lost fifth- and sixth-century Germanic lays about the fall of the ruling house of Burgundy. The oldest existing version is the Eddic poem *Atlakvida*, recomposed in Norway in the late ninth century.

There is often a hardness about these women in literature. Gudrun murdered her two sons by her own hands in revenge against her husband Atli who had killed her two brothers, and fed him the corpses before killing him. Impregnating women, inside or outside marriage, was often presented more as a conquest than a courtship, indicating that women were there for men's use. Occasionally, however, softer feelings, including the suffered hurts of unrequited love, come through – otherworldly Fand, returning Cú Chulainn to his wife Emer, says 'Pity the woman who loves a man/when no love invites her./ Better for her to fly from love/if, unloved, love bites her'.[9] Castelloza anguishes over her lover preferring a better born lady. Married love is acknowledged in the gnomic verses from the Old English Exeter book, singing of the Frisian wife's welcome of her husband home from the sea with his salt-stained laundry, giving him 'what his love bids'. Not surprisingly a common theme is the divided loyalty of a woman, such as Sigrun, to her birth-kin and to her husband, termed by Jesch 'the classic dilemma of woman in a heroic society'.[10]

It would be wrong to say the early literature is less sophisticated than the later, for it has complexities of structure, and the hearer/reader was evidently interested in the claims of kin by birth and marriage constraining the actions of individuals. The later literature, however, is of a type more familiar to the modern reader, especially if later medieval literature is kept in mind as a bridge. Here, for example, we find much more ambivalence about adultery, presumably reflecting the tensions between more demanding church teaching and natural temptations. Iseult, from Thomas Beroult's twelfth-century treatment, is a healer and admired as an ideal lover, but reviled by some for unfaithfulness. Chrétien de Troyes' Guinevere, first adulterously linked to Lancelot in the *Chevalier de la Charrete*, is a more complex mixture of unfaithful wife and devoted lover. There may be moral excuse for Tristan and Iseult because they are the victims of a potion and cannot help themselves falling in love. Guinevere selects an adulterous path. Are these characters simply the outcome of male clerics fantasising about women? Or are they early explorations of the theme of sexually transgressing queens which flourished into the fourteenth century when, as Peggy McCracken argues in *The Romance of Adultery: Queenship and Sexual Transgression in Old French Literature* (1998), reality caught up with fiction?

3

THE PRACTICAL SITUATION: WOMEN'S FUNCTION IN RURAL COMMUNITIES

Given the variety of agricultural conditions in western Europe, and the paucity and uneven provenance of source material from before 1200, it is a challenge to gather together and make orderly what can be found about the practicalities of women's lives in rural communities, the ones in which most women lived. Over the seven centuries there were many changes, with population growth and expansion of cultivation being major phenomena. These changes had consequences for women but they are not spelled out at all in the sources, and rarely receive consideration from historians. The population of Europe has been roughly estimated at 27.5 million in 500, falling to 18 million with the mid-seventh-century plagues. A period of population growth had begun by the tenth century and by 1000 CE approximations for France and Italy are 5 million each, with 3 million in Germany and 2 million in the British Isles. The population then continued rising and from 1050 to 1200 there was clearly pressure to expand settlement and cultivation to the limits of viable agriculture and animal husbandry. Pasture was ploughed up, forests felled, marshes dyked and whole new settlements created for inhabitants moved en bloc to them. Better understanding led to more three-field rotation and experiment with new crops such as legumes and there seems to have been a rise in productivity between the ninth and twelfth centuries, but nothing staved off the land starvation and its consequences were beginning to be noticeable by the end of the period. It is usually considered that about 90 per cent of the European population lived in the countryside, so this chapter is reviewing a huge number of women who were the bedrock of the whole subject. En masse, they were constantly the bearers and nurturers of the next generation.

What did rural women do in and for this period, and what did it do for them? The variety of climatic and geological conditions, settlements, and ways of exploiting natural resources over the continent was huge and unevenly distributed. Lombardy had wider variations of elevation, climate, soil and vegetation than the whole of Germany. In the Iberian peninsula, Compostela had 213 centimetres of rain a year and Barcelona about 10. The mixed races inhabiting what were to become politically identifiable countries such as France and Germany must in this chapter be viewed differently as occupants of areas too wet for vines and cereals (mountain areas and the Atlantic seaboard), areas very dry in summer, needing irrigation, and sometimes, perversely, drainage, as when upland snows melted and rushed down (the Mediterranean zone), and areas irregularly wet (elsewhere). Across highland and lowland zones land was variously exploitable as pasture land, arable plains, vineyards, woodlands. Human effort to wrest subsistence and, above this, a profitable living from land could do nothing to influence climate, but it could learn from experience to work with rather than against normal conditions, and further achieve some amelioration of circumstance by drainage or irrigation. The lie of the land could not be altered, but its use could be apportioned practically, using the higher ground for pasture and the lower ground for cereal crops and the lushest for meadow, and moving animals seasonally.

Alongside cultivation practices dictated by conditions, there was more deliberate human design of estate organization. The Roman empire had been Europe's first common market, large and powerful enough to organize suitable specializations and massive movements of products (particularly corn) within its territory. This facility of international exchange collapsed with the political fall of the Empire, and during our period long-distance trading was less regular and had to be re-evolved as opportunity arose. The Roman villa system provided in some areas continuity of estate exploitation and ancestry for some medieval manors. The manor is a portmanteau word for a very widespread institutional arrangement for estate management, best known from the recorded estates of ecclesiastics, particularly Benedictine monasteries, and essentially characterized by the coexistence of land exploited entirely for the landlord's benefit (his demesne) and land sublet by him to tenants of varying status, who worked on their tenancies and, by their labour services, rents in kind and eventually increasingly rents in cash, provided or paid for the labour on the lord's demesne. These characteristics were widespread. From Italy and eastern Gaul and south and central Germany seigniorial estate management spread to England and Denmark and was copied to some extent east of the Elbe, but it did not spread to Friesland or Norway or much in Sweden. The polyptych of St Germain-des-Prés from near Paris is the most famous of the continental surveys, showing peasant holdings and renders on its estates c.820. Documentation is rare between about 900 and about 1150, but then manorial customs began being set down in greater quantity. The relative proportions of demesne and tenant land were constantly changing on and between manors. Even before 1200 there was quite sophisticated realization of benefits from flexibility in arrangements and innovations in techniques. Usually innovation came from the landlords, as only they were empowered to effect it, but the toil to carry out projects came from the peasantry, nowhere more so than in the vast amounts of land reclaimed from forest and fen before 1200.

Though the terminology differs and is itself imprecise – the hide in Anglo-Saxon England, the *hof* or *hufe* in Germany, the *mansus* or *masure* in Italy and France – there was a common agricultural practice of defining a peasant farming unit and the dues arising from it. The unit had its origin in arable production, being the amount of land a plough could manage in a year. Holdings were being divided, even before 800, hence the half and quarter *mansi* at St Germain-des-Prés, and a sort of part-way stage is visible where the nominally unitary farm was being held jointly by two or three families. Fragmentation destroys viable units, and towards the end of the period there was more passing of the tenement to one son. Another trend was for labour services to be commuted into money rents but not necessarily irreversibly. Land newly brought into cultivation was usually available on lease rather than being integrated into the old service rent economy, and this made it particularly valuable for settling younger sons. Daughters' dowries might be a drain on family resources, and widows had to be provided for. Not all land was part of a manor; some peasants farmed small allods (land with no superior landlord) which can be inferred from documentation before 1100 and becomes clearer thereafter (but allods are not a feature in England).

In analysing documentary sources and considering archaeology and aerial photography, historians of economic development have been largely oblivious to gender. The politics of estate management and/or village community decision taking may be assumed to have been men's business, the heavy agricultural work obviously needed husbandmen, and policing the rural community was not women's work. Rural women were very much unrecorded and their normal activity even more unremarked. But they were everywhere, and must have been active: local communities could not afford drones. In fact, by piecing together scattered evidence we can become quite well informed about their activities.

Women's Work in Arable Economies

The polyptych of St Germain-des-Prés gives insight into peasant households in a well-populated zone where arable was practised on light soils. Entries survive for 1742 tenurial units, counting over 4000 males and over 3000 females, and it is assumed the listed people in each unit were coresidential. They are generally identified as man, wife and children, each parent carefully classified. Many families in these samples were cross-class marriages: a slave married to a *colona*; a slave and his *lida* wife, a *lidus* and his *colona* wife; a *colonus* married to a free woman.[1] Slaves were at the bottom of the social heap and were diminishing as a proportion of the overall population; by the late sixth century Merovingian lords had encouraged intermarriage among their free and servile dependents by offering emancipating sweeteners to freewomen marrying slaves. The difference between slaves and the people immediately above them shrank through movement in both directions. Christianity frowned on the enslavement of Christians but the church's moral distaste did not stop slaves being recorded on St Germain's and other monastic estates.

At St Germain, a couple was sometimes described as holding half or a quarter of a farm (*mansus*) but sometimes two or three families were described in one entry as holding one farm (between them). The survey gives the area of their holdings and lists the services due for them. Sample entries have been published in translation, though disconcertingly with differences of detail and punctuation derived from different reading of the original text. However, these differences do not greatly affect the total burden due from the farming couples. Three families in Neuillay, having between them a *mansus* with arable and meadow, owed a mixture of services – carting, manure spreading, fencing and ploughing and renders in kind, of sheep, hens, eggs, and wood products, planks, shingles, staves, and so on. They also paid 4 denarii each in head tax, a mark of unfree status. Standard assessments of work and produce were due for a *mansus* or fraction thereof. There is no place in the tenancy entry for indication of what areas of activity on the holding fell respectively to husband and wife. But there is a genderizing of work in the class-grouped entries for a particular place. At Neuillay the female slaves kept the chickens and made cloth if supplied with wool.[2] It would appear a fair assumption that the womenfolk kept the hens in other classes too – hens and eggs feature in the dues in kind. As for making cloth, regulations (*De Villis*) attributed to either Charlemagne or his son Louis the Pious refer to women's workshops (*gynaeca*) on the royal estates, instructing the stewards to provide them with raw materials at due times – linen, wool, woad, vermilion, madder, wool combs, teasels, soap, oil and vessels (containers) and any other small items necessary for the work. The list of provided items tells us the women saw the process through from combing the raw wool to brushing up the nap and dyeing the cloth. The king was evidently something of a 'benevolent employer', like later model factory industrialists mixing a concern for his workforce with the assumption that safe and happy workers are more productive. He instructed that the women's workshops were to be well ordered, with houses, heated rooms and cottages, and enclosed by good fences and strong doors, but all this was for a purpose: 'so that they may do our work well'. Weaving labour could not be demanded of free women. Thus we see virtually women's factories on royal and ecclesiastical estates in northern France in the early ninth century, and they lasted until the twelfth, weaving textiles and making clothing from the fabric. The workers were housed and fed but not waged. In Welsh law, a female slave's value was double if she sewed.

Herlihy drew on the St Germain survey to arrive at some conclusions about family size and resources. Holdings under 5 *bunaria* (each of c.120 ares) averaged under five members, holdings over 12 *bunaria* averaged over eight members. Only 26 women were identified as grandmothers and only two grandchildren were definitely so identified, therefore the family units were not here of the stem type. Where two or three families are listed on the one farm they seem to be the same active generation and some of the heads may be brothers or brothers-in-law as is sometimes stated. Of the 1401 households with male heads 43 per cent had more than one male head, so this was a common pattern and not an aberration.[3] At Coudray-sur-Seine the *colonus* couple Edimius and Electa shared a farm with another *colonus*, Frothardus, who is described as having his mother with him, apparently a rural widow living under her son's headship. Domesday Book, from England in 1086, treated mothers with similar anonymity: thus in Bedfordshire, in Stodden hundred, one Thorgot and his mother held half a hide (the Domesday hide being 120 acres) from King William in an unidentified place, assessed as one ploughland, with one plough, one villein and two bordars and woodland measured by pig capacity at four pigs. The value of this little holding was 12s in 1066 and 10s in 1086, and in 1066 it had been held by Thorgot's father, a thegn of King Edward. A 3-virgate holding at Wymington held by five brothers with their mother, all unnamed, is described as the mother's *dos*. Domesday Book and the St Germain survey were not attempting to identify the same ranks of tenantry, however. The named *coloni* and *lidi* and slaves at St Germain were the level of people anonymously recorded as villeins, bordars, cottars and (much more rarely) slaves in Domesday Book. The St Germain survey tells us the names of man, wife and children on the farm units so we can count them directly. Domesday's villeins and bordars have to be multiplied by an estimate of family/household size to arrive at an estate population figure, and the recommended multipliers have varied from 3.5 to 5. The named levels of society in Domesday Book are the crown's tenants in chief (including institutional ecclesiastical lords such as the abbeys of Westminster and Peterborough) and any immediate subtenants between those tenants and the basic villeins. Domesday Book is much less gender specific than the polyptych, but of course it is on a much greater scale. One could hardly expect an eleventh-century survey covering most of England to name every villein, bordar and serf and his wife and children: it would have required a database of about 2.5 million names. Because its focus is on the social level above the St Germain surveys, Domesday Book does not tell us the terms of labour service or rent owed by the agricultural tenants, but other sources from England do. Pre-Conquest surveys from Hurstbourne Priors, Hampshire, variously attributed to dates between 900 and 1050, and from Tidenham, Gloucestershire, attributed to c.1060, class the tenants but do not name them. Twelfth-century surveys from the monastery at Burton-on-Trent identify the villeins, cottars and rent-paying tenants and do throw up some pre-1200 statements about rural women. At Burton, in the teens of the century, the wife of Aldeon had to reap for one day. One Edeva, sister of Bruning, held a croft and one acre of inland on which she lived. Two women were identified only by their sons: the mother of Stainulf, who had one dwelling for 12d, and the mother of Richard the monk, simply described as living in the inland. A survey of Elton Huntingdonshire, a manor of the abbey of Ramsey, made in the reign of Henry II, includes an identification of a widow Gisla holding a virgate of land (about 30 acres) for 6s and by ploughing 6 acres (but of course she could have paid a man to do it). Gisla had apparently been in this situation since the time of Henry I, so over 20 years at least. The Boldon survey of 1183 from the bishopric of Durham has an entry identifying one Watling with Sama his wife holding 4 bovates (the bovate being about 13 acres) and rendering half a mark (the mark being 13s 4d).[4] Other holders are either named or occupationally described – the smith, the cottars, and so on – but with no reference to wives, so one wonders what was special about Sama: had she brought land to the marriage?

Women's Work in Pastoral Economies

All the estates mentioned so far were sites where a mixture of arable and animal husbandry was practised. This was a good symbiosis since the animals manured the ground when 'folded'. But there were areas where arable was so dominant that there were hardly any animals beyond the necessary ploughteams (for most of the period up to 1200 in the heavy soils of northern Europe most commonly teams were 8 oxen), and other areas where the ground was too high or uneven for arable cropping and where the economy was pastoral. For example, only 3 per cent of Norway's land is arable. Pastoral farming very commonly practised transhumance on a large scale, especially in the Iberian and Italian peninsulas. Here regulations were devised to control flock movement over long distances to and from mountain pastures. Animals were moved upland on to summer pastures and brought down again for winter, which in north-west Europe they had to spend indoors in stalls. It is generally considered that pastoral economies offer more opportunities to women, as milkers of cows, sheep and goats, as makers of butter and cheese, and as spinners of wool. Dairymaids are mentioned in the English Domesday Book, but the best illustration of women working in an early pastoral economy comes from Iceland, where Jochens says women and indeed whole families lived three or four months in the summer in upland cottages or shielings, milking the animals in the high pastures. Cows were milked there in the pasture, but sheep were milked in pens after being rounded up by the male shepherd. Up at the shieling the milk would be separated into curds and whey, but the cheese and butter production took place back at the main farm. This could not be managed where the home farm and the summer pasture were long distances apart.

Icelandic women in fact played an unusually important part in the whole country's economy. Homespun woollen cloth (*vadmal*) was essential for clothing, bedding, even sails and packaging, and indeed so vital to the economy that as silver became scarce the amount of homespun which could be bought for an ounce of silver passed into the monetary system as the law ounce of 6 ells. At the end of the eleventh century the first Icelandic property assessment, drawn up for tithing purposes, used the homespun unit. Standardizing measurements was a problem and the Althing in 1200 regulated the length of the ell and the cloth's width at 2 ells (1 yard). Women were involved in achieving these standards as they set up the looms and controlled the selvedges and tightening of the weave. The looms used were warp-weighted standing looms which were placed against a wall for use, but could be taken down. Weaving this way was a solitary occupation and was done by women in the home. One wonders how they ever had enough light in the homes of the period. (While the vertical loom was the norm, women were the weavers, but the introduction of the horizontal loom in Flanders in the twelfth century began the male takeover of the craft.) After being woven, homespun cloth could be used at once, but a better finish was achieved if the cloth was fulled and dyed. The Icelandic women's home-spun, produced in excess of family needs, created a valuable income to add to the mainly animal husbandry economy of that country. Hay was grown for winter fodder, and a little barley for human consumption. Women raked and turned grass as the men cut it, and they collected berries and the more accessible birds' eggs – men scaled the cliffs for eggs harder to reach. In Iceland neither sex could cope with farm life without the help of the other, married or hired. Law expected the woman to manage every-thing within the threshold, and the man everything outside. Housework was the only option for landless women, who had to enter service in a richer or larger household: in the smaller ones housewives had to manage with less or no help.[5] This underlines that most countrywomen every-where were not employed specialists such as dairymaids but were busy as farmers' wives with multiple skills, helping at lambing, and hand rearing sickly lambs and piglets, keeping a few hens, turning out to weed or reap as required, gardening, and gathering wild fruits and nuts. From the writ-ings of Alexander Neckham from the late twelfth century (a man familiar with England and France) comes a picture of the serving maid, who was expected to care for the hens, geese, lambs and calves, handle whey and curds, and feed the dogs. In ninth-century Russian graves scythes are identified with males and sickles with females, but whether this tells us anything about western practice is uncertain. Women ground grain while handmills were in widespread use. They fed their families a plain diet of soups and potages – a sort of porridge, the Italian polenta, and bread usu-ally made of inferior grains to wheat. Bread was not staple food in Iceland, where grains were short and what was available was consumed in potage or gruel. Famine was ever near, and the population was malnourished.

Women on the Manor

Because written records from great monastic estates dominate the early source material for rural life, the manor tends to be seen as the typical organization in the rural economy. The manorial unit was indeed long lived and widespread, but it was not standard in size or practices. Moreover, there were independent, freely held, or allodial, farms in many villages, and the independent agricultural families tended to be larger. Duby contrasts St Germain-des-Prés peasant tenant families consisting of just one married couple with children, with the situation on a *mansus* of about 68 acres of arable recently given to the abbey at Rônel, which at the time of the survey was still being farmed by the donor's descendants, amounting to 20 individuals, two brothers and their wives with three and five children respectively, a sister with six children, and an unmarried sister.[6]

For manorial tenants the relationship with the lord, both for free peasant tenantry and for bondtenants, brought extra constraints. The labour services and rents in kind have been shown already in the section on the arable economy, also there was obligatory use of monopolies such as the lord's mill or bakehouse/oven. The bringing into cultivation of new land not burdened with dues and services worked towards the lessening of existing obligations since lords had to compete to some extent with the attractive new opportunities. Labour services were lighter in Italy and southern France and heavier in northern Europe, but generally they were less burdensome in the twelfth century than they had been in the ninth. Commutation of labour services into money rents had freed up the tenants, but rents in kind were not as frequently commuted into money before the end of the twelfth century.

The manorial framework affected women in three areas: their work, their inheritance and landowning position, and their personal freedom. Manorial obligations bound them to weigh in with the required agricultural work and to do specific tasks of their own. The following examples are all taken from Duby.[7] At Friemersheim at the end of the ninth century the obligations on the *mansi* specified that when dayworks were being performed, the wife must bind the sheaves and pile them up in five stacks, being allowed four sheaves herself. St Germain's weaving requirements have already been illustrated, and twelfth-century ordinances from Münchweier say the *mansus* holder's wife must come to the monastery and receive from the provost a load of wool or prepared flax and make from it a linen or woollen cloth 7 ells long and 3 wide; she was given one *émine* of wine and a loaf at the start and two loaves when she returned with the cloth. In terms of inheritance and landowning, the manor interfered with what the peasant family might have wished, imposing conditions generally for the benefit of the lord and his staff. Around 1160 the Cistercians of La Ferté recorded that a piece of land let for 20 sous per year must not be given as a dowry to daughters. In terms of personal freedom, the manorial tie could be very restricting. In 1144 Louis VII of France and the abbot of Chartres simply exchanged two female serfs. In 1158, a redefinition of obligations on dependants of the manors of Efferen and Fischenich ordered the steward to take the best animal, or best of a man's clothes if he had no animal, and 6 deniers on the death of a man, and similarly the *schultheiss* to take her best garment and 6 deniers on the death of a woman. Both sexes had to pay 6 deniers for permission to marry. In 1176 at Haversford, a manor of the abbey of Corvey, the marriage of girls was commonly called *beddemunt*. Both sexes owed chevage (a poll tax), as at the manor of Zissen where it was 6 deniers according to a record dating from after 1163. In the later part of our period the lords were acquiring more jurisdictional powers over their dependants.

Rural Women in the Home

The classic rural settlement was the village, with a nucleus of clustered homes and gardens surrounded by arable fields worked in rotation and further ringed by wasteland and woodland which was in common use but often allocated according to the arable share. If the village coincided with a single manor there was just one community. But often things were less simple – a village had more than one manor, or parts of more than one manor in it, with different lords and their officials exacting seigniorial dues. Marrying an 'outsider', another lord's dependant, added to the complexities and was more likely to occur where different lords' properties were mixed up in one geographical location. Topographically village shapes varied, from being strung along roads to being ring-fenced around a green or pond. There were villages where the lord's demesne was an enclosed bloc, and villages where it was scattered in strips intermingled with those of the tenants. (The tendency was for the lords to move towards the first practice where they could.) There were villages where the tenants' strips occurred in the same order in different fields, giving them consistently the same neighbours; in origin these seem to have been laid out following the movement of the sun and are known by the Swedish term *solskifte*. Other villages had no such order. Still others had more consolidated tenant holdings, and there was the radial type where the holding ran from the house in the village centre out continuously to the edge of the cultivation – this is the *waldhufendorf* found in Germany and also in France. Then there were 'daughter villages' – the thorps of Denmark and the English Danelaw – secondary settlements sprung off from successful ones, and of course there were hamlets of just two or three households and even solitary farms. All of these arrangements had consequences for the women who lived in them, although this was not the focus of any contemporary attention and we have to think imaginatively to realize them. In the sizeable nucleated settlement women would have other women around them and activities such as fetching water, laundering in streams, and berry picking could easily become socializing experiences, leading to meeting others and engaging in conversation and co-operation. An activity like home brewing, where the product had a limited shelf-life but was best made in some quantity, could be made into a sales product if there were potential purchasers around. The woman in the hamlet had a more constrained circle of associates and opportunities. Those dwelling in isolated farmsteads had to be more self-reliant. The single woman who came into tenancy of a holding either as heiress or widow would probably have been better able to cope in the heart of a village community with more male assistance to hand and to hire. Though women tended to stay 'at home' more than men – it was the men who roved a-viking and the men who left the villages to labour in the towns in the off-peak seasons of the agricultural year – some women were more uprooted than others. Most women married – about 90 per cent. Most of these moved to join their husbands' establishment, perhaps within the same village, perhaps not. How long a woman lived in a place would affect her integration into the community. Some must have accompanied husbands attracted to new enterprises – recruited by locators for new developments east of the Elbe in the later twelfth century, or directed willy-nilly by overlords to new territory. Flemings were pioneering movers into Germany; William Rufus transplanted peasants to the Carlisle region in the late eleventh century and Henry II moved settlers into Pembrokeshire in the late twelfth. The move we can be most sure of was the colonization of Iceland between c.870 and c.930, where 10–20,000 Scandinavians are thought to have been involved, and with no native inhabitants there to marry with, incomers of both sexes were essential in the first generations. However, it is generally agreed that frontier settlement attracts male pioneers disproportionately, and thus creates zones short of women.

Archaeology tells us that most habitations were small. Early Irish house sites were only 6–7 metres across, amounting to 300–400 square feet for a family of five or six. There might be only a single room, with a hearth in the middle, with a cooking pot suspended on a chain, and beds round the windowless walls. To have two rooms was luxurious. The law tracts of the seventh and eighth centuries suggest that normally three generations lived together and the women span, wove and cooked. At Deer Park Farms (County Antrim), in use from the seventh to tenth centuries, three or four houses at a time were in use within a 25-metre enclosure, and these were for high-status inhabitants who could use clients and tenants to dig their ditches and pile up their banking. The conditions these lesser folk lived in are lost. According to a legal tract, household goods comprised such things as a griddle, sieve, kneading trough, cooking pot, cups, dishes, beetle, bucket, scale and pillows. A wife would bring cattle, clothing, pots and pans to the marriage, a husband ploughshares and oxgoads. She could expect hard work in the farmyard and house. Bitel describes every wife in early Ireland's cattle-based economy as a milker, churner and cheesemaker (or if upper class, manager of her dairymaids), producing for home consumption. They also penned the piglets and calves, feeding and fattening them, but not herding them further afield, which was men's work. The Irish women made cloth and clothing right through from the raw wool and flax, combing and spinning the wool, dyeing the yarn, and weaving with it. Flax they rippled, retted and washed before hackling or combing it, dyeing it and making thread. An eighth-century legal tract goes into great detail over cloth production and equipment.[8] As in Iceland, the weaving took place in the house. Textile working offered flexibility to home workers since it could always be left and resumed if more urgent tasks intervened. On the continent the long house, around 30 metres in length, was rectangular or boat-shaped, and made of wood, turf or wattle with a central raised hearth. Some of the long farmhouses had in effect a transverse passage dividing the animal end from the human, in which part would be a hearth and possibly a partitioned room. Smoke from these hearths simply found its way out of a hole in the roof.

At Ribblehead in north Yorkshire a Viking Age farmstead had three buildings all with paved entrances from a farmyard. The main farmhouse was roughly 19 metres long and 4 metres wide, with doorways in the two short sides, and it is thought likely that it had a partition in the middle. There are traces of the kerb of a wall bench. The second building was roughly rectangular, 6 metres by 3.5 metres, with one doorway. There seems to have been an oven or kiln in the corner opposite the door. A rotary quern, the oven/kiln and butchered adult animal bones suggest this was the kitchen. A third building, further away, is another rectangular one, 9 metres by 5 metres, with one paved doorway. There was a sandstone hearth in the middle, and as two slipper-shaped stones were found there, this is thought to be a workshop, possibly a smithy. All three structures would have had ridged roofs, thatched or turved. A small (50 millimetre) clapper bell, possibly a cowbell, and part of a horsebit, knife blades and a socketed spearhead and lathe-turned stone spindle-whorl were found on site, and four coins, of which two certainly and probably a third came from the third quarter of the ninth century, provide, from their placing, a date for the start of the structure. This comes from the period when the Danish Great Army began settling in the Danelaw territory and it is not possible to identify the site as definitely Viking or Anglo-Saxon, but this is of no relevance to us, as we can accept it as a working farmstead of c.865. Ribblehead is a high site 340 metres above sea level but in the pass between Wensleydale and the Lune valley. It is therefore at once both 'remote' and on a routeway. The women living there must have had a limited field of action and life style. Housework in such conditions was obviously small scale, but Ribblehead's inhabitants are lamented for their fastidiousness which has left little domestic debris for archaeological analysis.[9] Slopping out the cattle byres was men's work, if the Icelandic sources speak typically.

Icelandic literary evidence suggests the existence of specialist pantries and curd rooms and Ribblehead's food preparation building, if such it was, was a specialist area. Bathing and hairwashing feature in Icelandic terminology and sagas. The country's hot springs and warm streams were advantageous for both laundering and bathing, and hygiene in Iceland seems to have been well advanced for the time.

The Life Cycle of Rural Women

Having observed the countrywoman meeting the demands put on the farming wife and family in different types of agricultural economy and circumstance over the centuries, wherever the disjointed sources give us access to her, it seems attractive to terminate this discussion with a review of her life cycle, recapitulating in a revised order the aspects of her life previously treated in other contexts.

Life expectancy at this period was about 30–35 years at birth for both sexes; by around 20 a man could hope to live about another 25 years, but a woman's average expectation was then only 17 years. Those who made it to 40 might manage another 15 to 20 years. Childbirth and its complications may have taken 10–15 per cent of women's lives. At birth, the girl children of the rural poor seem to have been at least at more risk of infanticide than their brothers. Naturally around 105 boys are born for each 100 girls, and presumably roughly the same proportions were born in these centuries, since abortion would be random as to the (unknown) sex of the foetus. Were as many girls allowed to live? The sex ratio among the serfs on the estates of St Victor of Marseilles in 813–14 was 102, indicating no sign of female infanticide there. But Emily Coleman noted that the sex ratio on the St Germain-des-Prés estates varied from 110.3 to 252.9 and averaged 135; at 135, about a third of the girls born were being lost. Coleman suggested that the surge in population growth in the eleventh century might have been partly promoted by then allowing more of the girls to survive. Herlihy, however, argued for a less lurid explanation of the St Germain imbalance: that some men were recorded twice, once with their wives and children on the farm where they resided, and the other time alone, all that was necessary for identifying their responsibility for some particular rent. Excluding the 616 solitary men, and 44 solitary women in the record, who are only known as rent payers and might have family listed elsewhere (or not at all because these people were not personally manorial dependants) brings the sex ratio down to 119, still high but not unknown in other times and places. Analysing the records, the sex ratio at St Germain is found to be higher for children, at 141 (but 20 per cent of the children listed are not identified by sex at all); it is higher still at 159 for the intermediate *lidi* class of adults, and highest of all at 266 for the slaves. Some of the 'missing' women from the *lidi* and serfs are likely to have been attached as unidentified residents at the manor house. (Herlihy points out that on a manor house belonging to the monastery of Farfa c.800 the women servants outnumbered the men by 73 to 23, so this is not an unlikely assumption.) Among the children, the girls are also the more likely to have been removed from their homes into service. Right into the eleventh and twelfth centuries lords recruited first slaves and then children of their hutted dependants as live-in domestics.[10] We would like to believe Herlihy's explanation for the imbalance of the sexes on St Germain estates but there cannot be a complete removal of suspicion that either more girls were deliberately abandoned by exposure, or that in their early years more girls were neglected, possibly through comparative malnutrition if preferential treatment was given to their brothers when food was short. Some skeletons show shrinkage in height in greater percentage in females than males, a sign of chronic malnutrition. Thus by the time they died some women's shrinkage suggests that they more than men went chronically short of food, and we do not know how young this gender-selective starvation set in. Mothers tend sacrificially to go hungry to feed children and husbands, but did they also starve daughters? In pagan Scandinavia a newborn had to be shown to and accepted by its father for it to be allowed to live, and infanticide of the unaccepted by exposure or abandonment was lawful. Christian laws against infanticide took time to be made effective.

Where a girl lived in the parental home we can visualize her life with the aid of a few supplied facts. At Coudray-sur-Seine, for example, a *colonus* couple, Gerbertus and his wife Adalgundis, had two children, Bismodus and Gerberga. The father held one free farm with 11 *bunaria* of arable and 2 arpents of vineyard. He paid in army tax half an ox, two measures of wine in pannage, and ploughed 7 perches. He paid an arpent of wine, 3 chickens and 15 eggs. He performed manual labour, wood cutting, cartage services and handiwork as required, and paid for wood due 1 foot (of wood). It does not take much imagination, or surely lead us far astray, to suppose Gerberga might be set quite young to feeding hens and gathering eggs. Later she would be able to tend vines and tread grapes. She would have learnt these skills from her mother and other village women by example and instruction. Her father, meantime, would be bringing her brother up to help him with heavier jobs. The reference to pannage indicates the family had pigs, and the smaller farm animals such as pigs and sheep (boisterous enough to control but not like a bull) might be managed in certain respects near the home by girls and women. More distant herding, and cattle herding (but not milking) were male responsibilities. None the less, as noted above, Jochens found women in Old Norse society out in the shielings, and she cites a saga reference to a wife with two young daughters with her in the pasture. In another saga a 12-year-old girl was described as giving birth to an illegitimate son, and in another a woman delivered twin sons, in both instances in the fields. Assuming the teenage peasant girl survived, she might be married at about 20, the calculated age of marriage on Farfa estates. On the shared farms and half and quarter farms of St Germain, provided the co-resident families got on reasonably, there would be female associates at hand. Out at Ribblehead there would have been less female company around.

Of course some peasant women outlived their husbands and saw their families grow up and produce children. It is tempting to cast old peasant women as prematurely aged, wizened (from exposure to weather), arthritic (from hard labour in the same weathers) and malnourished as they came to the end of their lives – to be buried with sickles, spindle whorls and weaving battens. It is hard to conclude other than that the countrywoman's life was hard and lacking in luxury. *Sturlunga* saga has a picture of a woman nursing a swaddled child as she raked behind her scything husband. Famine was fearsome, but the food these countryfolk prepared and ate was at least natural and seasonal, or preserved by drying. Human nature being remarkably resilient, the countryfolk of both sexes made social highlights out of the church calendar and village community activity, which lightened the routine heavy drudgery. In the latter half of the period there was a great population surge and it was the sheer numbers of this class of women who achieved it.

In the most unpromising circumstances they managed to bring enough children into the world and rear them to adulthood to keep the demographic graph rising. What checked population growth in this period was infectious disease – malaria, tuberculosis and plague. Though malnutrition lowers resistance to illness, it is only in a series of dearths that mortality is noticeably affected, whereas plagues are more devastating. The sheer population growth testifies to things not being as bad as we might imagine for the countrywoman and her family.

4

THE PRACTICAL SITUATION: WOMEN'S FUNCTION IN URBAN COMMUNITIES

After the fall of the western Roman empire, towns in Italy and Gaul continued to exist as administrative centres, especially where they were seats of bishoprics. The barbarian kingdoms utilized them in this way, but were less impressed with the municipal aspects of Roman civic life such as baths, amphitheatres and basilicas. The civic and corporate splendour of Roman cities fell into decline, especially in those furthest from Rome. Old town walls, however, still protected the inhabitants from marauding troops in the sixth century, for example at Arles, Avignon and Pavia. The seventh-century onslaughts of the Arabs in the Mediterranean, and those of the Vikings in the north, becoming serious in the ninth century, disrupted local conditions and connections but gave rise to more systematic fortification which eventually lent itself to settlement supporting trade, and in this way towns characterized by trade were developed by both the invaders and their resisters.

In some instances towns' extension of their walls allows measurement of their growth. Cologne, for example, had about 100 hectares enclosed in the tenth century, 185 by 1106, and 320 by 1180, when its estimated population was about 32,000. Bologna in 1200 is estimated at 208 hectares, with a population of around 70,000. Pisa was the largest city of Tuscany in 1200, with perhaps 12,000 plus in its 114 hectares. Cities with populations of 10–20,000 were large for medieval times and thin on the ground, although there was a concentration of them in Flanders by the end of the period. Less famous small towns were scattered – about 10 kilometres apart was a good distance for trade – and mainly distinctive for their markets, usually weekly, which provided opportunities for nearby villagers to sell surpluses and buy the things they could not produce at home. Some

63

towns were the site of the nearest mill for their surrounding villages. Mills were profitable to their owners, and the Docibilan dynasty ruling in Gaeta did their best to keep them in the family, enjoying a monopoly until their fall there in 1032. Within the family, however, they were not averse to some female ownership. John I gave 4 months and 20 days use of a mill to his daughter Bona in 933. In both Gaeta and Amalfi mill ownership came to be characterized by what Skinner identifies as a sort of timeshare system. In 1079 Maru, an Amalfitan widow, sold off a portion of a mill in Atrani bequeathed to her by her mother and described as 1 month and 5 days, helpfully enlarged as meaning the month of May and 5 days of July.[1] More peaceful times, from the tenth century, along with climatic improvement and population growth, saw an outburst of surpluses, trading and credit activity in the last two centuries under review, enlivening towns in the economy and giving birth in northern Italy to the city states such as Genoa and Pisa.

Historians of early medieval towns have been interested, for the most part, in their constitutional and commercial development, and Heath Dillard was able to extract a very full picture of women of the Reconquest Castilian towns largely from twelfth- and thirteenth-century municipal law codes. The more fully organized, and better documented, towns of the later middle ages do offer more information specifically relevant to women and there is plenty to learn there about the way women were treated by the gild organizations, widows' rights to real property and to continue in their husbands' trades, age at marriage, rates of dowries, sumptuary laws, service occupations and involvement in parish and charitable activities, all of which are treated in the forthcoming *Women in Late Medieval and Reformation Europe*.[2] Undoubtedly much that can be seen in the later period grew out of what pertained before, but it is not satisfactory just to suppose this. What can be put together about our earlier period?

Sources include literary works, such as Gregory of Tours, who mentions in passing mercantile activity in, for example, Bordeaux, Marseilles, Paris and Verdun; early laws, such as those of the Visigoths, and later laws from eleventh- and twelfth-century Spanish 'reconquest' towns and twelfth-century Italian communes; other legal records, notarial records, wherein land and business transactions show women often managing their deceased husbands' estates, for example in Ravenna and Genoa, and engaging in complex business transactions in twelfth-century Genoa, Venice and Piacenza; and archaeological evidence such as that from Dublin, Hedeby and York.

Variant Opportunities for Women

There was a huge variety within the genus town: a variety of origins and development, function, practices, size and environment. At different times and places aristocrats lived in, or shunned, towns. They became distinctive residents of Italian towns in particular, but in northern France and England the nobility preferred country seats. Women of the aristocracy in Italian cities were subject to some politically motivated control by the city. In 1146 peace terms between the Count of Ventimiglia and the city of Genoa bound his sons to marrying Genoese women and his daughter was expected to take a Genoese husband. The different urban environments in administrative towns, episcopal towns, those at monastery gates and those with trading facilities at harbours, river crossings and route junctions produced different opportunities for the townsfolk of both sexes.

Italian cities led the way in sophistication. Rome, after the fall of the western empire, had continuous history because of the presence of the papacy, and it had international pull in the Christian west as a place of pilgrimage. The half-million population of Rome in the third century had shrunk to 400,000 in the fifth and to no more than 20,000 by 700. There must always have been work in Rome for providers of services to religious tourists. Venice, because of its strong trading links with Constantinople, had a head start in east–west trading and was well placed to make capital out of the opportunities for transporting crusaders from 1095. The women in Venice or Genoa lived in an environment watchful of tides and seasonal trades, and regularly preparing for the departure of convoys and reception of returning and visiting ships. There was work in provisioning ships and making sails. The buzz of a Mediterranean seaport would be felt in places such as Bari, Tarentum, Naples and Amalfi in South Italy, in Marseilles, and in Barcelona. On the Baltic, North Sea, Channel, Irish Sea and Atlantic coasts as Viking activity swung from raiding to settling and trading, Hedeby, Hamburg, Bruges (replacing earlier Quentovic and Duurstede), London, Dublin, Bordeaux and Lisbon dominated their areas. Gnomic verses from the Old English Exeter Book capture beautifully the seafarer's wife's reception of her husband, placing it on the North Sea coast: 'her beloved is welcome to the Frisian woman (wife) when the ship stands [at anchor]. His keel has come and her man/husband (*ceorl*) has come home, her provider (*aetgifa*, literally feeder); she invites him in, washes his dirty clothing and gives him new: she gives him on land what his love bids.'

To and from the coastal and river mouth ports goods travelled inland and towns manufacturing goods for trade, particularly cloth, flourished.

Inland from Bruges, whose walls enclosed 90 hectares in 1127, were the Flemish towns of Ghent, Tournai, Lille, Ypres, Douai, Arras and St Omer, clothmaking centres from Roman times and the home of the Frisian cloaks referred to in Carolingian documentation. On the main northern rivers were Cambrai and Valenciennes on the Scheldt, Mainz and Cologne on the Rhine, Dinant and Huy on the Meuse, Rouen and Paris on the Seine. Mid-way between Bruges and Venice there sprang up in the twelfth century the fairs of Champagne at Troyes, Lagny, Provins, and Bar-sur-Aube, spread between January and October. These fairs did not create permanent large towns but the temporary concentrations of merchants made demands on local provisioning and accommodation. In the Iberian peninsula there were unusual conditions as the reconquest of the territory from the Arabs evolved. Fortified sites on the moving frontier were encouraged to develop into permanent settlements, creating somewhat unique conditions as new young settlements were added to earlier ones which were maturing with the pacification of the earlier frontier zone. In the first generation of the process women were in short supply in these towns and exceptional measures were needed to attract them and keep them, including welcoming settlers with kidnapped brides, but treating severely any men who tried to abduct a woman from the town.

Not all towns were administrative centres, or centres of manufacturing, or densely populated with large numbers of people. All had many rural characteristics, with agricultural land and vineyards surrounding them, hens and pigs kept in backyards and roaming the streets, and many of the goods exchanged there were rural in origin or purpose – grain and dairy produce from the local villages, and metalwork for agricultural implements produced for cultivators. In this respect there was not as great a contrast between the life styles of townswomen and countrywomen as might nowadays be expected. In Castilian towns, Dillard paints a picture of housewives and domestics dealing with home-grown grain, wine and garden produce from the family plots and gardens, home-produced meat reared in private meadows and town commons, and local fish and game taken from streams, forests and mountain wastes.[3] The first written lease from Amalfi, according to Skinner, dated from 1029, records Drosu widow of Leo letting empty land to the son of Ursus Calvelli to cultivate with vines for 4 years at 2 solidi per year. Thus their rural surroundings impressed themselves on the towns. However, the sheer size of the larger cities made for very different conditions for the woman living among thousands compared with the woman of hamlet and farmhouse. In terms of manufactures, the two early town specialities were metalwork and cloth. Metalwork was not a women's occupation and the clothmaking in towns may have been less women's work than it was in the countryside.

Unforeseen disasters such as plague, fire and assault beset towns. Gregory of Tours tells how a plague came to Marseilles in 588, brought by a ship from Spain, and how similar epidemics occurred several times between then and the time of writing. Such eventualities would throw extra nursing burdens on the women of the town, as well as the grief of bereavement and fear of succumbing to the disease, shared by both sexes. Fires spread quickly in closely built housing with much timbering and thatch or shingle roofs: Gregory tells of conflagrations at Orléans and at Paris, where a woman resident prophesied it and advised evacuation but was ignored. Clermont Ferrand was ravaged by Theuderic's troops and the environs of Nîmes, including olive groves and vineyards, by Guntram's; what terrors were experienced in a rapid attack must have been multiplied in a siege of any length. When this happened, the women starved with the men – and probably worse, since the onus of defending the site physically would fall on the men who must have had prior claim on dwindling food stocks to keep their strength in any form. When things were desperate, women as well as men resorted to prayer and public ritual. When Childebert and Lothair besieged Saragossa in the mid-sixth century the men dressed in hairshirts, abstained from food and drink and marched round the city walls singing psalms and carrying the tunic of the martyr St Vincent. Their womenfolk, according to Gregory, followed them, weeping and wailing, dressed in black garments, with their hair flowing free and ashes on their heads; they might have been thought to be burying their dead husbands, so funereal was the scene. Fearing black magic, the besiegers were unnerved, and learning from a peasant that the saint's tunic was being used as a banner and the citizens were begging God for mercy the troops withdrew, scared.

Women's Role in Urban Trading and Craft

Town sites in Italy and Gaul had a sense of history, which continued to impress itself on their inhabitants through an ongoing relationship with the local protective saints and the security of the surviving walls. They were ready for a take-off of trade with the economic upturn from the tenth century. However, from Scandinavia, with no tradition at all of urban-centred episcopacy, a new impetus for trading towns was independently making itself felt from the ninth century. Excavations at Birka

(Sweden), Kaupang (Norway), Ribe (Denmark), Hedeby (Germany), York and Lincoln (England) and Dublin (Ireland) have all contributed to our understanding of trade and manufacture from the late ninth to twelfth centuries in the towns of the Viking world.

Viking trade was very long distance, and not just in goods which had to be transported afar because they were not locally available, such as eastern silks and spices. A complete cooking pot, found in a male cremation of the later tenth century at Birka, seems from analysis to be of English manufacture and similar to a product from the Lincon Silver Street kiln. Distant items found in urban centres need not, of course, have been fetched there from their place of origin by one merchant. The local trader may have been responsible only for the last leg of their journey, and it may be purely accidental that the goods never moved on elsewhere. Still, exotic items are an impressive proof of very wide-ranging activity. Whether women played any professional role in this business is totally unknown. All that can be said is that men took women with them into the trading outposts in Russia, where their burial suggests expatriate communities of both sexes on the trade routes. In *Women in the Viking Age,* Jesch, drawing on a story from the *Vita Anskarii* of c.875 showing the Christian Frideburg of Birka leaving her wealth to be distributed as alms at Dorestad by her daughter Catla, comments that it shows that women could control considerable property in Birka. She assumes that this wealth had come from some form of trade, pursued by Frideburg since, as she says, no husband is mentioned. But a daughter is, so Frideburg's resources may well have been those of a wealthy widow. The connection with Dorestad is interesting because apparently this was where Birka Christians used to go to hear about Christianity before St Ansgar's second mission. (It was of course a major trading centre before the Vikings damaged its trade.) So the Birka inhabitants who picked up Christianity there were probably in the town on business in the first place. Catla, who had been with her dying mother in Birka, went physically to Dorestadt to carry out her mother's bidding. Thus mobility is indicated as feasible for women in trading communities. Moreover, weights and balances have been found in women's graves at Birka.

Turning from trade to crafts, we know that Viking towns worked metals, wood, leather, textiles and substances such as amber, ivory, bone and horn, also glass and pottery. Gold and silver was worked for the luxury trade in jewellery and there were cheaper ranges of jewellery in lead, and copper alloys. Iron was used for tools, such as axe blades and horse furnishings, and keys and locks. Such items are found complete in urban archaeological sites, but more valuable signs of their local manufacture include remnants of furnaces, crucibles and half-finished items such as part-made copper alloy garment hooks from Lincoln. There is nothing to show women's participation, or lack of it, in these crafts, and any attempt to assign gender roles in production must remain speculation, but it is possible that they did jobs such as polishing the jewellery, though less likely that they did full stamina blacksmithery. Wood was used for building and shipbuilding – presumably male trades – and for making hooped staved vessels and lathe-turned ones, again likely to have been male production lines. Leather was tanned and stretched and made into footwear – shoes and ankle boots – and scabbards. Cobblers' lasts have been found at York, Hedeby, Oslo and Wollin. Bone and antler horn were made into combs, pins and skates, and the survival of items from earlier stages in the manufacturing processes at York, Aarhus, Ribe, Hedeby and Dublin proves the local manufacture. There is, however, no evidence of women's involvement in these crafts, even as sweepers of the shop floor, although perhaps this may be assumed where the craftshop was in the house. On textiles we are on slightly firmer ground. Spindle whorls are pretty ubiquitous in urban archaeology and spinning was widely regarded as women's work. The loom weights found on several sites are for warp-weighted weaving on a vertical loom, the sort of loom visible in the reconstruction of a Hedeby house at Moesgård, and the sort described in Jochens's account of the rural women weavers of Iceland. There is no evidence that pottery was made in Viking York, but Lincoln, Stamford and Torksey were pottery-producing centres, and several kilns have been excavated. Glass beads and pendants were widely manufactured and at York, jet. It should be remembered that spinning and weaving were women's crafts for centuries, partly because they could easily be put aside or left and then resumed as other domestic demands intervened. Other crafts where smaller, nifty fingers might suggest women's advantageous employment do not have this adaptability. One cannot leave a hot crucible or a half-thrown pot and come back and find its condition unchanged for work to resume. On the other hand, there is no reason at all why York's women could not have participated in family expeditions out into the nearby forests to locate naturally shed antlers for bone working.

In the sophisticated Italian cities the communal civic organization was dominated by an adult male elite which provided the officials. In Genoa, consuls had to swear their wives not to accept anything worth more than 3 solidi which might be the consulate's. Wives of citizens, however, as their relatives, could engage in trade – a ruling of 1157 from Genoa banned the members of the *compagna* from buying or selling any sable fur worth over 40 solidi, adding that they were not to let their wives and children do so either. Impressively, women were involved in 24 per cent of the Genoese *commenda* contracts between 1155 and 1216, benefiting from the survival there of Roman law in the city's custom.[4] Epstein claims that Genoese women participated in everything in the town, but his book *Genoa and the Genoese 958–1528* is not as rich in illustration as one would hope from this remark. The commune of Siena adopted Roman law in 1176, freeing up women there from the constraints of Lombard custom. They invested in business ventures by *società*, and in money changing and money lending. At Venice, too, women, seemingly largely widows, made sea-loans from the eleventh century. All these activities are comparatively advanced commercial transactions.[5] In Amalfi, Skinner shows merchants' wives and mothers dealing with business back home while their men were at sea – Leo de Rini confirmed an exchange made by his wife Anna while he was in 'Babilonia' (Cairo) in 978, and Drosu, the Neapolitan wife of Mauro the Amalfitan, had to contest some of his property in Stabia while he was absent at sea in 1007. Generally, the gilds in the Italian city states denied membership to women, but there is assorted evidence of individual participants in trades and crafts in different places, spinning, weaving, making clothes, soap and perfume, for example, in southern Italy. In Castilian towns women were into spinning and weaving and carpet making, they were involved in innkeeping, and sold goods for a living.

Service Functions of Women in Towns

The attraction of country girls to household service in towns has been studied in various places in the later middle ages, so it is naturally of interest to see how far back this can be traced as a feature of town life. The answer is well back, and though we do not have the data to see a career pattern or a catchment zone, we can see in the earliest evidence one of the dangers faced by women servants in households throughout time: namely the sexually voracious master. According to Gregory of Tours the married Eulalius, count of Clermont Ferrand, was in the habit of sleeping with the women servants in his household. Gregory does not say whether these were free or servile, but domestic labour was usually female and servile in the medieval Italian communes such as Genoa in the twelfth century, and many slaves were working in towns through the period in domestic capacities. Muslim slaves were sold in the Spanish peninsula and sometimes given as wedding presents from husband to wife. Female slaves were subject to abuse: Skinner considers impregnation by the household master an occupational hazard.[6] Lombard law acknowledged that female slaves bore children of their masters. Some female slaves were bequeathed in wills; an example comes from Lucca in 768. To use a different sort of evidence, slaves of both sexes were mentioned in Genoa's 958 charter, and Epstein cites a charter of 1005 noting the sale of a Burgundian woman slave, Erkentruda, to a couple for 10 solidi. Wills might free slaves, but sometimes only conditionally. Skinner provides two examples. A will of 1024 manumitted five personal slaves of the testator, as long as they did not take servile spouses, and offered his heirs chickens every year. Three of the slaves were female and were to serve the testator's daughters until the latter married. In 1067 Leo Caracci left 3 modia of land in Tremonsuoli and a small piece outside the city gate to John Gutium, described as his *clientulus*, but he was to serve Leo's wife Matrona and only to be freed on her death. In 999 the bishop of Gaeta was claiming some of his famuli to be slaves, which they disputed. Two of the related group, John and Anatolius, sons of Passari Caprucci, offered an oath that their mother Benefacta had been free and their father was not bound to the bishop. Skinner suspects the pound of gold they offered may have spoken more effectively than the oath, and wonders even if the large sum may have been raised by another landowner willing to buy them out to secure their services to him. This must remain speculation, but the case is worth citing to show that both parents' status was relevant in such matters.

Some female servants, whatever their status, were remembered in their employers' wills. Epstein gives the example of the Genoese notary Giovanni Scriba, whose cartulary contains documentation from 1154 to 64, who left his servant Adalasia some rabbit and sheep skins; his bed and 17 solidi to her son Ribaldino, and some clothing and 2 solidi to her mother Serra. One domestic employee whom it was particularly desirable to protect from sexual molestation was the wet-nurse, for contemporary belief was that intercourse could contaminate her milk, and Castilian towns fined men as for homicide for this offence and banished them. Spanish wet-nurses were taken into the family home for a contract period of three years, and supplied with a room, board and a fixed wage. Incidentally, the house-hold women servants in some Castilian towns were favourably placed compared to male agricultural workers because if they left before the end of their contracts they were paid for the days they had worked, whereas men got no pay for the period since the previous pay day. This preferential treatment, explained by the constant nature of women's domestic work in

contrast to the seasonal variety of men's agricultural labours, applied in
Cuenca, but not in Zamora.

The concubine occupied a grey area between being servant and family.
By the twelfth century Lombard law in southern Italy gave the children of
their father's concubines some inheritance rights, whereas in the north
they had no right to any part of the patrimony, although they should be
supported. Skinner cites the 1135 will of the Gaetan Jacob Maltacias, which
left his concubine Matrona Capomazza 3 pounds and his bed and bed-
clothes. After some bequests, the executors were to sell his remaining
property and pay his debts, then divide the cash between his daughter
Bona (who had already received 3 pounds as a specific bequest), his
nephews and Matrona Capomazza's daughter. In Castile, the term *barragana* was used to describe the openly cohabiting mistress or concubine of
usually a bachelor or priest, and her position, and that of her children,
was rather better than that of a more furtively kept mistress with merely
bastard children. Town laws preferred couples bound by matrimony (more
stabilizing), so the *barragana* was not the equal of a wife, but Dillard suggests the attraction of being kept in this way by a prosperous citizen to a
girl whose alternatives were hard work, a marriage in comparative poverty,
or public prostitution, particularly since there was always the hope the
man might marry her.

The *barragana* was essentially one man's temporary wife, and 'acceptable' in a way the prostitute was not, though it was realized the latter provided an expected service in a town, and serving a multiplicity of clients
was her hallmark. Some Castilian towns certainly in the thirteenth century flogged and banished prostitutes, some merely disadvantaged them
by a failure of protection – for example their clothes could be stolen without redress, and only a few towns, including Toledo, made their rape a
punishable offence in this period. However, elsewhere in southern Europe
by the twelfth century prostitution was being regulated, for example at
Pisa, but much more is known about this aspect of town life from the later
middle ages.

Domestic and Family Activities of Townswomen

Excavations at Hedeby, Dublin and York suggest that Viking town houses
were about 3.5 metres wide and anything from about 5 to about 17 metres
long, and usually rectangular in a proportion of roughly twice as long as
wide. The houses were set with the short side (gable-end) to the street and

the length running back into the plot, which was itself fenced. The York Coppergate house was sunk a deep 1.5 metres below the surrounding ground level, and had squared timber uprights and horizontal timber planks holding back the earth. It is not certain whether such a house had a second storey. Roofs could have been thatch, timber or shingle tile, with thatch thought most likely. At Dublin the houses were above ground, rectangular with rounded corners, built with posts and wattle infill, with steep thatched roofs carried on internal posts independent of the walls, some of which were double with fern insulation – early cavity wall insulation. The layout of what Wallace identified as the Dublin 'Type 1' house (which constitutes 75 per cent of the five building types identified in Viking Dublin) had a fireplace in the middle of a central strip running longitudinally from door to door, and on each side strips for bedding and sitting.[7] Much this pattern is to be seen in the previously mentioned reconstruction of the Hedeby house, with its vertical loom against one of the short side walls, next to the door. A hanging cauldron could be suspended over the hearth. The bigger houses seem to have been homes and workshops. There were other structures in these towns too, down to mere huts or pigsties. The Dublin houses had a lifespan of only 10 to 15 years, and were rethatched within this period, suggesting the housewives might have had recurrent problems with leaky roofs. The Dublin houses date from the tenth and eleventh centuries, and at York two distinct building styles can be seen each side of the mid-tenth century, the earlier like Dublin's a construction of posts and twigs and clay infill, the latter as described above. All the excavated towns and indeed their topography and some street names still, suggest concentrations of trades in particular streets. It was the coopers (barrelmakers) who gave Coppergate its name. At Dublin Fishamble Street seems to have had a concentration of amber jewellers and woodcarvers. This means that the craftsmen would have had occupational links – whether co-operatively or in commercial rivalry – with their neighbours, a connection not necessarily shared between their respective wives. However, in Naples Skinner suggests the smiths were in one street and gradually intermarried, creating a clan based on a profession.

Conditions tested housewifely skills. York has been portrayed in the Viking period as a town of rotting wooden buildings with earth floors covered by decaying vegetation, surrounded by streets and yards filled by pits and middens of even fouler organic waste, at least in the environs of Coppergate and Pavement. Both York and Dublin appear to have been infested with beetles, and conditions at York in 6–8 Pavement have been described as 'clearly unsavoury by modern standards but . . . tolerable, even cosy, by the standards of the time'.[8] (If these were ground floor work-shops with rooms over, the higher rooms could have been sweeter smelling.) Damp would be a problem in swampy York's deep-dug buildings and under Dublin's renewable thatch; Italian and south French towns might have had less of a problem in this respect, though there were plenty of malarial swamps in the low-lying coastal areas. It is obvious that keeping food fit to eat (even by contemporary standards) would be quite a problem. But at York the diet was varied – wild blackberries and hazelnuts, carrots, celery, bras-sicas, apple, and prunus fruits, oats, beef, pork and lamb (pig remains are especially noticeable at Dublin), chickens, cod, herring and shellfish. The Viking port sites being on or near coasts are likely to have had more fish in the diet than inland places more dependent on freshwater fish.

Housework included laundering and linen was smoothed using whale-bone plaques and glass smoothers. The richer townswomen of Birka and Hedeby had quite impressive wardrobes. Their better tunics were decor-ated with tablet-woven braiding in linen or silk and even with a metallic weft. Outdoors they wore a sleeved caftan or cloak, and at Hedeby the wealthier had ankle-length coats of felted wool, lined or often quilted.

The Italian cities, with their resident aristocrats dominating family dis-tricts and centred on their towers, had a social layer above those found in Viking towns. At the top, the local dukes had urban palaces. The will of the Gaetan ruler Docibilis II in 954 mentions a palace with baths, houses, separate kitchens, aviaries and courtyards – very pleasant living conditions, but ducal servants in 980 were crammed into a wooden house 7 metres by 6. As no urban land transactions are recorded from the coastal sector of Naples, Skinner wonders if the entire area may have been in the palace complex. Beneath dukes and counts, untitled nobles and their relatives lived in towers and substantial houses. Pitru daughter of Kampulus, of the Neapolitan family of John 'miles', described by Skinner as the best docu-mented woman from medieval Naples, brought a court case in 963 to get her neighbour's window blocked because it looked directly into hers. There is plenty of evidence of the town elites holding property and their womenfolk taking advantage of it. Bona, widow of Anatolius Cotina, in 1108 gave a house and a warehouse (*pothega*) next to the seashore in Gaeta and land in Scauri to the bishop of Gaeta. The house had a cellar, a *medi-aloca* and a *ventum* or top floor. Such houses seem to have used the lower section for shops, the middle section for storage and the top for living accommodation. Genoa was similar: Epstein believes living quarters there c.1200 were mostly over shops and storage areas on the ground floors, and faced with stucco and plaster, but nearer the heart of the city largely

wooden housing in blocks of three to four storeys brought fire hazards. In
Gaeta, cellars were traded, and by women – Maria, widow of Docibilis
Caracci, bought a cellar there in 1119 and sold – at a profit – in 1125.
Urban families competed and feuded, and marriage peaces were uneasy,
especially for the bride, often married in her teens. Commenting on Genoa
in *Women in Medieval Italian Society*, Skinner points out that the male head of
the family retained authority over his children of both sexes, even a married son brought his wife to the family home and had no control over his
own property or his wife's dowry until he reached 25. At least couples of
good family could marry while their parents were still alive: at the artisan
level couples might have to wait to inherit before they could afford to marry,
especially when the dowry was expensive, or they might end up living with
the bride's parents in their old age and supporting them. Even in one city,
customs could treat the female in-law differently, with 10 per cent of the
documented wills leaving artisan-level wives as their husbands' heirs but
none of the aristocratic ones. In that class, as Skinner chillingly puts it, the
wife was 'a temporary stranger tolerated for her childbearing capacity'.[9]

In the Castilian towns studied by Dillard, women's position in the family was good. Daughters in towns shared the parental inheritances, in real
estate and movable goods, equally with their brothers, inheriting separately from the mother and the father in the Visigothic tradition. A married couple's property was seen as identifiably his, hers and theirs. 'Hers'
included her *dos*, known as the *arras*, trousseau, and all her pre-marriage
possessions, and all this could revert to her relations, just as his property
could revert to his. 'Theirs' embraced the acquisitions of the marriage,
and these were divided by half, either at the first death or after both had
died. Inheritance flowed up and down the generations because a parent
was preferred to siblings for some part of a dead child's inheritance. In
Castilian towns women could own their own houses, and be treated like
any other responsible householder, or indeed more favourably in some
cases since widows might be excused all military dues or be charged at a
lower rate. With a married woman householder, however, her husband
was expected to take on the householder's role. As a housewife, the Castilian
townswoman did the laundry in assigned areas and could be fined for washing too near a spring. She took grain to the watermill, and made bread at
home but took it to bake to a municipal oven (in private ownership). The
town's baths were also in private ownership but under public regulation
and there were fixed days assigned to the two sexes. Some housewives did
all their own housework, cooking, cleaning, getting provisions; some were
helped by daughters and the better off had a staff of maids and nurses

perhaps under the supervision of a live-in housekeeper. From the eleventh century weekly markets and seasonal fairs opened up, and there were permanent shops and warehouses providing a wide range of goods by the end of the period – southern delectables such as figs, pomegranates and sugar, northern fabrics from Flanders and northern France, raw mercery goods for home use and ready made items such as chemises and the coifs, which were such an important part of a woman's dignity that at Laguardia in 1164 there was legislation against a woman knocking off a married woman's coif and tousling her hair. Pottery, matting, bedding, combs, mirrors, leather goods and even Muslim slaves could be bought. The women did some of the selling, especially of staple goods and sometimes their husband's produce, such as cheese he had made, or fish he had caught. Dillard raises the modern-day concept of flexible skills, and the value of being able to adapt say bookkeeping from the father's business to the husband's. Women in Castilian towns do not seem to have been involved in the long-distance trade caravans but were involved in innkeeping and are visible in this capacity on the Santiago route, a pilgrimage focus. In the towns respectable women did not frequent taverns and barmaids were socially inferior. Dillard's study shows us the variety of experience (and variety of women) in towns, combining the desired inaccessibility necessary to protect girls from abductors with their respectable association in public spaces more or less monopolized by women – laundry areas, ovens, courtyards where they might spin in company. Class made a huge difference within the town, the wives and daughters of the respectable citizenry being well protected by the law, but the lower class women being roughly treated without redress. There was no precise term for rape in Visigothic law, but convicted rapists were punished in the laws of Palanzuela (1074), Lara and Baltras (1135) and the death penalty was invoked for the crime at Toledo in 1118.

Life Cycle

There are few insights into the birth or childhood of normal or typical urban women in this early period. The *Liber Pontificalis*, constructed in the ninth century, claims sixth-century famines in Milan and Rome were so bad that women were driven to eat their own children, but this seems extreme. The account of Ibrahim b. Y'quib's tenth-century visit to a large coastal town thought to be Hedeby mentioned the practice of throwing unwanted children into the sea to save the costs of rearing them: infanticide was not

confined to the less sophisticated countryside. Dillard believes twelfth-
and thirteenth-century Castilian towns were less inclined to infanticide
than in Visigothic times.

There is little solid evidence of educational provision for girls in towns.
Dillard's reference to Toledan women of the late twelfth century remembering schoolmasters in their wills is about all. A Venetian father left his
daughter as a pledge for a loan of 40 solidi, redeeming her from one
Michael of Padua in 1180; presumably she had been in service to Michael
during the loan period.[10] Domestic and agricultural tasks appropriate to
their age, with or without loans, must have been the lot of many. One
glimpse of sharp practice in Clermont Ferrand shows Andarchius, a former (well-educated) slave who had risen in King Sigbert's service, trying
to marry the unnamed daughter of a Clermont citizen called Ursus by
tricking Ursus's wife into agreeing in her husband's absence, and setting
up an elaborate identity fraud to dupe the king to agree. (Nobody seems
at all concerned about the daughter's feelings and daughter and mother
are completely lost sight of as the tale unfolds.)

In the northern Italian cities couples who could afford it married in
their teens, with 12 the minimum age for the girls. In Genoa up to 1130
the girl's parents handed over a dowry, and the groom and his family a
counter-dowry (*antefactum*) and the new wife was promised a third (the *ter-
tium*) in the event of widowhood. From 1130 the counter-dowry (usually
about half the dowry) and third became negotiable, and in 1143 wives
were deprived altogether of the right to the third, and the counter-dowry
was limited to under 100 lire. (This prejudiced the widow's rights but
allowed the children to inherit more of their father's property at once.)
Ingone della Volta, consul in 1158 and 1162, a man at the top of Genoese
society, married his daughter Sibillia in 1156 to Oberto Spinola with
a dowry of 200 lire. In 1171 in Gaeta, Pasca, widow of Constantine
Baraballu, and her sons John and Nicholas provided a dowry for her daughter Trocta: the groom Bonus Campello acknowledged receipt of 8 pounds
of tari of Amalfi (the tari was a quarter dinar), some silk and a pair of gold
earrings, which Skinner describes as a standard sort of southern
trousseau. In Castile, where a woman's majority was 15 in many Leonese
towns, but could be as low as 12, a woman was endowed with a *dos* (*arras*),
when she married, and this varied from a tenth to half of the husband's
property or expected inheritance. It belonged to her, but if she had children they were entitled to inherit three-quarters of it. If she died childless
it reverted to the husband or his relatives. *Cartas de arras* (charters of
endowment) from the ninth to twelfth centuries endow women with land,

houses, villages, livestock, slaves, saddled mules or horses, clothing, hides and tithes. From the mid-twelfth century the arras began to be limited, for example to 20 maravedis, or differentiated according to the status of the bride, town girl, village girl from the alfoz, or widow for example, furthermore a third of it could be spent on the celebratory feasting, showing it was no longer filling the function of a substantial endowment for the widow and children. The Castilian towns in this period did not have a customary dowry or marriage portion, and parental wedding gifts had often to be taken into account when the parents died as advance shares of the inheritance. For marrying without her family's consent a daughter could be disinherited altogether. Marriage did not always follow the desirable polite courtship. Abduction could be against the woman's will or with her connivance. Women's fates after such eventualities varied considerably. In some towns the abductor was forbidden to marry the woman, to deter others from attempting to achieve their purpose by the same offence, but abductors and their prizes might be welcome scot free elsewhere, and other towns had procedures for negotiating a marriage to regularize the situation: Calatayud had this operating from 1131. In Aragonese and Navarrese towns rapists were positively required to marry their victim, as at Jaca from 1063. (It should be remembered that Reconquest Spain was subject to unusual pressures.) In 1099 Miranda de Ebro imposed the death penalty for rape or abduction. The ideal tradition, from Visigothic law through to its translation in the thirteenth century, was that a father married a daughter to a man whose proposal he accepted. But the mother had considerable input, and if widowed, the same power her husband would have had. Marriage was the central event in a woman's life, and a widow found it comparatively easy to remarry, as long as she waited a year from her husband's death.

The maintenance of separate property entitlement and the sharing of acquisitions made for unusually favourable conditions for the wife in the Castilian towns. Wives were seen as stabilizing influences, as well as maintainers of the population and producers of valuable fighting sons. Men had to be encouraged to marry and settle down, and wives to come to the town and not run away from it. These conditions fostered a more companionable collaborative partnership. The wife was empowered to shoulder her husband's debts when he was absent, though in places such as Leon she was protected from certain legal procedures in this vulnerable time. Because of the sharing of acquisitions, any value she added to her husband's property was booked to her or her heirs' credit when partitioning followed death. But there was a downside that she also shared responsibility for her husband's debts and fines, although some towns halved the debt and assigned the husband's gambling debts, pre-marital borrowing and certain other personal commitments as obligations on his heirs; similarly some towns, such as Leon, protected a convicted killer's wife's 'half' and the family home before confiscating the remainder. In normal circumstances, the balance in the marriage favoured the husband, as elsewhere, showing that he was at base the 'senior partner'.

In much of Europe, it was most markedly as a widow that townswomen had much proprietorial capacity. It was as a widow that the wife of St Namatius, late bishop of Clermont Ferrand, built the church of St Stephen in her old age in the suburb outside the walls. Wishing it to be decorated with coloured frescoes, she sat in the church, in a black dress, 'far advanced in age', reading (note!) from a book stories of long past events and telling the workmen what she wanted painted on the walls. Mistaken for one of the needy poor, she was given a piece of bread by a pious visitor, and graciously thanked him for it and ate it daily instead of other food until it was used up. This was the point of the story for Gregory of Tours, though we would prefer to know more about the bishop's widow's literacy, wealth, and influence. In 1004 Matrona, granddaughter of Kampulus the Prefect, a member of one of the leading families in Gaeta, gave three estates and other land, movable goods and property in Gaeta to her daughter Euprassia for a pension of 20 modia of corn, 10 modia of beans and peas and 30 jars of wine, necessary clothes, and a slave. Skinner speculates that if Euprassia was unmarried at the time, this could be a dowry incorporating an insurance for her widowed mother's old age, or it could be a simple lifetime gift to ensure the property got into the right hands before death intervened. It resembles the corrodies often met in medieval peasant family arrangements. There was a widespread tightening of inheritance more favourably to the male line in the twelfth century. In Castilian towns, the Visigothic tradition of gender-unbiased inheritance was fairer to daughters, compared with other customs, and the acquisitions custom had some practical sides in allowing for the value added to one partner's property by the other's efforts, but the outcome could be less secure for widows, who saw their husband's property pass to his heirs if partition was immediate. The widow was usually allotted the marital bed, but customs varied on the important matter of a house. If the husband had had an earlier wife or wives the distribution in places such as Cuenca disadvantaged the final widow and her children. (The making of a will of Roman type to make the widow heir to her husband's estate only became fully legal late in the thirteenth century.) Children could be forced to care for an impoverished parent, as at twelfth-century Daroca, but this would not be exactly a comfortable insurance. The Reconquest towns, eager to keep their populations up and settled, tended to favour a widow's remarriage, but remarriage could trigger the personal effects allowed to a widow being returned for partition in the family. Even at death, sex dictated difference of practice: at Salamanca the church bell tolled twice for a woman, but three times for a man.

5

WOMEN AND POWER: ROYAL AND LANDHOLDING WOMEN

'Women and power' has been a fashionable subject of investigation in recent years, although increasingly the topic has been modified by redefinition transforming 'power' into more restricted 'agency'. In secular affairs formal empowerment only came to women through birth or marriage, and in the religious sphere through a career bringing abbatial authority (often also dependent on privileged birth or following the ending of a high-ranking marriage) or a life demonstrating extraordinary sanctity and hence attracting influence. Private influence exercised by sheer force of personality within a woman's own circle must always be allowed for, but is rarely recorded and almost always unquantifiable.

It used to be a simplistic categorization that medieval women had no, or few, public rights and responsibilities but could be influential in the private, domestic sphere and, it being generally supposed that public rights and responsibilities have always been what constituted real power, the woman in the home could only exercise a pale imitation of it in her limited sphere. Even queens could be fitted into this view, as primarily mistresses of the royal household, ensuring domestic order round the king. Hincmar of Reims' treatise *The Government of the Palace* allocated it to the queen to 'release the king from all domestic or palace cares, leaving him free to turn his mind to the state of the realm', but Janet Nelson criticizes the distinction, commenting 'palace cares were political affairs and intimately affected the state of the realm'.[1] The power of personal influence (even of women over men) is almost impossible to assess from sources which give little psychological insight, but some medieval women may have manipulated affairs successfully behind their more visible menfolk. In the last 20 years the relevance of a public/private distinction has been increasingly denied, especially before the middle of the twelfth century, though there have clearly been variations in the legal capabilities of women in different societies.

If we concentrate on power's traditional association with having input and decisive action in public affairs, then it is clear that women came to any such influence chiefly through being born into, or married into, families wielding authority, usually via possession of land. Much evidence has been found of women placed in power by these means wielding it successfully and acknowledged as doing so by contemporaries. One of the best declarations to this effect is Count Philip of Flanders' reference in a charter of 1168 to the time when his mother Sybil of Anjou, wife of Count Thierry and regent in his crusading absences, 'strongly governed the principality of Flanders'.[2] Though some customs regulating inheritance of land and goods allowed partibility, royal, ducal, comital and knightly families alike normally passed authority undivided down the generations through males. In times of migration and invasion there was a premium on male rulers. Over the period reviewed, a comparative free for all within his kin at the death of a ruler gave way to the widespread practice of primogeniture, ensuring succession most commonly to the eldest male heir. Fiefs became widely heritable in the tenth and eleventh centuries, at least in direct male line, and by the late eleventh century in many parts of western Europe an heiress can be found inheriting a fief in default of a male heir and performing homage for it herself, but her great desirability in the marriage market underlines the fact that her husband was expected to gain power over her inheritance and the chance to sire heirs to its descent. Throughout the period it was less common for a woman to inherit and exercise power. If there was no obvious male heir but there was an heiress, she would carry the power to her husband, or pass it down to her son, though a characterful heiress might share rule with husband or son, as Baldwin II's daughter Melisende of Jerusalem did with each in turn.

Queens

The most important, and the most visible, exercise of authority was royal, so it is sensible to focus first on queens. The vast majority of queens in this period were not queens regnant but queens consort. When a reigning king married, his wife was not necessarily recognized as queen immediately, or indeed ever, and some recognized queens waited a long time for consecration: Charles the Bald's wife Ermentrud was consecrated as queen over 20 years after their marriage. Thus along with queens consort the position of women who were merely kings' wives or indeed concubines has to be considered here. The king's widow also mattered, as marriage to her might strengthen a claim to the late king's realm. (This was presumably Merovech's motive for marrying Brunhild, though the ploy did not succeed.) Emma of Normandy's remarriage, as Ethelred's widow, to Cnut of Denmark is represented in the *Encomium Emmae* – which she commissioned – as a cementing factor in Anglo-Danish society in England. The power queens wielded came to most of them either as a particular king's wife – ending with his death not theirs – or as the next king's regent mother – usually meaning their power was terminated by the son's coming of age, or soon after. To some degree there was always an element of the king allowing his wife a certain role, or delegating certain areas to her, and if by contrast he chose to constrain her activities, even to imprison her or repudiate her, he usually succeeded: Philip I repudiated Berthe de Frise in 1092 and imprisoned her in her dower chateau Montreuil-sur-Mer, appropriating Bertrade de Montfort, the wife of the count of Anjou, in her place. A queen's power derived from marriage could be precarious. As for the queen-mother, she faced a potentially bleak prospect of future ingratitude from the next king, and challenge from his wife. Furthermore, any power a queen held temporarily as widow during a period in which she remained available for remarriage would generally be taken up by a successful suitor. Many Anglo-Saxon, Lombard and Frankish queens retired into religious institutions, though not necessarily into fully vowed seclusion. Whether they went voluntarily is not always clear, and in Visigothic Spain the kings Ervig (680–870) and Egica (687–702) forbade the remarriage of royal widows, forcing them to enter religious life immediately. Altogether, queens were rarely able to put the stamp of their own personalities and preferred policies on a realm for long. A queen actually ruling was an abnormality, and where a king had the misfortune to leave no male heir, any daughter's role was likely at best to be to carry the crown to her husband or son, thus restoring 'normal' conditions.

Medieval queens received in their lifetimes far more attention than was proportionate to their numbers in society, and in the last two decades they have similarly received a perhaps surprising amount of attention from historians. Have such abnormal individuals as queens any relevance to the study of women overall? Because individual women feature so little in the mainly male-authored sources for the period, historians have to make what they can of the few that do, and inevitably these form a totally unrepresentative cross-section of medieval women. Queens do actually appear in chronicles and histories, kings' lives and saints' biographies, and they also appear in charters and other diplomatic documents and occasionally on coins and in art. Attempts have been made to treat these visible queens as illustrative of wider generalities. The argument that the greatest opportunities were offered to queens in those societies which also treated female rights rather better at all social levels offers the identification of a powerful queen as a pointer to such a society. The crediting of Christian queens with the conversion of their husbands, the founding of religious houses, or generous alms giving can be viewed as church propaganda defining a conversion role for women, and follow-up activities, displayed as examples for others to follow where empowered to copy. The frequent promotion of daughters of the nobility to queenship invites consideration of common experiences in aristocratic and royal circles, thus closing the social gap between queens and noblewomen, and widening the size, and therefore the significance, of the sample. The sources, however, did not generalize about women from queens, and nor can we.

Visibly influential queens may have been particularly decisive characters whose husbands were either henpecked personalities or characterful enough to recognize wisdom and welcome it, even from a wife. Individual cases do not reveal how common shared counsel between husband and wife might be. In Bede's *Ecclesiastical History*, for example, he shows two occasions when the unnamed wife of Redwald of East Anglia (a bretwalda or overking) influenced her husband, taking the moral line that it was improper for an honourable king to hand over a friend for gold, and later sowing seeds of doubt in her newly converted husband's ardour for Christianity. What is lacking at these points is a comment from Bede somewhere on the scale between 'on talking this over with his wife as prudent men do' and 'foolishly mentioning his intentions to his meddlesome wife'. Was consulting one's wife normal, rare, or totally extraordinary, in kings or at any other level? Bede's failure to comment at all might indicate that wifely input was normal.

The way queens are handled in the sources deserves attention. Only occasionally does a woman herself have any control over her own image, in letters or charters emanating from her secretariat, or works commissioned by her such as Emma's *Encomium*. Often, a queen is presented to us by an ecclesiastic who has a particular agenda and treats her accordingly. He needs the queen to fit a particular role (often biblically based) and to persuade his readership to see her in this light. She has, however, to be presented plausibly by the standards of the day, and she may be used, if necessary, to point the moral of a tale. It may be more in the representation of queens that we can hope to find what was expected of them than in the more prosaic record of their acts. Investigation reveals that the representation of queens in legend, law and political narrative is actually perhaps surprisingly homogeneous.

The prime purpose of royal marriage was of course to preserve the dynasty by the production of a legitimate male heir. Overthrowing a dynasty was a dangerous precedent, so a new family's early generations usually were particularly careful to strengthen their line. If a dynasty was toppled by outside invasion or palace revolution, the incoming monarch tried to secure his own dynasty by all possible means. It is not surprising that the first recorded coronation of a Frankish queen was that of Bertha (Bertrada), wife of the first Carolingian king Pepin, in 754, three years after her husband, the dynastic mayor of the palace, had deposed the last Merovingian king. In the royal family the heir's mother did not have to be the queen, but she was certainly better placed as the king's wife than as his concubine. In Pauline Stafford's book *Queens, Concubines and Dowagers*, subtitled *The King's Wife in the Early Middle Ages*, she shows that in the Frankish, Italian and English milieux studied, concubines were particularly features of a king's pre-marital and pre-accession career, or alternatively of his older age. The prince took a concubine in his adolescence, while remaining formally unmarried and under his father's control. The concubines of this youthful period tended to be from socially high-ranking families. Occasionally one became the king's wife by subsequent 'proper' marriage. The sons of these pre-marital concubines were treated as royal heirs until a more legitimate son was produced by a full wife. In the middle period of a king's life he married a specific wife, or succession of wives, whose sons immediately took precedence over any previous offspring by concubines. When the succession was secured by one or preferably two but not too many lawfully begotten heirs, a widowered older king might prefer concubinage to another marriage.

For the accepted continuity of the dynasty the king's wife had to be chaste. To accuse the queen of adultery was to shatter confidence in the succession. Hence, whatever the behaviour of the queen, such accusation was a political gambit. The case of Judith, wife of Louis the Pious, will shortly be reviewed. Other queens who had the accusation made against them include Brunhild and Fredegund in the sixth century, Richardis wife of Charles the Fat in the ninth, Emma wife of Lothair in the tenth, and Edith wife of Edward the Confessor in the eleventh. Eufemia of Kiev, second wife of Colomon of Hungary (1096–1116) was apparently sent back home pregnant accused of adultery. These examples, drawn from 'factual' history, are paralleled in literature in the stories of Guinevere and Lancelot, and Iseult and Tristan.

It was important that kings should be able-bodied males, and that their deaths be followed by a rapid and smooth passing of royal power to a successor with whom the people could easily identify and around whom they could rally. Long before royal primogeniture became the normal determinant of succession a new king was sought among a circle deemed to be throneworthy, normally defined in terms of relationship to the late king. Royal blood was crucial and prolifically spread due to early kings' life styles involving concubines and serial wives. While this pattern prevailed, there was some opportunity for a king's current wife to favour the promotion of her own son(s) above any older stepsons. Emma of Normandy, twice a second wife, is credited with the foresight of getting her sons recognized as heirs before their birth. The *Life* of Edward the Confessor (written half a century later) claims that when Emma was pregnant with him, all the men of the country swore to accept the child as king of England, should it be a boy, and the *Encomium Emmae* has her stipulating, on her marriage to Ethelred's supplanter Cnut, that a son of theirs should have the succession over the son of any other wife. Ethelred's mother, Ælfthryth, widow of King Edgar, became more sinisterly associated with manipulating the succession: her stepson Edward the Martyr, who had succeeded Edgar in 975, was assassinated visiting his stepbrother Ethelred and his mother at Corfe in 978; however the first written accusation of her plotting the murder only came in Osbern's *Life of St Dunstan* dating from c.1090. Even where only a share in a partitioned realm rather than a whole kingdom was at stake a stepmother queen was suspect, especially when she had a son of her own. Louis the Pious' three adult sons by his first wife Ermengard rebelled in the early 830s purportedly to rescue their father from the evil influence of his youthful second wife Judith, whose young son Charles the Bald represented a dilution of their inheritance. The queen was accused of adultery and incest with Bernard of Septimania, the court chamberlain and Louis' godson, but after ups and downs her son got his share – ruling the West Franks – and, by outliving Lothair and Louis the German, eventually inherited the imperial title in 877. In 856 he married his own daughter Judith, at 12, to the widowed and son-rich West Saxon king Ethelwulf, taking the precaution of having her anointed as queen (the first known medieval example of this) at her marriage. (This Judith was on better terms with at least one of her stepsons, who married her on his father's death.) The younger Judith's wedding at Verberie on 1 October 856 gave rise to two valuable written comments. The Annals of St Bertin recorded the event and commented on Ethelwulf's honouring of Judith with the name of queen, 'which hitherto had not been customary with him and his people'. The biography of Judith's stepson Alfred attributed to Asser adds useful context, showing disapproval of the West Saxon practice by claiming it contrary to the practice of all Germanic peoples, and dating it to the appalling tyranny of Eadburh, daughter of Offa of Mercia and wife of Beorhtric of Wessex (who died in 802 allegedly of poison which she had prepared for another). Charter and Anglo-Saxon Chronicle evidence seem indeed to combine to bear out a decline in the status of the king's wife in Wessex in the ninth century, compared with the eighth and tenth, when queens do appear. The tyrannous Eadburh has her parallel in literature in *Beowulf*'s tale of the early habits of the continental Offa's wife Thryth, a 'proud young queen' who had members of the *comitatus* executed for looking at her. Apparently her husband tamed this shrew into a well-loved queen.

A second purpose of royal marriage was advancement of the king's dynasty, and therefore the choice of a bride was often motivated by current international politics, or if more advantage was to come from strengthening alliances within the kingdom's nobility, from internal selection. When queens were 'foreigners' in their realms they were open to suspicion of favouring fellow countrymen, or introducing unpopular customs or fashions. An international rapport could moreover become outdated, its bridal proffering yesterday's woman, and the mixing of her genes with the royal stock could become a liability on changed conditions. An internal alliance could also come unstuck, if members of the bride's family became too big for their boots and brought discord to court, or if a rival clan became an urgent priority to appease. In two of the alleged adulteries mentioned above the queen's family suffered with her; Judith's brothers were removed and tonsured by her stepsons, and Edith's brothers were exiled and she, like Judith, sent to a nunnery. Royal bridal selection was a constant readjustment of status, the lesser families seeking enhancement by linking themselves to the currently powerful dynasties, the latter deciding whom to honour by the bestowal of affinity, weighing up whose future support might prove useful, whose territories might advantageously fall in to the superior power's hands in the future through the marriage link. The same game was played internally, and here inevitably magnates in border territories, who were often among the most powerful in a kingdom anyway, had an advantage when offering their daughters, or threatening to marry them to the adjacent power. Marrying internally was for those unable to woo on the international stage, or for those who might normally do so but had at a particular moment a perceived advantage in choosing a local wife. It was in fact the nobility of the kingdom which supplied most kings' wives in Stafford's areas of study.[3] Marrying externally, especially if within a traditional circle, raised the king and his children above the taint of involvement in internal noble squabbling, and renewed old alliances. Marrying externally into a new area or higher level carried more prestige. The first western king to obtain the most socially exclusive wife, a Byzantine royal, was Otto II. Two abnormal situations need consideration here: the Merovingians' occasional resort to wives of servile origin, and Charlemagne's reluctance to marry off his daughters at all. Both situations may reflect the monarchs' perceptions of superiority. The Merovingians may have thought themselves above needing the support of noble in-laws, and Charlemagne did not need to use his daughters to enhance his position. Of course, more obviously, marrying a slave did not embroil a king in the interests of her father and brothers, and not putting out daughters to client husbands left the king much more in control of his own policies. The fathers of the illegitimate children of Charlemagne's daughters had much less significant relationship with the king than they would have had as sons-in-law.

Charlemagne's own marital career is an object lesson in the opportunities and expectations of the times, and the difficulties of interpretation posed for historians. As only the second generation of the crowned Carolingians he might have been expected to marry circumspectly for the stability of the dynasty. Hardly so. There is disagreement, for a start, as to whether Himiltrude, a Frankish noblewoman, was his concubine or his legal wife. Their association dated from c.768 and she bore Charlemagne a son who was named Pepin after Charlemagne's father. After his father's death Charlemagne repudiated her, with the encouragement of his mother, and married a daughter of the Lombard king Desiderius. Within a couple of years this wife, whose name is not even recorded, was also repudiated, to her father's fury, and Charlemagne married Hildegard, the daughter of Count Gerold and Imma daughter of Gottfried Duke of Alemannia. Over 12 years this queen bore Charlemagne four sons and five daughters, dying at 25 in April 783. In the following autumn Charlemagne married Fastrada daughter of the East Frankish Count Radulf; she died in 794 after bearing only two daughters. Liutgard, of noble Alaman stock, was his last full wife, though she seems to have begun the association as a concubine. After her childless death in 800, Charlemagne had a series of concubines, four being named by his biographer Einhard. He had also had concubines during the period of his marriages, and had children by them. Was Charlemagne just so powerful he could do as he pleased, canon law on marriage notwithstanding? His reputation held up – he was the king crowned emperor by the Pope in Rome in 800, and eulogized as one of the nine Christian worthies. There was more to this marital career than personal fancy. The marriage to Desiderius' daughter came of an alliance with the last Lombard king, while the choice of her successor from Alemannia was part of the policy of maintaining influence in the part of Pepin's subsequently divided kingdom allocated to Charlemagne's brother Carloman, and the selection of Fastrada from East Francia brought support for Charlemagne's campaigns against the Saxons. Repudiating a wife was always a risk since it created bad feelings in her family circle, and divided loyalties at court, so Charlemagne was perhaps politically lucky to lose his later wives by death, which left him able to update his matrimonial policy advantageously without upsetting the supporters of the late queen.

Hildegard was fecund, a great advantage for a queen. It was a personal disaster with political consequences if the king's wife failed to bear children, and little better if she bore only daughters. This fate befell the Supponide Angelberga, wife of Louis II, who was crowned empress in 858. According to Stafford, who summarizes her career, Angelberga was active in all areas of Louis' rule, negotiating with other Carolingian rulers, accompanying her husband on campaigns in central and southern Italy, acting as his regent in northern and southern Italy, and dealing with leading churchmen. Coins were struck in the joint names of husband and wife, and she intervened in charters, appearing in official documents as *consors regni*. After her husband's death she called the Council of Pavia in 875 to resolve the succession, and only disappeared from the political scene in 888, living thereafter in the nunnery she had founded at Piacenza. But Angelberga was extraordinary for her time, and even this positive career had its downsides. In 872 Louis briefly divorced her to marry a noblewoman from central Italy where Angelberga herself was unpopular. Her failure to provide sons may have been a contributory factor, and certainly later there was a story of her attempting to seduce the count of the palace and accusing him of the attempt when she had failed. (A motif found in literature, see *Lanval*, as well as in the biblical episode of Potiphar's wife.)

Angelberga had been a truly power-wielding queen in Italy. A century later, another such was the empress Adelaide, third wife of Otto I. A Burgundian princess, she had been betrothed at 6 and married at 16 to King Lothar of Italy in 947, widowed, and imprisoned by the court official who then became Berengar II. She escaped, and was taken up by Otto at 21 in 952 to facilitate his taking over the Italian kingdom. She was crowned empress in 962, and like Angelberga, her name appeared jointly with her husband's on coins struck in Italy. Adelaide intervened in charters, and was a patron of Cluny, whose abbot Odilo wrote her biography, *Epitaph of Adelaide*. For a year spanning 973–4 she ruled with her son Otto II, but his Byzantine wife Theophanu soon came into her own, and apart from a brief moment in 984 it was only after Theophanu's death in 991 that Adelaide became regent for Otto III. Stafford describes Adelaide as a personification of queenly power throughout the Ottonian empire but particularly in Italy. Adelaide was well connected from birth, and she became even more so. Stafford counts up that she was daughter, sister and aunt to three consecutive rulers of Burgundy, sister-in-law, mother-in-law and grandmother to three successive kings of France, wife, mother and grandmother of three Ottonian emperors, and mother or aunt to a host of abbesses and bishops. This was a veritable 'grandmama of Europe'. If Adelaide was a queen *par excellence* her daughter-in-law Theophanu reached in Stafford's words 'the peak of dowager achievement, regency in the fullest sense of the word'.[4] Adelaide and Theophanu were the only two German empresses to be consecrated in the tenth century and their careers stand way above others. Active as Otto II's wife, Theophanu was even more powerful as Otto III's mother, associated in his official documents, negotiated with by foreign rulers, and an issuer of charters in her own name in Italy, one even styling her emperor. By the end of the tenth century regency in this governmental mould was a possibility, but it was not always thus. One of the earliest queens to exercise regency was Brunhild, the Visigothic princess who married the Austrasian Sigibert in 566, and whose complicated career is discussed by Janet Nelson.[5] Her husband was assassinated in 575, and it was ten years before her son Childebert II came of age (at 15) and when he died in 596 Brunhild took up a regency role once more. Theudebert, his 10-year-old son by a concubine, inherited Austrasia, and Theuderic, his 9-year-old son by his wife Faileuba, inherited Burgundy, which Childebert had inherited three years earlier from his childless uncle Guntram. But Theudebert kicked against Brunhild's control on coming of age in 600, and ejected her from Austrasia, taking as wife (and queen) an ex-slave of hers, Bilichild. Brunhild was, however, welcomed by Theuderic who remained unmarried, it was said due to her influence; he did have concubines and left four sons when he died in 612. Brunhild, trying to hold together the inheritance for Theuderic's 11-year-old son Sigibert, was murdered by her nephew Clothar II of Neustria in 613. Her story is not edifying. It does little to illustrate any formal or constitutional aspects of a queen-mother's regency. Moreover, the contemporary and near contemporary sources, Gregory of Tours at the time, and Jonas's *Life of Columbanus* and Fredegar a generation later, and the *Liber Historiae Francorum* in the early eighth century, are open to different interpretations and there has been much speculation among historians in attributing motives and policies. What Brunhild's career does clearly illustrate is the violence and vengeance of Merovingian royals. In times like these one cannot expect child kings to grow up in a calm and wisely governed kingdom (yet Gregory the Great praised Brunhild's governance), with their regent mothers respected by a chivalrous aristocracy. Everyone took what chance they could, including Brunhild. She is credited with stopping Childebert's betrothal to the powerfully connected Theodelinda and approving his marriage to the less grand Faileuba, his concubine, to suit her own interests. The constant thread in her life seems to be the desire to avenge her murdered sister Galswinth, the one-time wife of Chilperic, and her vendetta on this account with Chilperic, his next wife Fredegund, and their children. This is where the Merovingian personal infighting took precedence over consideration of the interests of particular kingdoms. These were barbaric times, but a little of the more civilized aspects of a regent's behaviour might be seen in Brunhild's influence on episcopal elections and her so called 'foreign relations' which were extensions of family relations in her case. In the tenth century Theophanu's regency took place against a rather more civilized background. But all the time we must remember that monarchies and especially minorities depended on the support of sufficient nobility of the kingdom to survive.

Queens had quite an influential role in creating and preserving good relations with the nobility, for they undoubtedly headed the social side of the court, winning the admiration of the young bloods of the *comitatus* who moved out to be the regional aristocrats as they aged. Imma, a Northumbrian prisoner of war released to raise his ransom, was said by Bede to have gone to King Hlothere of Kent because Hlothere was the son of Queen Æthelthryth's sister, and Imma had been one of Æthelthryth's thegns. In *Beowulf* queens Waltheow and Hygd are seen graciously hosting court feasting; small wonder Thryth's behaviour was so objectionable. The queen's central position at court was not a feature of romantic literary imagination, for it is robustly enough entrenched in Hincmar's *Government of the Palace* and in the Welsh laws of Hywel Dda.

The migratory conditions in early medieval Europe enabled warrior leaders to acquire kingly status, and long afterwards the prime role of the king was as war leader, successfully defending his people and aggressively enlarging his operational territory. We do not see much of early queens as war leaders, but the siege warfare of the tenth century brought a few to the fore. Emma, the wife of the West Frankish usurper King Ralph, defended Laon in 927, took Avalon from Gilbert son of Manasses in 931 and in 933 besieged Chateau Thierry which was surrendered to her. Laon was also defended by Gerberga, wife of Louis d'Outremer, in 948, when her husband was held in Normandy. Queens can be seen on campaign with their husbands, for example Angelberga with Louis II in Italy, or keeping near to him with the resources of the royal treasure, but at a safe distance, as Brunhild did. In the twelfth century Louis VII's wife Eleanor of Aquitaine accompanied him on Crusade. In literature the queen's role is sometimes to encourage or embolden the king to make war, sometimes in vengeance for sufferings of their own kin, and Brunhild's feud with Chilperic and Fredegund was of this nature.

Women of the Landed Nobility

Beneath the royal families of Europe, intermarrying with them, and on occasion supplanting them, was a vast range of nobility with a confusing variety of titles. Noble dynasties, like royals, hoped to keep power within the family down the generations. But social conditions were changing in ways generally thought detrimental to women, necessitating different strategies for achieving continued family prosperity. As monogamy became the norm and divorce and remarriage less easy, from the early ninth century, dynastic marriage strategies became more disciplined because there were fewer second chances to get it right. Compared with the earlier migration periods, conditions were more stable and the warrior elite had to give more attention to living off estate rentals and less to making a fortune from looting on frequent campaigns. It has long been argued that around 1000 CE patrilineage began to become much more dominant, especially in elite circles. To prevent family estates fragmenting among the children of each generation, the preservation of the patrimony for the benefit of one male heir, usually the oldest son to whom the fief descended, became common. Daughters' dowries, and inheritances for younger sons, were ideally provided for out of lands acquired, or resources otherwise developed, within the immediate family, which could be safely distributed within the family without damaging the patrimonial inheritance. Allodial land could be divided between equal heirs, but as excessive fragmentation brought problems there were moves to keep the property whole but in joint possession, or to restrict sons' marriages, and by the twelfth century to fulfil obligations to daughters by means of money dowries in lieu of a share of the land. However, women could and did inherit allodial land. A further development viewed as damaging to women during the period covered by this study was the tightening of bonds between these noble families and their overlords and associates of lesser rank in various forms of the relationship characterized as feudalism, a system wherein family heads were vassals of an overlord and responsible to him for the provision of the services allocated for the holding of the vassal's fief (most commonly military service owed in return for land). In very general terms the increasing feudalization of western European society has been seen as disadvantageous for women, because feudalism was a gearing of society for war, and as women did not fight, they were rendered automatically into inferior status. It is significant that though there are feminine forms for aristocratic ranks such as duchess, countess, marchioness there is no feminine form for knight. However, here too recent research has found women well enmeshed in the feudal chain, performing homage to overlords and receiving it as 'lords' of their own men. As fiefs became heritable, which was normal by the end of the period, inevitably the problem of sonless generations cropped up and in most west European countries in the central middle ages women could inherit a fief, despite earlier legislation to forbid this in some places, such as Conrad II's 1037 Italian edict. When women could and did inherit fiefs, however, their overlords developed more interest in their marriage and in the choice of the husband who would perform the service due from the fief and supply the future dynastic identity of the fiefholders. Lordly intervention in this area was most invasive in the areas of Norman influence, Normandy, England and Sicily. Recent work on particular regions of France suggests women's inheritances were not being automatically absorbed into their husbands' patrimonies. It was also possible to will property to women by testament disregarding residual inheritance custom.

Feudal conditions preset matrimonial strategies in ways which resulted in the higher nobility having perhaps less freedom of choice of marriage partner than any other social class. Families were jostling to preserve useful traditional alliances, open up new dynastic possibilities, and come to terms with old rivals and enemies. Marriages were normally within the same overall class, but in some areas it was more usual for the men to marry upwards: this was the pattern in northern France, but the reverse applied in England. Much depended on the chance of opportunity. Marriage was certainly too important for families and overlords to be content to leave it to the personal inclinations of the individuals concerned, and marriages were generally arranged, the outcome of negotiation and even sale. To get it safely sorted at the earliest possibility noble children were frequently betrothed as infants, and if, after this, both were to be brought up together, it was normally the prospective bride who was sent to the groom's family, not vice versa. The increasingly effective international disciplinary power of the church brought some protection for the child spouses by insisting that the marriage could not take place until the girl reached 12 and the boy 14, and that both parties had to consent before the marriage could be performed. How free the participants really were to dissent is questionable, and there must have been instances of bullying and duress. However, in the long term the ecclesiastical insistence on consent as the most essential validating condition of marriage did restrict the power of parents and feudal lords.

Matilda of Tuscany (1046–1115), variously described as countess, duchess and marchioness, sole surviving child of marquis Boniface II (assassinated in 1052), and his second wife Beatrice, was a powerful noblewoman. Beatrice rapidly remarried and ruled with her husband Godfrey IV the Bearded of Lorraine until his death in 1069 (an instance of marriage with a widow bringing power over her late husband's territory). Beatrice then ruled alone until her own death in 1076. Beatrice and Matilda both took the papal side in the investiture controversy, which involved them in politics at the highest level. (It was at Matilda's castle at Canossa that the famous reconciliation of the emperor Henry IV and pope Gregory VII took place in 1077.) Strategically located, with an army, Matilda played a part in the military and political development of the next two decades. When she died, a life of her was being written by Donizo, a monk of St Apollonius at Canossa, a house Matilda had refounded. Just as Matilda echoes queenship in her exercise of power, so her biographer echoes the ecclesiastical agenda which, as remarked above, often influenced the monastic interpretation of queens' lives, glorifying his house's patron, by stressing her ancestry and praising her pro-papal policies and making her out to be eloquent, a gifted linguist, intelligent, and politically skilled. He chose to give prominence to her rulership and play down her sex, whereas other Italian and German commentators viewed her through the more usual perspective of being someone's daughter, wife or widow. Even they, however, had to account for some of her bold actions which they characterized as 'virile'.[6]

Matilda inherited her power and exercised it through two marriages to some extent because her husbands were weak. Eleanor of Aquitaine (d 1204) inherited power and exercised it during and beyond two marriages, but charter evidence suggests she was less independent in her duchy during her two marriages, but then her husbands were more powerful, being kings. Recent work on Eleanor's charters for Aquitaine (where she had her own seal) concludes that she had a relatively limited sphere of action while married to Louis VII (who gained extended power over the duchy through the marriage), enjoyed the most substantial power of her married life between 1168 and 1173, when in effect Henry II sent her to govern the duchy in an abandonment of his centralizing policies (though even here after 1170 she had an enfeoffed son Richard to challenge her independence), and only attained real power in widowhood.[7] It is often argued that widowhood was the time landowning women exercised real power, but this was not always the case. Somewhere between 1024 and 1033 a widow Gise, described as noble and free, and widow of a noble and free man, gave herself to the abbey of Saint Mihiel in the diocese of Verdun after suffering many outrages from the inhabitants of her village. The bailiffs of a local lord had demanded dues and rents from her for lands which she held, and had held before her husband's death, as her own allod, free of all rent.[8] Taking advantage of a woman in a weakened position seems likely to have happened quite often. But for some powerful widows, the role was only an extension of the authority they had exercised as wives.

Matilda of Tuscany and Eleanor of Aquitaine were heiresses. Matilda's mother Beatrice, by contrast, acquired her power in Tuscany by marriage, held on to it successfully when her husband died, carried Tuscany to her second husband, but apparently shared rule with him, and held on to power again when widowed for the second time. When a male of the ruling classes died, that was final and arrangements had to take off from there, but when such a ruler was merely absent for some reason his wife might be expected to manage his affairs until his return. This activity became more widespread with the Crusades. One of the earliest noblewomen to rise to this challenge was Adela of Blois (1058–1137). Adela, youngest daughter of William the Conqueror and Matilda of Flanders, married Stephen, eldest son of Count Theobald III of Blois, Chartres, Meaux and Troyes, a man at least 18 years her senior, in the 1080s; he succeeded his father in 1089. Thereafter Adela seems to have been routinely consulted by him, joined with him in all aspects of comital administration, and took decisions independently besides implementing joint ones. Letters Stephen sent her while on crusade show his regular confidence in her, and during his crusading absences and after his death at Ramlah in 1102 Adela ruled as countess for over 20 years. The couple's oldest son, William, was about 15 when his father died, and had already been given the comital title, under-age, to ensure his succession if his father died on crusade, as happened. By the end of 1104 he was married, but far from Adela subsiding into dower retirement, events took a different turn. William disappeared into obscurity in 1107 and was replaced by his younger brother Theobald, who was given the comital title and associated thereafter with his mother in the administration until her retirement to the convent of Marcigny in 1120. That Adela was responsible for changing the succession is generally accepted by historians. William apparently acquiesced in his demotion which gave Theobald an easier ride; curiously Theobald was the one pushed out in the succession crisis after Henry I's death in 1135 when the Norman barons about to elect him as duke abandoned his candidacy for Stephen's after the youngest brother's coup in London. This is presented as a baronial decision, not Adela's doing. The two displacements are proof that seniority of birth among brothers was not always the guiding principle in succession disputes. The baronage would seem a more likely source of intervention at such moments than the fiat of the former ruler's widow, which leaves the attribution of William's displacement to Adela all the more striking.

Matilda, Adela and Eleanor belong to the period after 1050, which is better evidenced than earlier times. Are there earlier noblewomen to cite, even if admittedly as outstanding rather than as typical members of their class? Ermentrud, a Parisian noblewoman, left landed estates and property in a will of around 700. The brotherless Plektrud, wife of Pepin, mayor of the palace, is an example of a desirable heiress, bringing her husband lands between Rhine, Moselle and Meuse. The ninth-century Countess Gisla, daughter of the Saxon Count Hessi, was an active widow who travelled around supervising her and her son's estates. Dhuoda, the wife of Bernard Count of Septimania (mentioned earlier as the alleged adulterer with Louis the Pious' wife Judith), wrote the remarkable *Handbook for William* and is treated below in Chapter 7. The active career of Bertha (d 925) daughter of Lothar II, and wife to Adalbert II marquis of Tuscany, from her marriage around 895 to her widowhood in 915, is used by Skinner to show that women were not passive bystanders in politics, but rather, in her case, a major force.

Of course the noble classes, of both sexes, also behaved squalidly. There is nothing uplifting about most of the characters in Gregory of Tours' story of Count Eulalius and his wife Tetradia; she was described by Gregory as a young woman of noble blood on her mother's side but humbler on her father's. Stretching over 15–16 years this tale covers adultery, wife beating, theft, bigamy, murder, nun-abduction and other crimes, neither party being guiltless.

Superiority is relative. Beneath the higher aristocracy was a mass of lower lords, jostling for status in military and administrative careers and as landowners – a class more often found resident on their estates and practically involved in the supervision of their manors, which their wives and brothers managed when they were absent. From the viewpoint of their tenantry, these were lords too, and their wives expected the same respect. These women appear in charters, supporting the grants made by their husbands to religious houses. The three examples which follow come from Duby's *Rural Life*. The knight Josseran de Cipierre and his wife Odile gave a demesne to Cluny in 1089, with their two sons' agreement, and the charter refers to the wife's aunt Amelie previously giving part of the demesne to the monks with the approval of her two sons. Bertrand de Cortevaix's grant to Cluny around 1130 of wine, wheat and beans from his allod in exchange for 700 sous was done with the approval and consent of his wife Julienne. Wives exercised subtle influences: when the canons of Soissons settled their disputes at Ambleny and Chelle with Nivelon de Pierrefonds, sire of the local castellany, in 1089, they recorded that he had abandoned his unjust demands at Chelle visited by the grace of God, the council of his horsemen, and the prayers of his upright wife. Thus the moral superiority of the wife was set down for posterity. Noble families in towns tended to participate in mercantile activity as Epstein noted in Genoa in the twelfth and thirteenth centuries. By the late twelfth century the Castilian municipal knights were acquiring privileges and their widows were prickly about losing their status and in some places managing to hold on to it, but the widow who had her husband's tax exemption lost it at Palencia by 1181 if she remarried to a man not eligible for it.

The Life Cycle of Queens and Noblewomen

Infanticide in this period was probably less common in the nobility where family prosperity could provide for more mouths. Richer families tended to have, or at least succeeded in rearing, more children. The way the nobility kept check on unbridled multiplication was not by tackling the birth rate but by customarily restricting the marriage rate, by not allowing younger sons to marry, and by marrying as many daughters as possible into other families and relegating surplus daughters to nunneries. Noble husbands' absences from their wives cut the size of their families, as with Bernard of Septimania and Dhuoda. Noble children of both sexes were not generally suckled by their own mothers, so the typical noblewoman began life with a wet-nurse. That wealthy mothers did not normally breastfeed their own offspring is known because the practice is commented on as a rarity when it did happen, as with Ida of Boulogne, wife of the crusader Godfrey de Bouillon. The nurses were usually socially inferior to the family, but this was itself relative. In literature princes' sons were suckled by the wives of knights.

Noble infants of both sexes were raised in infancy within the family household, and there most girls stayed until marriage at 12–15 unless placed in convents or sent as children to the homes of their betrothed, which fate befell Marie of Champagne, daughter of Louis VII and Eleanor of Aquitaine, at the age of 8, and her sister Alice at 3. Matilda, daughter of Henry I of England and Matilda of Scotland, born in 1102, was betrothed at the age of 7 to the German emperor Henry V and sent to Germany in 1110 to be educated in the customs and language of the country, being married at Worms just before her twelfth birthday. Where a western princess was married into a country with an unrelated tongue such as Magyar, she must have had even more difficulty.

The education of high-born girls seems actually to have been better at times in this early period than it was again for several centuries. Amalasuntha (d 535) is credited with knowledge of Latin and Greek and her native Gothic tongue. Dhuoda's education will be commented on in Chapter 7. Hraban Maur, the great scholar, dedicated commentaries on Judith and Esther to Judith, wife of Louis the Pious, daughter of Count Welf of Bavaria. The linguistic abilities of Matilda of Tuscany have been mentioned, and Hugh of St Marie presented his ecclesiastical history to Adela of Blois. In the twelfth century aristocratic and royal wives were often better educated than their husbands. Gisela, wife of Conrad II, was more literate than her husband. Some girls were sent to nunneries for education and by no means was this necessarily a prelude to their entering religious life. Ermengard, daughter of Louis II of Italy, was educated in the convent at Brescia before becoming wife to Boso of Vienne. St Margaret of Scotland, Malcolm III's second wife, another wife better educated than her husband, approved of nunneries as a place for educating her daughters, for one of whom, Matilda wife of Henry I, the *Voyage of St Brendan* and the *Life of St Margaret* were composed; this Matilda corresponded with Anselm.

Parental betrothal of minors bound girls more strictly than boys. When marriageable age was reached, the wedding could be expensive. Gregory of Tours' full report of the departure of Rigunth, daughter of Chilperic and Fredegund, to marry Recared, the Visigothic king Leuvigild's son, in 584 states that 50 cartloads of gold, silver and other precious things set out with her, along with unwilling serfs and some people of good birth. When she stopped for a tented first night eight miles out of Paris, 50 of her escort slipped away, stealing 100 of the best horses and their gold bridles and two great salvers. All along the route members of the escorting party escaped, taking what they could. At Toulouse rumours of Chilperic's assassination reached the area, and Duke Desiderius, on hearing this, entered the city, impounded Rigunth's treasure and placed it in a guarded building, doling her out a meagre allowance, she having taken refuge in St Mary's church in Toulouse. This was as near to Spain as she got: her remaining treasure was stolen by the pretender Gundovald, and she was rescued at her mother's order by Chippa, the master of the stables, and brought home, as Gregory says, humiliated and insulted. Even this was not the end of her troubles: she fought verbally and physically with her mother, who at one point tried to slam a coffer lid down on her neck. Gregory comments on their continued quarrels that the main cause was Rigunth's habit of sleeping around. In the early part of the period some noble and royal women were seized and carried off by captors and married as spoils of war, as were Radegund of Thuringia and Swanhild of Bavaria, wives of Clothar I and Charles Martel. Judith's wedding to Ethelwulf in 856, accompanied by her anointing, would seem to have been a ceremony of some pomp, but this was not the norm. Marriage in ninth-century northern France hardly even involved priests and only queens had nuptial blessings at this time. In feudal times in some countries the first marriage of his eldest daughter was one of the critical events entitling a feudal lord to take an aid from his vassals.

Once married, noble wives and queens alike were safest if they bore heirs quickly. Charlemagne's Hildegard had nine children in 12 years, and the empress Theophanu five in as many years, the first four being girls. Several queens, Theophanu among them, are known to have taken themselves for confinement to religious houses. Matilda wife of Henry the Fowler bore two children at Nordhausen. Others opted for confinement at royal manors. Alfred's mother Osburh bore him at Wantage, Henry I's Matilda bore her daughter Matilda the future empress at Sutton Courtenay near Abingdon, whose abbot Fauritius was a distinguished physician. This level of choice was not available to those without wealth. Good birthing conditions may also have contributed to the size of royal and noble families, though it did not prevent women of these classes dying in childbirth. The use of wet-nurses probably tended to increase the size of these families also, since breastfeeding for a period of up to around 18 months makes conception within that time less likely and thereby spaces the family more widely. Barrenness was not a ground for divorce but it provided strong motive for seeking extrication from a marriage, not always achieved: Lothar II lost a protracted struggle to repudiate Theutberga. Bearing only daughters was also unsatisfactory, and this was Eleanor of Aquitaine's position as Louis VII's wife in 1152, after 15 years of marriage.

As this was the class most apt to rear its children by proxy, employing nursery staff at home or putting children out to other households, royal and noble mothers have attracted criticism in this area, on the lurking supposition that not caring directly for one's children means not caring so much about them. Upper-class families in this period, as later, tended to have more than one home, and to lead quite peripatetic lives. The parents therefore had the choice of leaving the children settled in one place if they themselves moved to another, or taking them with them. Eleanor of Aquitaine has been criticized for not having her children with her much, but certainly she did have some of them with her on recorded occasions, even involving Channel crossings.

There is not really sufficient evidence to show what we might call the sharing of parenting at this time. Although the stress in law on male rights would imply that fathers ruled their roosts, there is very little in fictional literature or epistolary or biographical material about deep-rooted affection between fathers and sons, still less about fathers and daughters. There is not much evidence of mothers and daughters being deeply devoted either, but there is a thread of the mother and son relationship being capable of depth. This is found in Scandinavian literature such as the *Vǫlsunga saga*, and in French and Italian reminiscences, for example Guibert of Nogent's memoirs. The mother is generally represented as the softer, more indulgent parent, sometimes interceding with the sterner father. This is partly, one supposes, derived from the role of the Virgin Mary as interceder with God the Father. It may also have sprung from the fact that mothers were generally younger than fathers, and in some cases noticeably closer to the children in age, and well-placed generational go-betweens.

During her marriage, a queen or noblewoman was expected to subordinate herself to her husband's interests. (This is where Eleanor of Aquitaine's alignment with her sons against their father went too far.) Matilda, wife of Henry V, between her marriage at 11 and widowhood at 23, is seen as throwing herself into the expected role, accompanying her husband to Italy and remaining there for nearly two years as regent when he returned to Germany to deal with rebellion there, only failing to bear him a surviving child (one chronicler suggests a child was lost). She showed plenty of spirit later, struggling to secure the English succession for her son Henry II. In this activity she was not so much identifying with her second husband's interests but rather looking to him to support hers. Her son was grateful enough and treated her with respect for the rest of her life, acknowledging her superiority over him as an ex-empress over a mere king. In the tenth and eleventh centuries noblewomen involved themselves in political affairs, appearing as military leaders, judges, chatelaines and controllers of property. The opinion that their rights were eroded and their roles became more private from the eleventh century is now seriously undermined. Ermengard of Narbonne was at sieges in the twelfth century, and Sybil of Anjou in her husband's absence on the third Crusade defended Flanders from invasion.

In life and in fiction a queen or noblewoman had considerable input into household management. Throughout the period, they were the mistresses of the household, which involved a supervisory relationship with the young military followers of their husbands. It was not just in chivalric literature that the knights honoured their lord's lady. In earlier times the lady with the mead cup swept graciously through her lord's hall, as Waltheow in Heorot, and Hygelac's wife Hygd, also in *Beowulf*. The knights of Kriemhild's escort to Hungary were a force at her command in the *Nibelungenlied*. Arthur's Guinevere was of course too receptive to Lancelot. As noted above, Hincmar's court treatise made the queen responsible for maintaining there an atmosphere conducive to government. Although there is a more critical analysis now of the supposed courts of love of Eleanor of Aquitaine in Poitiers, there was undoubtedly some civilizing culture in the courts and households of the great, even though these were also organized for war. Charlemagne's court attained high cultural standards – alongside the king's sexual exploits and his daughters' lovers and bastards. The Ottonian renaissance marks another high point, and the troubadour culture of the *langue d'oc* spread over Europe bringing the veneer of chivalry and courtly love which underpinned a core of European literature for centuries. Noblewomen had an input into this, as readers of and listeners to romances, dedicatees of treatises and poetry and even writers of it: consider the patronage of Ermengarde of Narbonne (d c.1196), the works of Chrétien de Troyes dedicated to Marie of Champagne, and those of Wace, dedicated to Eleanor of Aquitaine, and the works attributed to Marie de France, treated in Chapter 7 below.

Many individuals of both sexes married more than once, after suffering the death of a spouse, for the risks of war, tournament and chase scythed down the men in their prime, and childbirth, gynaecological problems and dietary iron deficiency in particular sapped the women. A good length for a marriage before death intervened was 10–12 years. Widows were under various pressures to remarry, even though they were by laws and customs provided for through the dower their husbands assigned to them, which their sons or stepsons ought to respect. This dower was most commonly a third of the lands her husband had held, and if she was an heiress in her own right her estates, which her husband had managed in his lifetime, came back to her on widowhood (sometimes this led to reduction of dower). As early as Merovingian times widows enjoyed a surprising amount of economic power.

Widows were an attractive remarriage proposition. Remarriage after separation/divorce was resisted by the church in the ninth century and may seem commoner than it was because this is the class where named examples were recorded and remembered. Divorce was rare among English kings, but every French king from 1060 to 1223 had at least one divorce. Royals and nobles still treated marriage cavalierly in the early eleventh century and the church had often to admit defeat, its disapproval simply disregarded. In high circles wives were repudiated and cousins married, with only courageous churchmen offering resistance. The breaking of a marriage was more often initiated by the husband because it was frequently more in his interests than his wife's. If the marriage was barren, he, wanting heirs for the line, could hope for success with another partner. He was the more likely to see political advantage in discarding a wife from an outdated alliance and binding himself matrimonially to a new alignment. At the end of the period under review Ingeborg of Denmark was fighting tenaciously to preserve her nominal marriage to Philip Augustus and succeeded in being restored as queen but not into the king's affection, leaving her vindicated but scarcely any happier. Although women divorced against their will invite sympathy, there were worse alternatives: incarceration by the husband (Philip I's imprisonment of Berthe de Frise has already been cited), or worse, murder (for example Bilichild's by her husband). The open keeping of concubines in the eighth and ninth centuries, and long after this in Scandinavia, and the continued resort to mistresses by their husbands was a fact of life for many wives of this class. The children of these unions were acknowledged and married only marginally downwards. An illegitimate daughter of Henry I was married to Alexander I of Scotland. (Henry had plenty to negotiate with, being credited with nine illegitimate sons and twelve illegitimate daughters; ironically only Matilda survived him of his three legitimate children.) William the Conqueror was born of such a union, for which there was a term '*more Danico*' (Danish fashion) which suggests that it was identified, in the Latin cultural zone, with the Vikings. Nobody tells us how these 'Danish' wives felt, nor the 'second class' wives of the Irish polygamists, nor concubines and mistresses. The primary wife was allowed to feel resentment, indeed both Irish and Welsh laws allowed her to injure her husband's mistress, the Welsh laws even to kill her. Concubines and mistresses were publicly known – thus Harold's concubine Edith Swanneck was reportedly the woman sent for to identify his body after the battle of Hastings, not his wife, the daughter of the earl of Mercia.

At their husbands' deaths, royal and noble widows on the whole entered a phase of their lives when they were comfortably maintained and well respected. How they got on with their children, stepchildren and grandchildren, as in all families, made a difference to their security in old age, as we saw in the case of Brunhild whose two grandsons treated her very differently. Retirement to a nunnery was quite common among high-class widows, and as remarked above, was by law required of widowed queens in Visigothic Spain. Those who entered convents by no means always took vows or left the world. Angelberga is such an example. Royal and noble wives who survived their husbands were able to busy themselves with the commemoration of their spouses in a variety of ways. In Denmark one Gyda erected a stone commemorating her husband Thorbjorn, whom she described as a very noble thegn. Edith commissioned the *Vita Edwardi*, which is a curious analysis of her own family at the end of Edward's reign, tied up with proofs of his holiness. Eleanor of Aquitaine interested herself in the development of a Plantagenet mausoleum at Fontevrault. These are the kinds of commemoration we might expect. As to longevity, the average age at death of 47 female descendants of Charlemagne over four generations has been calculated at 36, and only 39 per cent of the 47 lived to 40 or more, compared with 57 per cent of the 53 men, but in Saxony men were dying younger than women in the tenth and eleventh centuries.[9]

The Transplantation of Women and Ideas

Kings in particular, and to a lesser extent their aristocracy, sometimes looked far afield for wives. Distant marriages held out advantages of peace making, alliance binding and territorial aggrandizement or its potential. The migration period literature constantly classifies women as peace weavers, pledges of good relations between tribes. The poets are not convinced that the peace will last, 'even though the bride be fair'. In *Beowulf* the fight at Finnsburg episode shows the disastrous outcome of the Danish Hildeburh's marriage to the Frisian Finn, when she is eventually taken home from the slaughter having lost husband, son and brother. The poet calls her heartbroken, and later epics expound the dreadful tussle between natal family obligations and marital family duties. The tensions on such a wife were enormous and her chances of effecting better intertribal/interstate relations by her own diplomatic behaviour were minimal. What really lay behind these diplomatic marriages in the early centuries was more the hope that two peoples would warm towards the children and further descendants of the joined couple, and build on their loyalty to one of the parents to extend amity to the other, and perhaps accept rule by a future descendant. This probably worked better at a local level: the lineages of Ardres and Guines eventually came together through marriage after a century of fighting and by the 1190s could commission a history glorying in both sets of ancestors. As time passed, kings and aristocrats collected a wide range of titles and scattered estates through cognatic inheritance.

As kingdoms and major fiefdoms emerged from the disorder and fragmentation of the early centuries there emerged also an international tier of personnel who performed on the widest stages throughout western Europe and the crusading area. For this international, essentially military, elite the attracting of a wife from afar brought status to both sets of in-laws. Alfred and Edward the Elder laid the foundations of West Saxon success against the Vikings in England, and it is no coincidence that their children commanded international respect and were sought in marriage alliances on the continent. A century later the ealdorman Ethelweard, a descendant of Alfred's brother king Ethelred, sent a Latin translation of the Anglo-Saxon Chronicle to the abbess Matilda of Essen, a descendant of king Alfred. Ethelweard knew that Alfred had married his daughter Aelfthryth to Baldwin [of Flanders] and that Edward's daughter Eadgyth, the abbess's great aunt, had been married to Charles [the Simple, king of the Franks], Eadhild her sister to Hugh [the Great, duke of the Franks], Eadgyth (the abbess's grandmother) to Otto I, and that Athelstan had married another unnamed sister to a king near the Alps about whom Ethelweard had no information because of the distance in time and place. (Hrotsvit of Gandersheim names this foreign bride, enabling her to be identified as Aelfgifu, wife of Conrad of Burgundy.) Two more sisters were Eadgifu who married Louis of Aquitaine and another Eadgyth who married the Viking Sihtric of York. (The stepsisters sharing names were by different mothers.) At the end of our period a royal family with a clutch of daughters to spread in adjacent territories and further afield can be illustrated by Eleanor of Aquitaine's daughter Eleanor and her husband Alfonso VIII of Castile: their daughters married kings of Leon, Portugal, Aragon and France. Some international marriages had both immediate and lasting results: the marriage of the emperor Henry VI to Constance of Sicily established the Hohenstaufens as rulers of Sicily for four generations. By contrast the hopefuls who married the heiresses to the kingdom of Jerusalem in the twelfth century did not succeed in establishing their own lines there and the individual queens did not succeed in disposing of the succession themselves (unlike Adela of Blois), but suffered baronial intervention.

The significant dynastic outcomes to such marriages, in which the transplanted wife's role is more as a breeding womb than as a personality, could take several generations to become clear but the coming of a foreign bride could have a more immediate impact of her cultural and or political background on the host country. Obviously we might expect to find a major impact at a pagan court when the incoming queen was Christian. Christianity was a proselytizing religion: its members believed they should save others' souls by converting them to share their own salvation. This made no role for the bride to keep her religion quiet and look after her own soul only. But it was impossible for her to convert husband, court and country single handed, or even with a little support (see the next chapter). Even a marriage of Christian royals could present problems of practice: Oswy of Northumbria was accustomed to the Celtic missionary brand of the faith, but his wife had been reared in Roman missionary Kent. So they kept Easter by different calculations at different dates. It took a synod to settle the matter, and the queen's Romans won the argument, although there is no suggestion that the queen did any of the persuading.

In a study of Hungarian queens from 1000 to 1386, Janos Bak viewed their importance as agents of foreign influence and immigration. Indeed, rather dismissively (from the viewpoint of the individual queens) he suggested that probably the most important aspect of the early medieval queens' careers was the fact that foreign knights and courtiers came with them to Hungary, citing examples in this period from the entourages of Gisela of Bavaria (d 1065) wife of St Stephen, Judith, daughter of the Emperor Henry III (d 1093/5) the wife of Salomon, Busilla of Sicily (d c.1102) wife of Coloman, Margaret Capet (d 1197) wife of Bela III, and Constance of Aragon (d 1222) wife of Imre (Emeric). In particular, considerable French influence is traced from Margaret's marriage, in the form of Parisian studies, Cistercian foundations and possibly also the western romances, resulting in the Hungarian aristocracy's assumption of Trojan names.[10] The natives, however, did not always welcome a foreign queen and her retainers, relatives or culture, and subsequently came to entertain xenophobic hostilities and rewrote their history to suit. Somehow or other Gisela became *non grata* amid anti-German feeling. Of course in

the *Nibelungenlied* Attila's Huns suffer a bloodbath as a result of the import-
ation of Kriemhild, with Burgundian knights who came to her aid in the
forefront of it. The marriage of Otto II and Theophanu brought considerable Byzantine influence into the imperial family and thence into
Saxony and can be seen at Gandersheim.

In Scotland, the marriage of Malcolm III to Margaret, Anglo-Hungarian
descendant of Edmund Ironside, led to the introduction of much Anglo-
Norman influence which was reinforced in the next generation by the
marriages of Henry I to Margaret's daughter Matilda, Alexander I to Henry's
illegitimate daughter Sibylla, and David I to Matilda, daughter of Waltheof
earl of Northampton and Huntingdon. Norman influence was on the
ascendant in the British Isles at this period and would probably have penetrated north of the border anyway, but the impact was more peaceful and
acceptable because change was introduced by royal patronage rather
than imposed by foreign power. Margaret, who had lived in England for
some 15 years by the time of her marriage, sought help from Lanfranc as
Archbishop of Canterbury for modernizing the Scottish church on the
latest lines flowing from Rome. Turgot, the prior of Durham, became
bishop of St Andrews (and ultimately Margaret's biographer in the work
for her daughter Matilda). Her son David in particular spent years at the
English court in his capacity as earl of Huntingdon *iure uxoris* and enthu-
siastically pushed feudalization in Scotland and encouraged the new twelfth-
century monastic orders' foundations in his realm. Malcolm Canmore's
first wife Ingibjorg is thought to have been the daughter of Thorfinn earl
of Orkney and had his ties remained in this location it is difficult to
believe that the Norman influences would have been felt with the same
speed and lack of resentment. Therefore we can link considerable political
and cultural change in Scotland to the coming of Margaret with her particular background, contacts and personality.

Eleanor of Aquitaine's marriage to Henry II must also feature in this
context. There was in the later twelfth century a great surge of literary
activity in France, which may be traced back to the southern troubadours.
Eleanor's grandfather, Duke William IX of Aquitaine, based at Poitiers,
was a composer and singer as well as a crusading aristocrat and seducer of
women. Bawdy songs and softer love lyrics came from this development
and importantly in the vernaculars of Occitan, Norman French (and later
English, Italian, Spanish and German). Classical myths and Celtic legends
had already merged in the *Brut* and other origin legends and gave rise to
the developed Arthurian canon, again in vernacular languages. Henry II
and Eleanor were in the forefront of patronage – for them Wace wrote in

Anglo-Norman the Normans' origin story, *Roman de Rou*, and the 'English' one, *Roman de Brut*, derived from Benôit de Sainte-Maure's *Roman de Troie*. Marie de France dedicated her *Lais* to a noble king widely assumed to be Henry II. Although scholars are less assertive now of specific patronage by Henry and Eleanor, it cannot be denied that England had a part in this literary outburst, which it would probably not have done if Henry II had married a Scottish princess or a more northerly French aristocrat from Flanders or Boulogne as his grandfather, great-grandfather and predecessor on the English throne had. The courtly love/romance had an importance that was much more influential than just the entertainment of the royal court. Nor did the influence stop at one generation: Parsons argues that Eleanor's daughters carried the Arthurian legends to Germany, Spain and Sicily.

6

WOMEN AND RELIGION

Consideration of what religion meant to women in early medieval Europe, what it did for them, and how it was influenced by them must concentrate primarily on Christianity and in particular the Roman-based church. There were of course pagan religions before the Christian conversion and some of their associated customs and beliefs lingered, especially in remote rural communities, well beyond 1200. Moreover, heresies periodically arose within nominally Christian communities, and there was the rival Islamic faith, physically attacking southern European territory and inspiring a more widely recruited aggressive response in the Crusades; the existence of widely spread Jewish communities in Europe has also to be taken into account.

At the starting point of this study, around 500, Christianity, though an old religion, with weighty tradition and already influenced by many of its most significant writers and saints, was unevenly embedded over western Europe. Roman Christianity prevailed among the old Roman provincials' descendants. The Visigoths, Lombards and Burgundians were Arian Christians, the Franks were being converted from paganism to Roman Christianity and the Angles and Saxons and all the Scandinavians were still heathen. By 1200, when this study ends, the church was a largely unchallenged cultural binding force in the west, expanding with the thrust of colonization, and mounting Crusades in the Holy Land. Within the period the history of the church is dominated by missionary activity and institutional reform and definition, almost wholly spheres of masculine activity within the church. So what was happening in the religious field for women?

The Effect of Christian Conversion on the Standing and Role of Women

Because the Christian church made such an effective official obliteration of pagan practices, and controlled so completely the writing down of both

108

record and opinion, it is practically impossible to see the effect of Christian conversion on the standing and role of women in the first generations, at any level of society. Christianity was in some central tenets a more masculine religion than classical and Germanic paganism had been: God the Father and Christ the Son were essentially masculine, where Juno, Venus, Frigg and Freyja were goddesses in their own right, demanding loyalty or propitiation. The Virgin Mary and Mary Magdalen were not to be approached the same way: they could at best only intercede with the one all powerful God. Furthermore, Christianity took a strong line against women preaching and still more acting as priests, whereas sybils and priestesses and wise women were established features of classical and northern paganism. However, Christianity also carried some germs of equality – equality of the soul regardless of gender, and individual equality before Christ, male and female, slave and free – but it did not quickly effect improved standing for women.

Many women, especially in England, Germany and Scandinavia, including Iceland, became first-generation converts over the period. Too little is known about their previous beliefs to assert how this changed women's individual lives. Perhaps thereafter more of them were allowed to live, as the church fought, though slowly, against abortion and infanticide. The new career option of entering a convent seems to have been more restricted to upper-class women than it was to upper-class men. For the majority of women, who did not enter convents, the change of religion brought some noticeable change to the principles of marriage, though not immediately. In *Women in Old Norse Society* Jochens contrasts the pagan marriage by capture or purchase arranged between males with the Christian free-consenting marriage, polygamous unions and concubinage with Christian monogamy, and easy divorce with lifetime union.

The sources illuminating the conversion process are class biased. A major theme of male ecclesiastical writers was 'domestic proselytization' – the Church's use of a Christian wife to work over her pagan husband to accept baptism. An early successful example was Clothild (d 544), wife of Clovis, who is presented in her later *Life* as starting on Clovis's conversion to her religion on their wedding night. She managed to get his agreement to the baptism of their sons before, eventually, in the crisis of a battle going badly, Clovis decided to convert. She then called upon St Remi, the Gallo-Roman bishop of Reims, to complete the conversion of the king and his men. Later, according to her *Life*, with Clothhild's advice the king destroyed pagan shrines and built churches and did other good works. The converting of Clovis took time and had its setbacks, such as the death of the first baptized baby.

Clothild's great-granddaughter Bertha, dispatched across the Channel to marry Ethelbert of Kent, made little progress in converting him and was chided for this by Pope Gregory in a letter of 601. According to Bede, Bertha's Christianity was useful to the Gregorian mission firstly because it meant Ethelbert had heard of Christianity, and secondly because the queen had been using an old church dedicated to St Martin, established in Roman times, which became an early base for Augustine. However, Bertha had obviously not familiarized the king with her religion since Ethelbert insisted on meeting Augustine out of doors, presumably to make it less easy to practise magic on him. This implies Ethelbert had no comprehension of his wife's religion and was up to this point suspicious of it. Allocating the queen religious space in a church on the east side of the city suggests the same superstitious distancing of the Christians. A generation later Boniface V wrote quoting 1 Corinthians to Bertha's daughter Ethelburga, married to the pagan Edwin of Northumbria, urging her to labour to effect his conversion and suggesting that without this her very marriage was insecure. It was not until after she bore her first child, a daughter, that Edwin agreed to conversion and indeed had the baby given to the church.

Historians have suggested that the role of such proselytizing wives may have been predetermined by politics and their very wooing may indicate deliberate movement towards their faith by the husbands. Clovis may thus have been looking for a Catholic wife to give him some edge over the Arian Visigoths and Burgundians in the eyes of the Gallo-Romans; Ethelbert may have been wishful for alignment with the Frankish royals and their religion. Nevertheless, not merely historical commentators such as Gregory of Tours and Bede, but the words of popes such as Gregory the Great and Boniface V, actually handling the situation at the time, stress the Christian wife's potential as a tool of conversion. Bertha and Ethelburga were Catholic Christian princesses married to initially pagan kings, furthering Christianity against paganism. Other Christian princesses battled with varying success for a particular form of Christianity, Catholicism against Arianism. These included Clotsinda, wife of the Lombard king Alboin, Clotilda, wife of the Visigothic king Amalaric, and Ingund, wife of the Visigothic prince Hermangild. Whether Clothild was converting Clovis from paganism or Arianism is not clear, though the sources imply paganism.

If queens and princesses were domestic proselytizers at the top, and Gallo-Roman wives of Frankish aristocrats in the middle, a role for women at the base of society is harder to see. Two of the fullest early descriptions of conversion procedures are in Bede's *Ecclesiastical History*. After Edwin's acceptance of Christianity Bede describes, almost in passing, an occasion when Paulinus, who had accompanied Ethelburga north, came to Yeavering with the itinerant royals and preached a conversion crusade to crowds of people from the villages and districts who assembled there to hear him and were baptized in droves in the river Glen. Again, an old man who had been baptized by Paulinus in the river Trent with a great crowd of people, in the presence of king Edwin, remembered that event and told it to an informant of Bede's. Bede's accounts make no reference to sexes, leaving it unknown whether women were present or not. The gathering at Yeavering was probably predominantly male, since the villagers attending the court would be more likely to be men offering military or escort service or rents in kind than whole families including elderly parents and small children. (The whole dimension of how far people travelled to attend and how long they remained in the vicinity would become vastly more complicated if the distance was beyond adult male walking range and men, women and children needed accommodating.) Teaching the men would be compatible with the teachings of St Paul which referred women to their husbands when they wanted things explained. These mass conversions were not entirely successful: on Edwin's death in battle Northumbria was overrun and eventually missionaries from Iona had to be sought to start again. A successful mission needed localized staff to nurture it and the early church in Northumbria was desperately short of personnel and dedicated churches. A few weeks after Paulinus' visit to Yeavering there must have been some garbled teachings and confusion in the vicinity and no one, apparently, to sort things out authoritatively. One can imagine this was often the case – a superficial conversion with complete lapses, or confused understanding.

The taunts of Christian converters, including Clothild, about pagan worship of stone, wood or metal images might reflect their knowledge of the pagans' actual practices but might only echo biblical terminology such as Psalm 115 on idols. Two letters of Gregory the Great gave contrary recommendations for pagan shrines: abbot Mellitus was instructed to tell Augustine to resanctify pagan temples so that worshippers could come to their familiar places, but the new convert Ethelbert was instructed to overthrow pagan shrines. Undoubtedly many pagan practices survived the conversion and remained in folk custom throughout the period – and surfaced in some witchcraft cases in the sixteenth century. It seems likely that more of these beliefs and customs lingered in rural areas amid agricultural practices than in the towns, where access to bishops and monasteries was easier, and movement of people and ideas brought greater sophistication. Superstitions relating to animal fertility and crops and weather would take centuries to root out. Countrywomen, routinely involved with the rearing of lambs, calves and piglets, and coping with curdling milk and problems with laying – or not laying – hens would be the more associated with folklore remedies. Churchmen who followed the same assimilative tradition as Gregory the Great found ways to preserve the feasting and floristry enjoyed by the pagans. Even the central Christian festivals slotted into the calendar without disruption: Christmas succeeded the earlier celebrations of the sun's rebirth for the northern hemisphere after the shortest days, and Easter the celebration of spring.

Professional Nuns

Nuns form the most visible professional group of religious women, vowed widows and virgins having a more fluid role and deaconesses being early disfavoured by Frankish councils. (The effect of their restrictions not only closed down opportunity for women to work pastorally, but also deprived ordinary laywomen of receiving the auxiliary ministry some women had been allowed to perform in the early church.) The withdrawal of pious men and women from the secular world into eremitical or communal living to promote more single-minded pursuit of the Christian religion began in the east by the third century. Pachomius (d 346) traditionally founded the first monastery, in Tabenesi, and wrote a rule for himself and his fellow monks and one for his sister and her nuns, who inhabited a separate but interlocking monastery. So female monasticism is as old as male. It reached Rome and the west in the fourth century. The women active in the early foundations were generally from wealthy and pious families, were often widows, and had powerful churchmen as friends and correspondents, patterns which were repeated in many circumstances through our period. An influential pair of siblings were Caesarius of Arles (d 542) and his sister Caesaria, for whom Caesarius compiled a rule for nuns which shows how far the organization of a women's monastic community had come early in our period. Already there were specialist offices to ensure the smooth running of the community, such as abbess, cellaress, porteress, and wool mistress.

There was much wisdom and humanity in Caesarius' rule, which is translated by Emilie Amt in *Women's Lives in Medieval Europe*. He was anxious that girls should not be admitted too young (his definition being under 6 or 7) or before they could read and write and obey the rules. Their entry was not to be a matter of shallow haste, it being generally a year before they could take on the nun's habit. They were to have separate beds in one room, with no private chests. Indeed, the sisters' total abandonment of personal possessions had to be understood clearly on entry, leading to consideration in the rules of how those who had wealth already, or expectation of it, were to divest themselves of it. Their clothing, which was not to be considered their own, was to be natural or milky white and made within the monastery, which itself was to be devoid of decoration. They had to read for two hours from daybreak, undertake duties by turn, and work wool humbly and industriously. The picture is of a wholesome life style. Caesarius was not so unworldly that he ignored the possibility of improprieties creeping in and there were warnings against the receiving or sending of presents or letters, the uttering of harsh words against each other, even thieving and hitting each other, recognition of the tensions which can arise in enclosed female communities. The admission of men on business was regulated, and a significant feature of the rule was the enclosure of the nuns 'perpetually in the cells of the monastery', a feature which the violence of the sixth century made an increasingly important part of the protection of women religious. The Arles rule was adopted by St Radegund (d 587) for her foundation, Holy Cross, at Poitiers, which later went over to the moderate and humane rule associated with St Benedict of Nursia (d c.550), whose vision of monasticism was favoured by Gregory the Great, and became the dominant influence on western monastic life.

In *Women's Monasticism and Medieval Society: Nunneries in France and England 890–1215* Venarde identifies the late seventh century as one of the two leading periods for women's monastic foundations before 1200 (the other peaking around 1150). Double monasteries were a feature of the early period, especially in Belgium (for example Nivelles) and England (for example Whitby). Three famous ones near Paris were Faremoutiers-en-Brie, Chelles and Andelys. In Germany Tauberbischofsheim and Heidenheim were double houses. Double monasteries benefited the nuns because they were associated with high educational achievements and offered powerful career opportunities for the abbesses, who were often influential in local politics. In the double monastery the women's abbess was generally the superior figure, hearing confessions, and giving absolution and benediction to members of the community of both sexes, until the Carolingian reform period when monasteries lost autonomy and women were pushed back from performing clerical functions. Nuns of this period also contributed to the missionary activities of bishops, especially in Germany, performing support services including copying texts and embroidering sacred textiles.

The 817 synod of Aachen approved a systematized Benedictine rule and similar rules were already prescribed for canonesses at councils of

813 and 816. But women's monasticism flagged and the Carolingian renaissance passed nuns by. Viking disruption did untold damage and where a nunnery had been destroyed, it was not infrequently refounded as a house for monks: such was the case at Fécamp. Venarde estimates that there were fewer women's houses in England and France in 1050 than there had been in 750, and that even a high estimate would be only 30 nuns to a house. Between 1080 and 1215 he estimates some 425 new houses for women were founded in England and France. By 1180 Louis VIII had limited Notre-Dame de Soissons to 80 nuns, Montmartre to 60, Faremoutiers to 100 and St-Jean-aux-Bois to 40; Hildegard ruled some 80 nuns when she died.[1] Neither before 1080 nor after were the women's foundations closely connected with the principal current reform movements in the church. It took Cluny nearly 150 years to found a monastery for women at Marcigny, and then it was for women whose husbands had entered Cluny.

Although Caesarius had visualized differences in monasteries for men and women in the early sixth century, any desirable or even only permissible difference between the application of rules in houses of the two sexes was lost to sight. Thus Heloise wrote to Abelard that the one Benedictine rule was currently kept in the Latin church by women equally with men, although, as it was clearly written for men alone, only men could fully obey it, and she argued against the yoking of 'bullock and heifer' since those whom nature created unequal could not properly be made equal in labour. Heloise knew enough about St Benedict to understand his enthusiasm for moderation appropriate to circumstances, and wanted Abelard to devise a rule suited to the nuns of the Paraclete. His response embeds some sound practical suggestions but is a poorly drafted text for its purpose, practically impossible to make reference to because of its lack of orderly divisions or logical arrangement, and though highly ornamental and erudite in parts it stops abruptly rather than being drawn to a close. It did, however, form the basis of the rule for the order.

In *Women and the Religious Life in Premodern Europe* Ranft succinctly fits the order of the Paraclete into the twelfth-century developments, giving it a little more space than the better known Fontevrault, wherein the abbess controlled the mother house and all its dependent priories, and the men in the order were there solely to provide spiritual and material facilities for the women. The English Gilbertine Order was a pragmatic evolution beginning with seven women hermits enclosed as nuns, and expanding to include lay sisters, lay brothers and finally canons. The extra divisions were added to serve the nuns' interests but unlike Fontevrault the women were never in control and later in the twelfth century the women's position deteriorated and before the end of the century some foundations were made for canons only. Some order can be made of these developments: basically women had to tag along in Benedictinism, fitted into double monasteries or provided with their own according to what churchmen of the day thought proper. In the early twelfth century Heloise reasonably voiced the unsuitability of this from the nuns' point of view, and separately some imaginative male founders – Robert of Arbrissel and Gilbert of Sempringham – arrived at dedicating men to the service of nuns in various ways. This subordination of men to women's interests was maintained at Fontevrault but the Gilbertines, tainted by scandal, pulled back. The Premonstratensians, favourable to women in their early years, were soon repelling would-be women members and Cistercians did their best to shake them off. With these generally repressive developments the existence of dominating abbesses and well-educated convents was adversely affected. By and large, conventual educational achievement was less widespread in the ninth and tenth centuries, though some German houses flourished without check, including Quedlinburg and Gandersheim. At Hohenburg abbess Herrad (d 1195/6) compiled her encyclopaedic *Garden of Delights* using a variety of sources including Arabic learning newly assimilated in the west. This testifies to her educational level, and the quality of the Augustinian canonesses' library.

Gandersheim, an imperial abbey in Lower Saxony in the Harz mountains, may be used to illustrate the developments possible in more peaceful situations blessed with political good fortune. It was founded in 852 by Liudolf and Oda, ancestors of the Ottonian emperors. Tradition says five of their daughters took the veil, three in turn becoming abbesses there. These first dynastic abbesses established the house as a centre of learning by the early tenth century. Otto I fostered the abbey, in 947 giving the abbess privileges including a seat in the imperial diet, and his niece Gerberga became abbess in 965. Under her the house maintained its high scholarly reputation and only aristocratic daughters were admitted. Otto II's 5-year-old daughter Sophia was sent to Gerberga to be educated. At this time the house contained its remarkable canoness Hrotsvit, whose poetry and drama are treated below in Chapter 7.

Throughout the period 1080–1170 houses in England and France were fostered notably by the lower nobility, and German convents were nearly all royal or noble. Neither papacy nor episcopate interested themselves much with them. This low level of prelate involvement causes historians to seek some explanation for the phenomenal growth of nunneries in the twelfth century in secular conditions – rising population, increased wealth, and feudal landholding patterns and their effect on marriage. The women entrants into monasticism were virgins, whose families were probably aware of their poor marriage prospects, and widows, who may have opted for (or been pushed into) the cloister to avoid remarriage, or in despair of it. According to Venarde, at Ronceray 27 of 78 entrants recorded in charters between 1028 and 1184 were identified as wives, widows or mothers: virginity might be the great ideal but the practical skills of women of worldly experience (in household and estate management) were consciously valued. The first abbess of Fontevrault, Petronilla of Chemillé, was positively preferred for her qualifications as a woman of the world. Some women were fleeing into religion as a refuge from husbands, and their reception varied. Robert of Arbrissel is said to have refused to send fleeing wives back to their husbands at the request of the husband or the local bishop, but the anchoress at Flamstead told Christina of Markyate that she was not in the business of receiving absconding wives.

Both married or widowed and virgin entrants were from the late eighth century likely to give land to the house on entry – such donations (dowries) constituted a significant portion of the house's endowment. Most new houses rapidly built up a landed estate mainly gifted from the local lower aristocracy. Some of these grants were directly bound up with the entry of a nun, some were perhaps made with an eye on the future with the expectation that in some generation ahead a daughter or widow might be the more willingly accommodated. Investment in a local nunnery could have been a sort of corrodial place reservation for some female in the family. Oblation of a nun was rarely the purely altruistic gift of a daughter. Some element of either motivation would fit with the predominantly high birth of twelfth-century nuns. Hildegard of Bingen defended her elitist establishment when it was criticized for its selective entry and luxurious conditions. The excess of marriageable women over marriageable men was not a natural situation but a societal construct. Men were removed from eligibility as priests and monks, or died in battles and on crusades, and younger sons were restrained from marrying and making claims on the patrimony: they could only marry heiresses.

The twelfth-century economic boom permitted surplus funds to be given to the church and devoted to the construction and maintenance of monastic houses for both sexes. The channelling of some of this surplus to women's houses at least indicates contemporary appreciation of the female religious, though men's houses outnumbered women's in most regions by ten to one.[2] The women religious were destined to become increasingly regulated. The rather idiosyncratic careers of individuals as varied as

Heloise and Hildegard of Bingen and Christina of Markyate began in an age when so much was undefined that imaginative flair could have play. Later, stricter claustration was enforced, orders like the Premonstratensians and Cistercians began to distance their women, Innocent III was keener to regulate than to encourage, and the expansion of nunneries was checked from around 1170.

Because the professional religious abandoned their individuality in the greater service of God in their house or order, they were unencumbered by property and should not have been excessively bound by friendships in any one place. Fontevrault and Prémontré and Cîteaux all arose from individuals leaving their fixed communities in search of a holier life, but this was easier for men. Religious women did move, however, at their own behest and that of others. In 748 Abbess Tetta of Wimborne sent St Boniface 30 of her nuns to support his missionary work in Germany; their leader was Leoba (b. c.700) who became abbess of Tauberbischofsheim. She retired to the nunnery of Schönersheim in 776 and died there in 780, being buried, as he had previously ordered, at Boniface's Fulda. Another of the exWimborne nuns, St Walberga (d 779), sister of St Wynnebald, succeeded him in 761 to the leadership of the double monastery of Heidenheim, where Huguberc wrote the *Life of St Willibald and St Wynnebald*. According to Leoba's biographer Rudolph of Fulda, writing in the 830s, Tetta was 'exceedingly displeased' at the departure of Leoba, whom Boniface had specifically asked for, but agreed because 'she could not gainsay the dispositions of divine providence'. Hildegard of Bingen was less reticent when in 1151 her nun Richardis of Stade was elected as abbess of Bassum in the diocese of Bremen where her brother was archbishop, putting up resistance to letting her go.

Recluses and Mystics

Medieval conditions made it hard for women to follow the more individual strand of eremitical life which was a less questioned option for men. The vulnerability of women living alone opened female hermits and recluses to societal discouragement on two fronts: criticism (and suspicion) of them for seeking a riskily improper life style, and well-meant smothering of them by over-protective males. Ranft argues that female hermits were known throughout medieval society, but her count of 8 in England between the sixth and ninth centuries and 12 in Ireland over a similar period, and 6 in sixth-century Italy, only underlines their infrequent visibility. There was however a strongly eremitical strand in tenth- and eleventh-century church reform, institutionalized in Prémontré and Cîteaux, and the startling *Life of Christina of Markyate* shows the lack of formal definition in religious life in early twelfth-century England. Even for women, however, the theoretical superiority of the reclusive life over communal religious living was accepted and so it was a progression for a nun to leave the cloister community for a recluse's cell, in her own monastery or elsewhere. Eve of Wilton in the late eleventh century left Wilton for St Laurent de Tertre at Angers.

Women hermits, as unprotected solitaries, disappeared as regulations tightened. The woman recluse, protectively embedded in a religious community, flourished especially in the twelfth century. Female anchorites attracted the attention of religious men, who devised rules for them reflecting the laxities they were designed to avoid. One of the more famous authors was Aelred of Rievaulx who wrote *De Institutis Inclusarum* for his sister.

Recluses meditated, read and prayed, practised penance, and uttered counsel and prophecy (in the sense of declaring divine message rather than foreseeing the future). The Austrian Benedictine Frau Ava (d 1127) wrote German poems on Gospel themes. Recluses' days were structured by the Divine Office, and their lives were virginal, removed from temptations of society and insulated from the day to day worries of getting their own food – a servant for mundane matters was allowed. The more rigid directions pressed against them teaching children or developing close friendships except with elderly women and their spiritual directors. Nevertheless, the successful outcome of some fosterings shows they did happen. Hildegard of Bingen began her career around the age of 8 with the anchoress Jutta, whose cell was attached to the Benedictine monastery of Disibodenberg. Christina of Markyate, fleeing an unwanted marriage, lived for two years with the anchoress Alfwen at Flamstead. Alfwen was under the protection of a hermit, Roger, who was a monk of St Albans who had been allowed out to live as a hermit. More startlingly, Christina moved in with Roger, hiding in a small room off his cell. Her career ended as prioress of the regular Benedictine community of Markyate but her biographer's balance of her innocence with the scandals thrown at her shows a career spiced with titillating episodes. Both Markyate and Disibodenberg grew into regular houses for women supervised by male monasteries, reflecting the twelfth-century tendency to regularize and formalize earlier more experimental set-ups.

Mysticism was a matter for the fervent, in or out of religious community life. Centring on an individual's personal knowing of God through religious experience, it was one of the areas of religious activity in which the comparatively unlettered could shine as impressively as the sophisticated theologian. In mystical visions and prophesying women might even be said to have had the edge over men. Though women mystics are mainly associated with the twelfth century and later, Suzanne Wemple identified three saintly Merovingian ones: Radegund, who lived in a cell adjoining her foundation at Poitiers; Balthild, Saxon ex-slave and Neustrian queen, who founded and lived at Chelles; and Aldegund, the virgin visionary known as abbess of her own foundation at Maubeuge.

Although outstanding women mystics and visionaries won enormous respect and were listened to by leading churchmen, secular political figures, and private individuals with problems, they had first to prove their credentials in the world and usually this required male assistance. Aldegund told her visions to Subinus, abbot of Nivelles; Elisabeth of Schönau's brother Eckbert edited hers. To be taken seriously these spiritual women needed as it were a reference from a male religious professional of proven capacity. This leaves a nagging doubt that some of these spiritual promoters may have manipulated their protégés for their own ends. However, the idea of Hildegard of Bingen being manipulated by anybody seems very unlikely. Although the women mystics say they are unlettered, and generally needed male writers to set down their revelations, they were not uneducated in contemporary religious thought. Elisabeth of Shōnau's visions were much derived from popular theology, the liturgy, and the Bible. One of her more extraordinary visions was of a crowned virgin interpreted as representing the sacred humanity of Jesus. A mystical marriage with Christ was an attractive topic for the imagination of women trained to think of themselves as brides of Christ. Hildegard's apocalyptic visions were on an altogether more inventive scale.

The best known female luminaries of the early middle ages came from noble or royal backgrounds and had fairly easy access to churchmen high in the hierarchy who were often their relatives. Elisabeth of Schönau, given to the double monastery there at the age of 12, was of noble origin and had a great-uncle who had been bishop of Münster and relatives who were nuns at St Andernach. She influenced her brother, previously a canon of Bonn, to join the monks of Schönau where he later became abbot. As her fame spread bishops sought her counsel. The 22 letters she left were addressed to bishops, abbesses and abbots, 3 being to Hildegard. Humbling themselves before their Lord, such women handled the affairs of this world with less hesitancy. Hildegard's correspondents – nearly 400 of her letters are known – included Frederick Barbarossa, Eleanor of Aquitaine, St Bernard of Clairvaux, four popes, two archbishops of Mainz, Philip archbishop of Cologne, and Hazzecha abbess of Krauftal. She was quite bossy with some. Cloistered women were not unaware of what was going on, nor did they hold back from weighing in with their opinions.

Laywomen's Religious Observances

Christianity operates through outward manifestations and inner convictions, in other words it requires both public performance and private attitude. The public performance embraces carrying out required activities and refraining from banned ones. The inner attitude involves understanding based on cognitive processes, and belief, dependent on faith. People can be observed going through the motions without it being certain that their inner convictions are secure. Indeed, in the early Middle Ages it is difficult even to see what the outward forms of normal lay piety were at any given time or place.

Lay people had to be baptized: converts at any age and after instruction, subsequent generations soon after birth with, ideally, instruction preceding their later confirmation. Received into the church, the laity ought to attend mass and receive communion, but how frequently they did so cannot be known. Their very access to priests is itself obscure. In Bede's *Ecclesiastical History* and the two versions he wrote of the *Life of St Cuthbert* Cuthbert was praised for travelling into wild and remote areas where others dared not tread. Cuthbert's preaching tours kept him away from his monastery one to three weeks at a time and occasionally for a whole month. Clearly the lay people he saw on these occasions were exposed only rarely to pastoral care. Bede says when a priest or clerk visited a village at this time all gathered at his command to hear the word, and gladly carried out in their daily living what they heard, and, a significant remark this, *could understand.* The process was interactive since they were urged to confess their sins and repent, and such was Cuthbert's charisma that they all made open confession. No reference is made to the sex of the hearers and penitents. By this period the earlier public confessions and penance of the early church were being replaced by privacy, and the allocation of appropriate penances was guided by manuals for confessors known as penitentials. Some penances are prescribed for particular female sins such as taking medicines to prevent conception or to procure abortion, lesbianism, and mothers having sex with young sons. By the 840s Dhuoda, instructing her lay son to keep the canonical hours and be corrected through penance, admitted that she had often been lax in praising God and slothful instead of doing what she should in the seven hours of the divine office.

Already in Bede's day laymen were founding churches on their estates and over the centuries a parochial network was established. Before this a district might have been lucky to have an oratory or an erected cross to mark where Christian ministry would take place when a visiting ecclesiastic came. Until the church was well staffed there were severe limits to the regularity of lay participation in services. In the towns of Italy and southern Gaul where there was continuity of urban episcopates the framework was already in place and the townspeople doubtless better instructed. Any supportive pastoral role ever borne by clerical wives was cut back by progressive legislation in favour of clerical celibacy in intermittent bursts of activity over the centuries. The 1215 Fourth Lateran Council's requirement of annual confession as a minimum for lay members of the church was clearly a tightening and not a slackening of moral discipline, indicating that the situation before this could not have been good.

The church calendar imposed a structure of fasts and feasts which was of general application though patronal feasts could alter the emphasis on celebrations in particular places. We know from the saints' lives that some laywomen were strict about fasting, though these examples are not typical since these women were later to opt out of the secular world for a life of religion and sanctity, and therefore might have been of above average piety before. Sadalberga, later abbess of Laon (d 670), was credited in her early two-year widowhood with keeping vigils and fasts and giving alms. She was at this stage of her life in secular dress, and in fact went on to a second marriage and bore five children before founding a convent in the lifetime of her second husband.

One chink of light on laywomen's receptiveness to Christianity, and belief in and respect for saints of the church comes from their incidental appearance in miracle stories told of holy men and women. In the *Life of St Wilfrid* there is a story of a woman who brought her dead unbaptized child to St Wilfrid and held it out for baptism. When he hesitated, she begged him to resurrect it in order to baptize it. The bishop, having achieved the miracle, demanded the child should be handed in to the church at the age of 7, to be brought up in the service of God. When it came to it, his mother, with her husband's advice, fled with the child and tried to hide him; the child had to be sought and fetched. Faced with the loss of the child's life the mother had tried to retrieve its salvation. Faced later with losing her healthy son's company, she tried to break her promise. Here was a woman who had not had her child baptized but was aware of the consequences when it died in this state, a moral Wilfrid's biographer Eddius was anxious to point out.

Other saints' lives tell of sick people of both sexes seeking miracle cures from saints' tombs, relics and places associated with their lives. Blind, paralysed, dumb and deaf persons were brought to saints' tombs and healed, while others were cured of fevers, ulcerous conditions and haemorrhages, specifically described conditions such as cancer of the breast, and the frequently mentioned possession by demons. As women were prey to all the ills common to both sexes, plus all the gynaecological ones, and infertility in a couple was usually blamed solely on the woman, it is not surprising they were frequent seekers of saintly cures. The childless prayed and fasted, sought the counselling of holy persons, and made pilgrimages to the tombs of saints. After successful conception there was still pregnancy and childbirth to get through and various girdles and belts of the Virgin or saints and even hairs of saintly heads were thought to help delivering mothers. Though saints were portrayed as weighing in at childbirth the church was squeamish about pollution of its premises and from the sixth to twelfth centuries argued about the uncleanness of the postpartum female and menstruating women, and about the burial of pregnant and newly delivered corpses, and unbaptized babies. Women must have been very much aware of their contaminating weaknesses in their fertile years. The sexual act, meantime, was forbidden for so many nights of the year, including the whole of Lent, that the population growth of the later centuries under review could hardly have taken place had the rules been taken seriously.

The saints' lives written about female saints in this period show plenty of women who were thwarted nuns and were cajoled or forced into marriage once or twice but eventually escaped into religious life, sometimes during the lifetime of a husband but more often in widowhood. These women, as will be shown in the next section, were often well born and sometimes able to dispose of inherited lands and wealth to found monasteries. Wills of women – most often widows – who did not achieve sanctity also show them leaving land to the church, or plate or vestments. Early charters show women involved in land grants, mainly as the wives of principal donors, but again sometimes as widows in their own right. However, the wills and charters reflect the rules of secular disposition of property rather than the actual level of piety of men and women donors.

Judging still mainly from the rather untypical examples of laywomen who went on to become saints, mothers were the spiritual mentors in the child's early years, but these duties were best fulfilled if the mothers were themselves pious and educated and with privileged access to chapels, religious personnel and psalters. There is insufficient evidence to show what more ordinary mothers, certainly lacking in Latin, managed to bring to the spiritual nurturing of their children, and least of all to indicate the pious aspirations of women of the rural tenantry and bondwomen. Women en masse, however, do appear at times of crisis, either rallying to the church's arousal of them or forcing themselves on to its attention. St Genevieve in the late fifth century was supposed to have called together the matrons of Paris to fast, pray and keep vigils in the face of the approach of Attila the Hun. Gregory of Tours' report of the role of the women of beseiged Saragossa when the community sought divine protection was described in Chapter 4 above.

Three Crusades to the Holy Land were mounted in the period covered by this book. The popes clearly visualized the early Crusades as male activities, viewing women as potentially negative factors, inhibiting rather than encouraging male relatives' participation. However, women could be positively decisive influences, urging their menfolk to take the cross and behave with valour. Adela of Blois is credited with stiffening her homecoming husband's backbone after his desertion at Antioch. Because of the Crusades' overlapping of holy war and penitential prilgrimage, women's participation in crusading fervour had to be given outlets, including permitted accompanying of the crusaders, financing suitable fighting men to go, and taking part in processions praying for liberation of the Holy Land after the fall of Jerusalem. Ordinary wives and daughters accompanying husbands, fathers and brothers seem to have been few, but such women as were with the Christian forces, from queens to washerwomen, found themselves at times in the thick of sieges, in the perils of deserted camps, and captured by the enemy. In these situations the elite might engage in diplomatic negotiation, the practical carry water to the troops and the pragmatic marry their captors.

Women were liable to find themselves at the receiving end of misogynistic preaching. They were perennially being harangued about vanity and beautifying themselves, and perpetually lectured about dutiful submissiveness to men. The church's representation of Judgement frightened them for their souls and its teachings on penance and purgatory tried to discipline their lives, although christenings and churchings increased their sense of belonging to a Christian community offering hope of salvation. When they died it buried them and prayed for their souls. For laywomen religion was not just something which they were aware of only on entering a church building and while staying within its walls. The church calendar imposed Lenten fasting and dictated the holy days, providing occasions for communal celebration. The church also involved itself in the intimacies of private life, laying down forbidden periods for marital sex and also venturing into parishioners' beds in preaching the dangers of overlaying babies. As the church sorted itself out in the eleventh and twelfth centuries the effectiveness of its teachings became perhaps most noticeable to laywomen in the increasing control it took over marriage and matrimonial litigation.

Women Saints

In a startling application of data analysis to the lives of saints, J. T. Schulenburg has calculated that women formed on average 14.9 per cent of some 2680 saints from c.500–1200 listed in the *Bibliotheca Sanctorum*. Dividing their distribution from 500–1099 by half-centuries, she displayed that some periods were proportionately better represented by women saints than others – they formed only single figure percentages for the whole of the sixth century and the period 1050–99, but 20 per cent or more from 650–749 and 900–49, and 19.1% for 750–99. Furthermore, some areas produced higher percentages over the period as a whole. Italy and France, though they produced more saints, averaged female percentages of 7.2 and 10.4, whereas Germany, Belgium and Britain, producing fewer in total, achieved female percentage scores of 21.2, 25.5 and 27.6.[3] The figures should not stand alone: we need to know also what a person had to do to attain sanctity, and whether either the definitions of holiness or the mechanisms for proving it changed. Clearly the period 500–1200 was productive of saints. Schulenburg obviously thought the overall female percentage was a poor showing in the face of the church's claims to spiritual egalitarianism, and concluded it was much more difficult for women than men to be recognized as saints, but it might seem surprising that so many were. In Britain nearly 40 per cent were female between 650 and 750.

The early middle ages did not look for the scientific explanation for abnormal phenomena. Such things were seen as acts of God. Floods, fires and plagues were deemed divine punishments. Unexpected reversals of dire situations – a patient recovering, a fire altering course with a change in wind direction – were seen as miracles. At this point in the unfolding of events people looked at the attendant circumstances and might identify a saintly intermediary. Practically everyone in the community had an interest in enhancing sainthood. Frightened people felt safer if they could identify with a patron saint of the church, locality, craft, or the affliction troubling them. Professional churchmen and women could spiritually enhance themselves and their institution by proximity to a holy relic, and more prosaically, look forward to an economic future made rosy by the offerings of pilgrims if a shrine became a well-known attraction. Kings embarking on wars and battles hyped up themselves and their armies with the support of local and national saints. The recognition of new saints, and continued signs of old saints' effectiveness, were positive boosts to everybody except the devil; an accumulating throng of good examples and interceders who were just that little bit more approachable to medieval mortals than Father, Son and Holy Ghost. Thus saints multiplied, not entirely by their own efforts, but according to how observers wanted them to be seen.

Schulenburg shows that early medieval male saints were largely recruited from the higher clergy, especially bishops and abbots. Female saints were drawn from women who had chosen pious lifestyles – consecrated virgins, nuns and hermits – and from those who had used power as queens or abbesses to found religious institutions and do good deeds beyond the normally expected levels of benefaction. Individuals with conviction and charisma ran risks for the establishment of the faith. Those who succeeded were viewed as apostolic in the areas they converted; those who lost were still salvageable as martyrs after death. Later, when the church was more firmly established, it was still fairly informally that sanctity was conferred on a person of locally holy repute. But later still, towards the end of our period, rules were devised for the canonization process, and proofs with some substance were required. At tombs, record of miracles was kept, to provide quantitative and qualitative evidence of the saints' miracles after death, and saints' lives were re-edited to buttress the case. By no means were all applications successful. The same developments which made sanctification more testing also made male dominance of the church tighter, cut the opportunities for inventive and original contribution, and imprisoned nuns in less noticeable and less influential activities within their cloisters.

Besides the saints produced in the period, there were saints inherited from the past. So great was the hunger for saints to cling to that saints from past times and other locales were also widely adopted as patrons and legendarily fitted into their new localities. All through the period relics multiplied and circulated, radiating holiness wherever they were brought. Bodily relics – saints' heads, arms, fingers, even hairs of the head – were 'rescued' from earlier resting places and split up by gift or theft among royal and ecclesiastical collectors. The Virgin Mary escaped this rough handling through her Assumption 'body and soul', but the volume of her attributed tears and milk remedied the deficiency. Then there were endless material relics – gravecloths, pieces of robes and tunics and girdles. Female saints, incidentally, were held in high regard by both men and women.

Some of the most popular women saints of the middle ages were inherited from earlier times, for example St Margaret of Antioch, whose legendary escape from the belly of a dragon may account for her association with women in childbirth. The Virgin Mary herself underwent a great growth in popularity from the tenth century. Mary was too perfect to be identified with, but her measureless grace made her the principal intercessor with God. Mary Magdalen offered by contrast, as she was presented, the ideal model of a forgiven sinner holding out hope to all. Her cult took off notice-ably in the eleventh century, and Vézelay was claiming to have her relics by the 1050s.

Paradoxically, the written lives of early medieval female saints have come to be valued by historians for the secular information contained in pass-ing therein. Episodes from saints' childhoods, perhaps their resistance to suitors (socially acceptable or not), a marriage or two (by no means were they all physically virginal), and their use of personal wealth have all been seized upon. The miracle records produce indications of the sort of sup-plicants who came to their shrines, identifiable sometimes by sex, age, place of origin or the nature of the cure sought, sometimes detailing how long the affliction had been endured. Light is thrown on the saints' parents (usually upper class) and siblings (often they came of a large family with more than one saint) and on the pressures of social conformity (for girls, to marry). This information is worth plucking from the sources but not here, where the focus is on saints in the context of religion. What saints of a period are portrayed as doing surely shows what they were valued for doing by their biographers. The lives of 18 Frankish female saints written by contem-poraries or near contemporaries have been edited and translated in *Sainted Women of the Dark Ages* from which all the examples given below (except the Hackness story) are taken. In her introduction, J. A. McNamara tells us the lives were written for reading within monasteries, and to a larger audience on feast days, including anniversaries associated with the saint. They were therefore very much for publication, angled to promote the public image of the saint and mould her public reception. The imaging of women saints was very much the work of male writers, a subject probed in Mooney's *Gendered Voices* (though this work is more valuable for the post-1200 period).

What example did female saints set? It was good to fast. St Genevieve ate only on Sundays and Thursdays and she ate barley bread and beans until persuaded to add fish and milk to her diet after she was 50. St Radegund, after taking the veil, ate only legumes and green vegetables. St Anstrude took no food or drink until she had chanted the offices of the psalter with hymns and canticles on solemn feast days, and took refreshment only at nones or vespers. St Eustadiola never took flesh of fowl or quadruped for her supper over a period of 70 years.

It was praiseworthy to keep vigils, regularly as a matter of course, and specifically in reaction to particular circumstances. St Genevieve kept vigil till dawn every Saturday night. St Anstrude exercised herself with nocturnal vigils and psalms. Saints saw visions. St Aldegund had nocturnal visions apparently as a matter of course. St Austreberta had a vision of her approaching death seven days before the event. St Sadalberga was shown the gates of paradise. Other people had visions of them, especially at their moment of death or after their deaths. Ten years after her death St Gertrude was seen on the peak of the refectory at Nivelles fanning back the flames of a fire with her veil, thus saving the monastery. Five days before St Aldegund's death, her sister had a vision of Aldegund being led to the celestial kingdom, and a sister at Nivelles saw bright light and heard psalm singing the night Aldegund died. At Hackness, 13 miles from Whitby, Bede tells us one of the sisters heard their passing bell toll for St Hilda of Whitby and saw her soul borne up to heaven.

Saints alive and dead performed healing. St Genevieve cured a paralysed girl. St Anstrude healed in her lifetime and her corpse began healing others even before it was entombed, as well as immediately afterwards. St Radegund took a dead child into her cell where Christ restored her to life. At St Monegund's tomb two mutes were given tongue. St Glodesind's tomb cured several blind people of both sexes, and, competitively, cured for free ('no money was extorted from them') three women with fevers who had paid much of their wealth in vain to doctors who had failed to help them.

Within their communities, saints performed the vilest chores. St Radegund scoured the nooks and crannies when it was her turn to sweep the pavements round the monastery, and cleaned the privies, and flung herself into her week's turn in the kitchen. Her reception of beggars extended to washing their heads and picking off worms. St Eustadiola washed the feet of travellers and cleaned their hair. Their rota-sharing humility was all the more commendable in women who had actually created the community by their own gifts and influence. Sadalberga, with the assistance of her second husband, started the building of a convent in the suburbs of Langres, endowing it with revenues of her hereditary patrimony, and had gathered over 100 women there before deciding it was too dangerous a place and moving the community to Laon where it expanded to 300 nuns in two adjoining monasteries. Here she still took her turn as cook for the week, though capable of higher things – her author says she was wise by nature 'in ordering the affairs of the monastery'. St Balthild built the convent of Chelles and the monastery of Corbie and gave woods and farms and wealth to other monasteries and churches, yet at Chelles she cleared dung from the latrine.

The saints were merciless on themselves to the point of mortification. As her biographer Baudonivia nicely put it, Radegund was generous to all but stingy with herself. Her other biographer Fortunatus tells us she tormented herself with iron fetters, haircloth and hot metal through Lent. St Rusticula alias Marcia had her bed made only once a year and declined the offer of softer straw on her deathbed. Gertrude secretly donned a hair-shirt, but let it be known when she declared she wished to be buried in only it and a cheap veil. St Rictrude concealed with fortitude over the Christmas celebrations her grief for her dead daughter Adalsendis, until Holy Innocents Day, when she sought a private place to mourn. Her biographer comments with approval that her manly mind overcame her womanly feelings. This sublimation of womanly sentiment is a feature of other female saints' lives too. The adverb 'manfully' is used with approval of Genevieve, Aldegund, Bertilla and Balthild, while Monegund's biographer sang the praises of 'members of the inferior sex . . . full of manly vigour' as examples to live by.

Saints also performed more whimsical feats demonstrating their favour with God. Genevieve lit candles by the touch of her hand, and Aldegund was similarly powered. Glodesind was instrumental in the sending of a self-propelled boat to a clerk of the monastery who had been waiting a long time on the river bank and had the wit to invoke her to ask God to send a boat. A chained boy captured by thieves was rescued through Gertrude, and a bound prisoner being led to execution was freed and allowed to run away after prayer to Anstrude.

A final recurrent motif in the lives of the *Sainted Women* is that disrespect for the saints, usually after their deaths, was punished (by God rather than by the saint in a fit of pique). A housemaid who had the audacity to sit herself upon St Radegund's high seat was set on fire by God's judgement and burned for three days and nights until confessing to Radegund and begging for mercy. Baudonivia tells us the community prayed for her 'as though Radegund were present (for wherever she is invoked in faith there she is)' – no better phrasing for the belief in the efficacy of deceased saints could be worded – and Radegund quenched the fire, leaving the girl miraculously unhurt. Glodesind's biographer said something similar in mentioning the monastery she had ruled 'and still rules though she rests in her grave'.[4]

The selected *Sainted Women of the Dark Ages* are portrayed leading holy lives in abstinence and prayer, proven meritorious by their visions and miracles. Otherworldly in their fasting and vigils, they also drew on their own secular possessions and ran their communities as abbesses 'manfully'. In modern parlance some are shown to have 'had it all'; their fortunate births to aristocratic families are meticulously recorded and some had enjoyed good and fruitful marriages. Sadalberga's second husband Baso was a 'worthy man' and she had five children after praying for a child when childless. The biographer of her daughter Anstrude calls them 'an elite troop of children'. Rictrude, of noble Gascon birth, married another saint, Adalbald, and had four sainted children. Rictrude's biographer is effusive: 'the man had strength, good birth, good looks and wisdom which made him most worthy of love and affection. And the wife had good looks, good birth, wealth and decorum.'[5] Then came a savage change of fortune – the husband was killed, ambushed by relatives of his wife. In penance for past pleasures she imposed on herself fasts and vigils and prayers plus a hair-shirt, and cast off the burdens of estates and the baggage of wealth, and aimed to be an example to all.

Women of other Religions

Within the geographical boundaries of western Europe populations belonging to non-Christian faiths existed in considerable numbers. Jewish and Muslim women demand our attention, and as it is in the context of religion that they contrast with Christian women, this is the place to give it. The concentrations of these non-Christian communities differed, with the Jews widely spread but scattered, largely in towns, and the Muslims concentrated in the Spanish peninsula and Mediterranean islands, where they were a dominant force for a large part of the period.

Jewish women

The Roman empire had facilitated the migration of Jews round the Mediterranean and into inland Europe. In a multifaith and multiracial empire they attracted little particular attention but the Christianizing of

Europe created polarization and the Christians were soon taking the offensive. Events recorded by Gregory of Tours show the Jews' association with towns, that they were traders, that their women were with them, that they had synagogues which were the object of destruction by Christians, and that their communities were pressurized to convert to Christianity.

Jews continued to spread in Europe, entering England in the wake of the Norman Conquest, and following the twelfth-century colonization into eastern Europe. In the twelfth century they were part of the philosophic and scientific renaissance, especially in Spain, Provence, then France and Italy. The Crusades beginning at the end of the eleventh century were disastrous for them. Mounted to recover the Holy Land from the Muslims, the Crusades fostered hostile awareness of the Jews, and their small communities became vulnerable to violent attack. Extracts from Hebrew Chronicles printed by Amt describe massacres and atrocities in Speyer, Worms, Mainz, Cologne and Trier at the time of the first Crusade (1096). Many Jews of both sexes committed suicide and killed each other for their religion. Mothers killing their children are described in these chronicles as 'merciful'. The Jews are often portrayed as cooped together in some insufficient refuge such as a courtyard or Christian bishop's palace. At Mainz the women, described as 'saintly', threw stones out of the windows against the enemy, and one sacrificed all four of her children lest the Christians took them alive; subsequently the Christians killed her and her husband killed himself. In the twelfth century Jews prospered with burgeoning trade but the second Crusade (1146) brought more anti-Semitism, and the Third Lateran Council (1179) called for toleration. In England the ferment of monastic foundation and crusading and the civil wars left many upper-class people in the hands of Jewish moneylenders (usury being forbidden to Christians) which increased hostility to them, and royal protection was bought at the price of special taxation. In 1189–90 England's Jews were subject to atrocities in London, Norwich, Lincoln, Stamford and York. The pattern was as above, a mixture of suicide within the group and slaughter from the outside.

Against such backgrounds the Jewish women in medieval towns lived out their lives, running with a different calendar. The Jewish family model descended from the traditions of the Pentateuch and the Talmud, complemented by rabbinical writings. Extracts from the code of Maimonides (Rabbi Moses ben Maimon) who was born in Cordoba in 1135 and died in Cairo in 1204, are quoted in Amt. He summarized ten obligations that marriage imposed on the husband and four it entitled him to from his wife. His ten obligations to her were food, clothing and sexual intercourse ('conjugal rights'), a share of his property assigned to her by marriage contract (*ketubbah*), treatment if she was ill, ransom if she was captured, burial if she died, maintenance from his estate and the right to live in his house in widowhood after his death, maintenance for her daughters by him from his estate, until their espousal, and inheritance of her *ketubbah* for her sons by him in addition to their share of his estate with any half-brothers. His four entitlements were her earnings, her findings, usufruct of her estate in her lifetime, and to be her heir if she died in his lifetime. As to how much clothing was to be provided and when, Maimonides remarks sagely that costs vary in places so the guide must be suitable garments for the rainy season and the dry season worth not less than any housewife of the particular country would require for her clothing. Besides clothes she must have house furnishings and the home where she lived; her husband must lease for her a house at least four cubits by four, with an outside yard and a separate lavatory. The furniture, utensils and toilet articles were summarized to be provided according to the husband's wealth. Given the commercial interests of Jews it seems surprising that Maimonides should allow the wife to restrict her husband in his business travel to nearby places only, so that he did not deprive her of her conjugal rights; he needed her permission to set out.

If the wife resisted intercourse with her husband and said that she had come to loathe him and could not submit willingly he must divorce her at once because she was not like a captive woman obliged to submit to a hateful man. However, she would forfeit her *ketubbah* in these circumstances. Those who rebelled merely to torment their husbands (an interesting suggestion) also forfeited their *ketubbah* if persisting in rebellion and after due process. Divorce was much more frequent among Jews than Christians.

Depending on the country, Jewish wives should weave, embroider or spin, and only spinning could be demanded of them if the local town custom did not include work of these kinds. Even if they were wealthy they should not sit idle, because idleness led to immorality. If they were poor the wife had to bake the bread, cook food, wash clothes, nurse her child, feed her husband's horse and see to the grinding of corn – grinding it herself by hand if this was the local custom. Wives had to wash their husbands' face, hands and feet and generally wait on them. Dietary and hygiene practices were distinctive. Women should not go out in the street with head uncovered, make vows or swear oaths and not fulfil them, have sex during menstruation, fail to set aside their dough offering, or serve their husbands prohibited food. Over their heads hung dismissal and forfeiture of *ketubbah* for 'ill repute'.

Maimonides' rulings were flexible according to wealth and circumstance. They were guiding rules for a people spread over different societies and not particularly wishing to stand out against local custom where it was not a matter of principle. The implication is that the Jews in Europe were taking note of where they were, and adapting to suit, but remaining conscious of being Jews and abiding by their ancestral codes' rules on personal relations and diet. Baumgarten's study of Jewish family life in Germany and north France (the Ashkenazim) indicates more shared facets of practice and belief among Jewish and Christian women than was earlier thought.

Muslim women

The prophet Mohammed (570–632) broke away from Judaism and inspired a resurgence in the Arab world which began to trouble Europeans seriously in 711 when the Arabs swept into Spain, defeating the Visigoths. The victory of Charles Martel at Poitiers in 732 saved France from invasion and confined the Arabs to the Hispanic peninsula where only the Asturias and Basques held out. The ninth century saw the Arabs take the valuable Mediterranean islands from the Balearics to Crete, and pillage Marseilles, Arles and Rome itself. The last major Arab fleet to attack the northern Mediterranean coast came in 1015. The Christian tip of northern Spain gradually recovered Muslim territory, growing as the kingdoms of Galicia, later Leon, later still Leon and Castille, Navarre, Aragon and the county of Barcelona emerged and the kingdom of Portugal. Soon after their conquest of England, the Normans conquered Sicily, and just after the end of our period, with the battle of Las Novas de Tolosa (1212) Muslim rule in Spain was confined to Granada.

This outline of the timing and locales of Muslim activity in Europe highlights Spain as the area where Muslim women (including local converts from Christianity and their descendants) call for attention over much of our period. However, there is disappointingly little published in English on medieval Muslim women in Europe. The Qur'an (though translations vary) shows what was demanded of Muslim women anywhere, and surviving local regulations from Spain reveal the practical means employed to preserve women in their place. Little was recorded in writing about Arab household matters which were the women's sphere. The Qur'an offers some illumination but its later interpretation tended to favour the men. Muslim men were seen as the breadwinners and had authority over and responsibility for the women, who were required to be obedient and could be disciplined for opposition. Muslim women had inheritance rights, but males got twice as much as females. A common heritage with Jews and Christians was that there was a forbidden circle within which marriage was not allowed. The main difference between Christian and Muslim marriage was that marrying more than one wife (in fact up to four) was permitted to Muslims. The single were urged to marry. Wives should be virgin when first married and live chastely as wives.

Muslim divorce was, for the men, comparatively straightforward and designed to be effected as smoothly as possible; there was a possibility of arbitrators from both sides. Indeed a 4-month cooling off period was part of the process. Thereafter the divorced woman had to wait three menstrual periods before remarrying; alternatively after this time she could remain 'amicably' in the same home, or leave. (Widows had to wait slightly longer, 4 months and 10 days, before remarrying. If they stayed within the same household they should be supported for a year.) If a man replaced a wife he could not recover gifts/dowry made to the first wife. Only in cases of proven adultery could gifts be forcibly recovered. There were scaled compensations for women divorced before they had been touched, or before they had been dowered. The terminology recommends gentle treatment, reiterating 'equitably' and 'amicably'. One wonders if it was so painless.

Muslims were slave owners and slave traders and this complicated the rulings on marriage. A female slave was entitled to a dowry from her husband but she was cheaper to marry than a freewoman; however, marrying a slave was a last resort 'for those unable to wait'. The Qur'an says a man should not force his slave girls into prostitution if they preferred to live chastely. Slavery and religion were mutually complicating factors in the Moorish occupation of Spain. Muslims and Christians alike thought it acceptable to enslave and trade in slaves from the other belief. As the Reconquest proceeded most of the Muslim women in Castilian towns were slaves or captives awaiting ransom, according to Dillard. Many Castilian towns burned both parties if a Christian woman fornicated with a Jew or Muslim, but Christian men could consort with Jewish and Muslim women. Muslims allowed Muslim men to marry Christian women, so long as the children were brought up Muslim, but did not allow Christian men to take Muslim wives. Muslim Spain and Sicily long contained Muslims, Christians and Jews (whose relations there were on the whole better than those of the same races on middle eastern ground). The emergence of the Mozarabic dialect was part of Andalusian multiculture. Among the Cordoban martyrs of the 850s in Eulogius' *Memorial of the Saints* were Maria, daughter of a Christian father and Muslim mother, and Flora, daughter of a Muslim father and Christian mother. The poetess Wallādah (b 994), daughter of the Cordoban caliph and a Christian slave, defied Islamic conventions.

In practice, Muslims believed in protecting their womenfolk by preventing them getting into harm's way. The regulations from twelfth-century Seville, published by Amt, show some of the mechanisms: keeping women from sitting by the river bank when men were there, and avoiding lime stores and empty places where a man might take a woman alone. Women at the bathhouse were protected from the man who ran it by the ban on him sitting with them. Women were barred from jobs that might endanger them, for example running hostelries. Danger and embarrassment could be avoided by stopping prostitutes from standing bareheaded outside houses, and decent women were warned against dressing themselves up to resemble them. These concerns sound not unlike those of many Christian city fathers, but a reference to dancing girls being forbidden to bare their heads conjures up a world of more sensuous delights. Seville reserved bitter vituperation against Christian priests whose relations with non-Muslim women were cast in a lustful light. (Remember Spain was the country of the tolerated barragana.) Muslim women were not allowed to enter Christian churches where the priests were deemed 'evildoers, fornicators and sodomites'. Of course Muslim women seemed safest shut up in their designated spaces, with daughters and sons up to the age of 7.

Women and Heresy, Witchcraft and Sorcery

A number of heresies, some of earlier origin, disturbed the Christian church in our period. The main ones were Arianism, Pelagianism and Monophysitism. Of these only Arianism has any interest in the context of gender, because, as seen above, there were several instances where Catholic Christian princesses were credited with converting Arian rulers who married them. (Brunhild, on the other hand, was an Arian who converted herself, to Catholicism, on marriage.) The Catholic princess Ingund, Brunhild's daughter, was savagely assaulted by her Arian Visigothic stepmother-in-law for sticking to her own religion, but this attack was probably not solely motivated by religion since there was a political intergenerational struggle in process in the family. More significant than Arianism, in terms of women's participation, were the twelfth-century heresies of the Cathars and Waldensians.

Cathars, identified by this name in twelfth-century Germany, were known as Albigensians in France because of the concentration of them in the region of Albi. Their dualist beliefs were akin to those of the Bulgarian Bogomils, but how much was directly derived and how much coincidentally rethought is not known. Cathars practised their religion and lives on different principles which the Catholic church could not approve. They rejected the priests and sacrament of the Catholic church, following the lead of 'perfects'. They condemned marriage and procreation, and the eating of meat. The perfect were those who had purified themselves from all matter (which was regarded as evil), and these received the *consolamentum*, the baptism of the Holy Spirit, which mere believers could only receive when close to death (after it they could take no food). All the perfect were superior to the mere believers, and although perfect men had seniority over perfect women, in their absence female perfects could lead the community in prayer. Eugenius III recruited St Bernard of Clairvaux to preach against Albigensians in 1145. Hildegard of Bingen urged the clergy of Cologne (where Cathars were noticeably active in the 1160s) to preach against them and did so herself there in 1163, just before some were burned alive. Church councils condemned Cathars from 1165 and Innocent III launched a crusade against the Albigensians in the early thirteenth century but this belongs to *Women in Later Medieval and Reformation Europe*, as does the evidence collected at Montaillou. Cathars in Germany, France and north Italy posed a threat to the established church because they appealed to common folk and particularly, as Hildegard saw, in the face of lax or inadequate Catholic clergy. So Cathars/Albigensians threatened the souls of those they seduced, and challenged the church, with their asceticism comparing favourably with the established clergy.

The Waldensians teetered near the border of orthodoxy. Peter Valdes, a rich merchant of Lyons, underwent a spiritual regeneration in 1173, distributed his goods to the poor and took up itinerant mendicancy. He soon attracted a following, known as the 'poor men of Lyons' but including both sexes. Scriptural teaching was a feature of this sect and went on in people's houses. As late as the Third Lateran Council (1179) the Waldensians won approval for their piety but by 1184 they were banned, along with Cathars. Among heretics, women were until recently thought to have had a less repressed position than in the established church, but this now seems less convincing.

The credulity of the age which embraced saints' miracles and prayed for divine intervention for personal benefits easily believed in the working of magic for good and ill. Pre-Christian practices survived right through the medieval period, some descending from rituals associated earlier with specific deities, others being more general superstitions and rites believed effective in matters of healing and fertility. Practitioners categorized as witches, sorcerers, diviners, soothsayers, spell-weavers, necromancers and such like, often without gender specificity, were condemned in the Bible and attracted adverse attention in secular laws and penitentials. An early sixth-century Salic law begins 'if a witch eats a man and it can be proved. . .'. Mid-seventh-century Visigothic law condemned in nongender-specific terminology suppliers of poisonous herbs, sorcerers and rainmakers ruining wine and crops, nocturnal sacrificers to the devil and his workers, and those using harmful spells. Charlemagne's edicts spoke out against making wax figures, summoning devils, using love philters, raising storms, cursing people, drying up milk and the like. Charles the Bald ordered the death penalty for men or women convicted of sorcery and witchcraft. Penitentials indicate that women specifically were prone to believe themselves riding through the air by night. Burgundian law allowed proven witchcraft by the wife as a ground for divorce. Allegations sometimes look political, for example when Judith, second wife of Louis the Pious, was accused of witchcraft and adultery, and Gerberga, the sister of Judith's alleged lover Bernard of Septimania, who was a nun at Chalon-sur-Saône, was drowned as a witch, thrust into a wine cask and thrown into the river, the first known execution of a woman on grounds of witchcraft in the Latin west. Diabolical monstrosities were reported in monastic chronicles – William of Malmesbury recorded the story of the witch of Berkeley in 1140, whose corpse was snatched from the church by her devil master despite the efforts of the ecclesiastics. Healing magic was likely to be associated more often with women since they were the countryside's healers of first resort. If the patient was cured no aspersions would be cast, but if the patient died it was easy for somebody to think foul play had been at work. The challenge to the church presented by Cathar and Waldensian heresy seems to have promoted emphasis on the more serious Satanic, anti-Christian aspects of witchcraft, and after 1200 a schematization of witchcraft was erected, including both sexes but eventually concentrating on women as the main perpetrators.

7

WOMEN WHO EXCEEDED SOCIETY'S EXPECTATIONS

The gender constraints inherited from the Judeo-Christian and secular Roman and barbarian past and the continuance of misogynistic formulations were reviewed in Chapter 2. Intellectual influences apart, the physical demands of agricultural work led to some division of labour between the sexes, which was considered in Chapter 3. Men's greater physical strength was a fact, one still demonstrated in athletic and sporting records. Women's comparative physical weakness was probably less of a disadvantage to them in urban environments, where there were economic opportunities for them as servants, jobs in other service industries such as inns and hostelries and laundry work, and suitable accommodation for single women – as 'live in' employees or in multiple-occupancy dwellings without the responsibility of the land which was attached to peasant crofts in the countryside. A clearer picture of an urban female underclass emerges after 1200, but did not then spring from nothing. Nor did opportunity for women in capitalist enterprises: there is evidence from the more sophisticated Italian cities before 1200 showing women participating in money changing and money lending and the investment opportunities of the *società*, and also owning houses, warehouses and shares in mills from the tenth century, as seen in Chapter 4.

In the elite landholding and higher aristocratic circles treated in Chapter 5 the women were born into better conditions and though most enjoyed any power under the shadow of husbands, fathers and brothers, a few were recorded acting more according to class than gender – for example Robert Guiscard's wife in armour, and Adela of Champagne and Blois governing her husband's territories in his absence and continuing long after her sons came of age. The Crusades drained aristocratic males

137

out of the west and left their womenfolk literally holding the fort. In these circumstances there were wives who escaped the normal constraints of the laws of property and contract and truly managed their husbands' estates, as in towns wives kept the business ticking over in merchants' absences.

In times before much mechanization and with secular laws stacked unfavourably against them, women's physical and legal disadvantages constrained their activities in fields requiring strength or authority. The church issued a mixed message of equality and inferiority, but was absolutely adamant against women as priests. This had a knock-on effect on the provision of educational facilities, which were to train boys for the church. Some upper-class girls reveal themselves as 'surprisingly' well educated in these circumstances, particularly in the early ninth and the twelfth centuries. But their education was not provided for by formal structures sharing or paralleling the boys' grammar schools and the universities taking over from cathedral schools. Tied up with this is the fact that there was no established way for girls to enter the professions of law or medicine, and few of them attained enough proficiency in Latin, confidence in the value of their own knowledge, and urge to communicate to others, to produce writers to compare with the large number of Latin male authors of the time. By the twelfth century the vernaculars were being used in literary composition but this had little effect on the proportion of known female writers.

Thus in a sense any woman who chose to communicate through the written word was exceeding society's expectations and in the rest of this chapter attention will be paid to five of them, who will be seen to be extraordinary in other capacities as well. It is to be observed that, to fit these women writers most easily into the established assumption that women's education was inferior and institutionally unstructured, editors and commentators have resorted to explanations invoking extraordinary times or conditions. Dhuoda is slotted into an assumed heyday of Frankish aristocratic female learning; Hrotsvit into a particular culturally eminent period at Gandersheim; Hildegard gets away with her boldness with papal support; Heloise just makes it into a period when, in Wheeler's perhaps exaggerative words 'a young woman might hope to be taught by the great masters of philosophy'[1] before the institutionalizing of universities froze women out; Marie belongs to a milieu of intense literary activity. It is as if no one can give credence to the possibility that, even exceptionally, women might have managed to acquire education and communication skills against a background of unremarkable times, fighting a tide rather than swimming along in an unusual current. By explaining away their existence as the product of fortunate times for their enterprise, historians continue to belittle these women's achievements. Examining them apart, surely a good deal of irrepressible personality and doggedness comes through too.

Dhuoda (fl. c.810–c.843)

Women were expected to be wives and mothers. Faced with the retirement of his mother into religious life when he was little more than 12 years old, Guibert of Nogent recollected staring into a void, facing 'the loss of all those precautions for the helplessness of tender years that only a woman can provide'. Guibert acknowledged his luxurious and pious upbringing with nurses in infancy and teachers in boyhood. Mothers were expected to be their children's early spiritual mentors and Guibert said his taught him how and for what he should pray to God, 'as often as she had leisure from household chores'.[2]

It was beyond normal expectation, however, for women's maternal duties to extend to writing down moral guidance for their older sons, in the enchiridion, speculum or moral mirror genre associated over the centuries with ecclesiastics writing for princes and sensitively responsible learned fathers for their sons. Dhuoda of Uzès, wife of Bernard Count of Septimania, did just this. Her *Liber Manualis*, or Handbook for William, has been increasingly widely known since its translation into French in 1975 and English in 1991 and 1998, and a large amount of interpretative work has resulted. The text cited here is Carol Neel's *Handbook for William*.

Dhuoda's work certainly exceeds our expectations of a Carolingian noblewoman's education, religious knowledge, practical acumen and drive to communicate. Our expectations may simply have been underambitious, but on the other hand this is a unique piece of female authorship. Dhuoda states that she began the book on 30 November 841 and finished it on 2 February, most probably 843. She tells her son in the work that she was married to his father in the palace of Aachen on 29 June 824, and that he himself was born on 29 November 826. Her only other child, a son, was born on 22 March 841. She did not even know this baby's name, as her husband had taken him away before his baptism. The son for whom the book was written, William, was between 15 and 16 when she wrote it, and had been handed over by his father to Charles the Bald as a hostage for Bernard's loyalty. Bernard, the son of St William of Gellone and grandson of Charlemagne's aunt Alda, had been made Louis the Pious' chamberlain in 831, but had been accused of adultery with Louis' second wife Judith, Charles's mother, in 832. The family's position was precarious and in the event Bernard was executed by Charles in 844 for treason, and William similarly in 850, trying to avenge his father. When she wrote these events lay in the future, but Dhuoda could see that William's position was difficult and she set down those he should love and serve – God, his earthly father, his king and lord (and the members of his family), magnates and priests, in that order. (The order is very different however, in her instructions to pray – for clergy, kings, his own lord, his father, and then generally for travellers, the sick, all the holy people of God and the deceased faithful, especially his dead paternal relatives.) Dhuoda hoped William would see to it that his baby brother benefited from the book in due course, and envisaged that others might see it. Dhuoda's authorship was therefore uniquely positioned. Any communication intended for her son had to be written because of their separation. His absence from her had obviously not relieved her of the parental responsibility she felt for his moral education. She clearly had doubts about her husband filling this void, for she told her son to pray for his father's dead relations, commenting that because of many pressing obligations 'your father does not do so now himself'.

Dhuoda knew what she was about. She called her work a mirror in which the boy could contemplate the health of his soul. She aimed to train him to please his fellow men as well as God, and win, by these means, earthly prosperity and divine exaltation. The demands she put upon the boy, a layman, were exacting. She urged him to pray not only in church but wherever he was, and gave him prayers for bed and rising, and instructions to keep the canonical hours and perform contrite confession. The boy's life was to be conducted with humility, doing good works, and learning from the counsel and example of worthy men. Priests were to be revered, though some would prove better than others. She assumed he had books for guidance and made recommendations of spiritual reading to him, ending the book with a recommendation of the psalms and the comment 'in the psalter alone you have the material for reading, study and learning' for life. Dhuoda had specific instructions, such as keeping away from prostitutes, and more general ones such as overcoming anger, loving fairness, and being generous to the poor. Thus far fairly positive, if demanding, in her recommendations, Dhuoda next turned to more difficult areas in life – coping with troubles and making amends for things done wrong. She hoped William would attain perfection and find eternal life with the saints.

Dhuoda began the work by calling it a little book branching out in three directions. She then told the boy to read it through, promising that by the end he would understand what she meant. She went on that she would like it to be called 'rule', 'model' and 'handbook', and then launched into a definition of hand, as in manual or handbook and so on. One can imagine the eyes of a 16-year-old boy at a royal court glazing over impatiently when presented with this Latin text. There is a vast amount of scriptural reference and a good deal of numerology which modern readers find tedious, but perhaps William would have been impressed. We are certainly impressed with Dhuoda's absorption of the Vulgate and Christian writings which reflect Alcuin's educational programme for the Carolingians, and her boldness in taking it upon herself to teach her son in this way. It has been generally agreed that Dhuoda's period was probably the pinnacle of Frankish aristocratic female learning. Dhuoda seems to have had scribal help in the writing of her book: at one point she says 'I am having this copied out as an example to you', and at another 'I have dictated [the words of this little book] . . . and have had them copied down for your benefit'. If the baby had been older, she says she would have another copy made for him. However, there seems to be a lot of herself in the wording.

Dhuoda emerges as a very strong woman morally. She obviously had a far from easy marriage with an often absent husband (whether or not he was adulterous with the queen) and rose to the challenge he left her of keeping his authority alive locally in the Spanish Marches. She admitted that in defending his interests she had fallen into debt and borrowed large sums from Christians and Jews. Some she had managed to repay, and intended to go on doing so, but begged her son to pay off creditors from her and his own resources if she died in debt. The impression comes through of a woman trying to hold a small family together under centrifugal pressures. She was trying to prevent William's filial respect drifting away, and to tie him to his infant brother in what she hoped would be their joint religious remembrance of their mother. Politically she believed people's behaviour had deteriorated. But Dhuoda's piety was not the hand-wringing of someone feeling powerless. She hung on, convinced she must pass on not only her faith but the wisdom of experience to her sons. It is possible that other women of the ruling class of her day entertained similar feelings for their politically entangled husbands and sons, but only Dhuoda left the surviving evidence we need to be able to prove that one of them really did.

Hrotsvit of Gandersheim (c.935–c.975)

Women were willingly recognized as professionally religious, as nuns, canonesses, and more rarely as recluses. But it was exceptional for one of them, in this context, to be in the forefront of literary achievement. Ranft, in *Women and the Religious Life in Premodern Europe* calls Hrotsvit of Gandersheim 'perhaps the grandest surprise in the cultural history of the early Middle Ages', identifiable as the first dramatist since classical times, and the earliest known poet in Germany.

Gandersheim was an exceptional community in many ways and has been called the cultural centre of Saxony in the ninth century. Its elitist entrants were able to study patristic and classical writings there. Hrotsvit was familiar with Terence, Virgil, Horace, Ovid and the Christian writers Prudentius, Sedulus, Fortunatus, Capella and Boethius – and not with just a passing acquaintance through others' citations, but well enough to play with Terence's style. This reflects the educational and library facilities of a women's house firmly connected to the Ottonian dynasty and not disturbed by Viking attacks. Hrotsvit was not exposed only to censored material suitable for an innocent virgin. She appreciated fully the situation whereby Christian writers might prefer for eloquence the 'uselessness of pagan guile to the usefulness of sacred scripture'. In effect she produced religiously orthodox messages about Christian virtues and forgiveness – especially in the context of martyrdom – in the Terentian style which was fashionable in intellectual circles but disapproved of for its pagan content. Whether she set out to do this entirely sincerely or as an elaborate literary contrivance makes little difference to our surprise at finding such intellectual free ranging in a tenth-century women's abbey. Remarkably well educated and with a rich literary heritage to hand (she said all her materials were in the abbey), Hrotsvit experimented boldly with a wide range of literary forms. She wrote six plays, eight sacred legends, two epics, one in praise of Otto the Great and one on the history of Gandersheim itself, three long prose prefaces, and many letters and shorter works. A quick taste can be acquired from Katharina Wilson's *Hrotsvit of Gandersheim: a Florilegium of her Works*. The legends embraced a wide range of subjects from the Virgin, and Christ's Ascension, to saints Basil, Theophilus, Denis and Agnes, the near contemporary martyr Pelagius of Cordoba (d 925), and the tale of the Frankish saintly knight Gongolf and his murderous wife. Focus on the Virgin, the Ascension and St Agnes is not out of character for a woman of religion, and the two Greek saints might be explained by the influence of Otto II's Byzantine wife Theophanu, a frequent visitor to Gandersheim; four of the legends and four of the dramas have roots in eastern hagiography. The Cordoban tale Hrotsvit said she had heard from a native of the city who had actually seen Pelagius the hero; it has been suggested this was probably Riccamund, Christian bishop of Granada and diplomat in the service of the caliph Abd ar-Rahman, who visited Otto's court. Thus the selected subjects show how Hrotsvit was inspired by the fortunate position of her abbey with regard to the legacy of the past and current cosmopolitan cultural influence. It is thought the legends were probably read out in the refectory at mealtimes.

The same influences lay behind Hrotsvit's plays, which are claimed as marking the beginning of nonliturgical drama in Europe. Astonishingly, given her background, she introduced a purely farcical episode in a pantry of pots and pans into *Dulcitius*, the play about the martyrdom of the Holy Virgins Agape, Chionia and Irene. The dialogue is rumbustious, and it is supposed these dramas would be performed or more likely read aloud, at court, although they were dedicated to Abbess Gerberga (II). The existence of twelfth-century copies of her plays shows they did not sink into oblivion at her death. The *Gesta* of Otto and the early history of Gandersheim (to 918) glorify the current dynasty and the writer's house which was associated with it, with a distinguished line of active women patrons and abbesses. The history of Gandersheim, finished in 973, was Hrotsvit's last surviving work.

The variety of Hrotsvit's work shows us that she was a writer in full control of her output, able to tackle a range of subjects in a mixture of styles. There is a distinct cleverness about the pieces, and a good deal of sex inversion, which lets us see that this canoness could see perfectly clearly the traditional misogyny around her and challenge it with boldness and humour. She also shows rhetorical skills and an interest in etymology, music and arithmetic, and names her first teacher Riccardis, and her last abbess Gerberga II, herself educated at Saint Emmeram, the Bavarian cultural centre.

Hrotsvit was not reticent in declaring aspects of her purpose and method in her prefaces. Dronke thought her claim that 'many Catholics' were troubled by the tussle between pagan eloquence and less literary scripture was a wild exaggeration and almost certainly a joke, but the problem existed and continued to trouble scholars and educationists.[3] Hrotsvit openly acknowledged that she had not been aware of some of her sources being considered dubious when she set out on the work, and her general attitude to this situation was unfazed: 'what appears to be false today may perhaps be proven true another day'. Referring to learned male patrons she used the usual self-deprecating vocabulary – 'Hrotsvit of little learning and worth', 'little work of a worthless woman' – but paradoxically declared, undeniably, 'I also know that God gave me a sharp mind'.

Hildegard of Bingen (1098–1179)

The structure of the career of Hildegard of Bingen is in outline not that extraordinary for her time, but the details of her achievements make her truly remarkable. Hildegard was born into a socially upper-class (free noble) family blessed with numerous children (she may have been the tenth), at least four of whom, two of each sex, entered the church, not an abnormal pattern. Her entry into the church was not out of the ordinary: given by her parents at around 8 years old, she was placed in the care of Jutta von Sponheim, living (from 1112 apparently) in a hermitage attached to the Benedictine male monastery at Disibodenberg, an association which developed informally into the nuns' part of a double house and burgeoned into a house of nuns of which Hildegard became head, moving the house to Rupertsberg near Bingen in 1152. (Thus far the outline is not dissimilar to the contemporary career of Christina of Markyate, apart from the fact that the latter entered the church in defiance of her parents' attempts to marry her off, and did it more scandalously, hiding in the cell of a male hermit.) What might be seen today to be Hildegard's 'clay feet', namely her elitist inclinations and her autocratic personal self- interest, come directly from her background. She admitted only well-born nuns to her community, and on feast days allowed them luxurious garb including crowns or tiaras; when criticized on these points by the canoness Tenxwind of Andernach she blithely defended both. When her favoured companion the nun Richardis of Stade was promoted to the headship of another abbey, in 1151, Hildegard raised all manner of objections to the young woman's departure, fearlessly identifying what was patently unacceptable to her personally as being a project unacceptable to God. (This was a battle she lost.)

Hildegard did not remain simply a professional churchwoman at the glass ceiling that a woman with birth and connections could reach in the twelfth-century church. She crashed triumphantly through, receiving express command from Eugenius III to produce further visionary work, and, extraordinarily, preaching to mixed audiences of churchmen and laity with the church's approval – four preaching itineraries, undertaken between 1158 and 1171, are known, and the fame of her sermons led to requests for copies of the texts. Her main works, in order of composition, were *Scivias* (*Scito vias Domini* – Know the Ways of the Lord) completed in 1151, her most famous visionary work, which Eugenius III commended in incomplete form to the synod at Trier in 1147–8, the *Liber Vite Meritorum* (Book of Life's Merits) completed in 1163, a further work of visions and commentaries, and a final visionary work *De Operatione Dei* (On the Activity of God) also known as *Liber Divinorum Operum* (the Book of Divine Works) finished around 1174. Her visions are described, then interpreted, and some manuscripts were pictorially illustrated. She also wrote the first known extant liturgical morality play, *Ordo Virtutum* (the play of the virtues), developed from *Scivias* and set to music of her own composition. Two very early manuscripts survive of her musical texts and scores, the *Symphonia*: one the Dendermonde manuscript prepared at Rupertsberg around 1175, and the other the Riesenkodex, prepared there in the 1180s after her death. Hildegard also attempted scientific writing embracing cosmology, theology, physiology and medical fields. Originally it seems known by the title *Liber Subtilitatum Diversarum Naturarum Creaturam* (Book of the Intricacies of the Diverse Natures of Creatures) the work is now known only from thirteenth-century texts copied after it had already been split it into two: the *Liber Simplicis Medicinae* (Book of Simple Medicine), known since the 1533 edition as *Physica* (Natural History) and the *Liber Compositae Medicinae*, since the 1903 edition known as *Causae et Curae* (Causes and Cures). Selections from this latter were published in 1999 by Margret Berger as *Hildegard of Bingen On Natural Philosophy and Medicine*, bearing a warning that the text's attribution has been undermined, being possibly a post-Hildegardian compilation. Hildegard also conducted wide-ranging correspondence with church and lay people, putting out letters which vary from bold criticisms of secular clergy, made to their faces, and reprimand of the Emperor Frederick I, to agony aunt advice to suppliants seeking guidance – some 400 of her letters are now edited. Her works are in Latin, though it appears that she was not, unaided, strong in syntax. Some of her preaching is expressly described as in Latin, but she may also have used German.

These achievements constitute a totally remarkable output in quantity and range for any twelfth-century writer, but from a woman truly phenomenal. There is no doubt that Hildegard's entire career was underpinned by the conviction, shared by herself and the highest church authorities, that she was merely the feeble vessel (she called herself *paupercula*, poor little woman) chosen by God as the conduit for his messages to humankind at that moment. With St Bernard of Clairvaux and Eugenius III sponsoring her, Hildegard could not have won higher earthly recommendation. Underlying misogyny might well have motivated attack on her had she given any ground for suspicion of her doctrinal orthodoxy, but Hildegard did not stray from the orthodox and indeed preached against Cathars.

Hildegard claimed to see it as her duty to convey God's utterances to the world but there was not the same compulsion directing her to enter the field of natural philosophy and medicine, subjects similarly rarely tackled by female writers. It was Hildegard's holy reputation which made her writings on any subject respectable. Very soon after her death in 1179 attempts were begun to achieve her canonization, including the collecting of her letters and preparation of illuminated manuscripts of her texts and the composition of a *Life* incorporating autobiographical fragments. The main proceedings belong to the 1230s and failed for lack of satisfactory evidence of miracles, but the single thirteenth-century text of the Causes and Cures has '*Beate Hildegardis Cause et Cure*' at the start of the text and she continued to be referred to as St Hildegard through the middle ages and indeed beyond: the 1533 edition of the *Physica* is entitled *Physica S. Hildegardis*. Thus the charisma of Hildegard as a holy woman made it continue to be worth associating her name with her works, adding value to them. Hildegard, in sum, shows how the career of a well-born woman entering the church could develop in the particular circumstances of the twelfth century, but also how this particular woman extraordinarily transcended so many of the normal restraints on such women, such as the bans on women preaching, and how she could be accepted and respected not only at the time but ever since. Over 300 years later the monastic humanist Johannes Trithernius accepted her medical writing, convinced that a woman could only have known such things from the Holy Spirit. The conviction of the God-given supernatural nature of her insights thus held even in the nontheological field. Her scientific works combine some interesting observation with much contemporary misinformation. Hildegard's ideas, despite idiosyncrasies, belong loosely to the twelfth-century cloister tradition, but she had some curiosity and independence in her treatment, and a surprisingly nonjudgemental attitude to sexual relations.

Heloise (d 1163/1164)

The story of Heloise, whose date of birth is unknown, is absolutely extraordinary. Initially educated by the nuns of Argenteuil, she moved to Paris to live with her uncle Fulbert, a canon of Notre Dame. In her uncle's house, she became the lover of the philosopher Peter Abelard, who moved into the house with the intention of seducing her. He (born in 1079) is imagined to have been about 20 years her senior, though she could have been anything from about mid-teens to late twenties when their affair began; she is usually imagined as being around 17. Their relationship was supposed to be that of pupil and private tutor. Preoccupied with a reckless affair, his public teaching tailed off and the scandal became widely known, though only belatedly discovered by the uncle. Heloise became pregnant and Abelard whisked her off to his sister in Brittany, where she had a son. Abelard and Fulbert came to terms, whereby Abelard agreed to marry Heloise but in the interests of his reputation insisted Fulbert keep it secret. When Abelard went to Heloise in Brittany to carry out the plan she at first resisted, claiming she would prefer being mistress to being wife. Abelard prevailed, and after the birth the couple returned to Paris, leaving the child with Abelard's sister; they married at dawn a few days later, separating to conceal the event. Fulbert soon began telling of the marriage, which Heloise denied, and Abelard presently delivered her to Argenteuil again, making her dress as a novice. Nevertheless, he visited her there and apparently they indulged in sexual intercourse in a corner of the nuns' refectory (in recollecting this episode his phraseology is coy, but he is acknowledging something shameful given the circumstances). Fulbert and his friends, feeling Heloise had been betrayed, took vengeance on Abelard by castrating him. After this Abelard ensured she became a nun and only afterwards became a monk himself. Some 14 years later he wrote down, in what purported to be a letter of sympathy to a friend, self-indulgent musings over the calamitousness of all this, and other troubles, *for himself*. In this *Historia Calamitatum*, the source of most of the above details (the rest being from their subsequent correspondence), he claimed that he had remained continent until deciding to bed Heloise, who was already renowned for her learning, and that he wormed his way into proximity by persuading her grasping uncle to take him as a lodger, who would educate the niece: indeed Fulbert gave him 'complete charge' of her. Some education!

A few years before penning the *Historia Calamitatum* Abelard discovered that the nuns of Argenteuil, where Heloise had become prioress, had been ejected and dispersed by Abbot Suger of St Denis, and he arranged to establish a group of them under her as abbess at his former oratory dedicated to the Paraclete, near Troyes. Eventually it seems some third party showed Heloise the *Historia* in which Abelard treated her so unaffectionately (if, as some argue, he wrote it meaning her to see it, it was heartlessly cruel). She saw through it at once – 'you wrote your friend a long letter of consolation, prompted no doubt by his misfortunes but really telling of your own', and she reproached him 'heal the wounds you have yourself inflicted'. She revealed how much he meant to her and how completely she lost herself in him; she had entered religion at his request only to prove his complete possession of her body and will; he still had her heart. She burned with shame at the distrust which had made him ensure that she had taken her vows before he did the same. In this first letter of the series of three she wrote to him at this time, she addressed him as 'master or rather father, husband or rather brother', and called him 'beloved'; he responded more distantly addressing her as 'dearly beloved sister in Christ' (as he might have addressed any abbess). In her second letter she called him 'my only love', and in replying he unbent sufficiently to call her 'my beloved' and 'my inseparable companion', but he refers a little testily to her bringing up the matter of their entry into religion as 'your old perpetual complaint'. She got the message and promised in her third letter to rein in her hand from writing in this vein, and she moved thereafter towards a relationship of two professionally religious individuals. Both of them achieved successes in the eyes of contemporaries, he as a philosopher, she as abbess, before their deaths some 20 years apart. The year after his death in 1142, Peter the Venerable, abbot of Cluny, took Abelard's body for burial at the Paraclete, of which he had been the founder. Heloise was later buried alongside, and after many vicissitudes their remains lie together in the Père Lachaise cemetery in Paris. A thirteenth-century manuscript of the Tours Great Chronicle claimed that she was buried in his tomb, and that his corpse raised its arms to embrace her when she was put in.[4]

Plenty is known independently of Abelard, who was the great unsettling thinker of his generation, and some independent information about Heloise exists, but the correspondence of the two, on which so much is built, is known only from late thirteenth-century and later manuscripts. The authenticity of the letters, particularly of hers, has been questioned, but current opinion is largely in their favour. Moreover, Constant J. Mews has recently opened up the case for identifying earlier love letters between the two (Heloise remembered he wrote incessantly to her when bent on sinful pleasures) in the text known as *Epistolae Duorum Amantium* (a text purporting to be letters between a male master and a female pupil) copied from a manuscript at Clairvaux in the late fifteenth century.[5] Even the better known original letters, without the reinforcement of the 'lost' set, present enough of a challenge to the commonly held assumption of male educational monopoly. The words attributed to Heloise are masterful, strongly argued and classically referenced. Whoever wrote them had an education the equal of any contemporary male. Would the young Heloise have received such foundation teaching at Argenteuil in the early twelfth century? Would a canon of Notre Dame have taken his niece into his bachelor household and planned continuing education for her? (Her mother's Christian name Hersinde is known, but her father is never identified and it is possible Fulbert was her father.) Would her continuing study with the foremost teacher of the day really have been his ambition for her, whether uncle or father? Did she actually learn much from Abelard except illicit sex? ('More kissing than teaching' was his recollection of their activity.) Would a pregnant woman in her late teens, or even late twenties, have reacted to her teacher's offer of marriage with the old argument of misogynists that scripture and philosophy do not go with babies and nurses and the muddle and squalor of small children, declaring that he must not bind himself to her and it would be better if their relationship remained one of free love rather than marriage? In some ways the whole construction seems 'over the top', yet the text shows awareness of what might well have been the attitude of the outside world and is not oblivious to the scandals caused. External sources testify to Heloise's contemporary intellectual reputation. Mews quotes Hugh Metel (d c.1150) writing of her surpassing her sex in her composing, versifying, and joining new words, 'making known words new'. Peter the Venerable of Cluny wrote to her after Abelard's death with flattering reference to her early 'name and reputation, not yet for religion but for . . . virtuous and praiseworthy studies'. He reminded her how she had turned her zeal for learning to a better direction, 'as a woman wholly dedicated to philosophy in the true sense' she had 'left logic for the gospel, Plato for Christ, the academy for the cloister'.

If Heloise wrote the letters attributed to her she can indeed be credited with complete mastery of the literary and dialectical skills of the day, learned without dilution in deference to her sex. Her letters to Abelard appear sharper, often less convoluted than his to her. It seems not untypical that all we know of their son, Astrolabe, in later life, is a long verse letter of advice to him from Abelard, described by Radice as rather platitudinous, and from Heloise a practical request to the abbot of Cluny to secure him a prebend. In the matter of the rules for the Paraclete Heloise could identify and analyse the problems; a later, undated set of rules reflecting Abelard's recommendations but by no means slavishly accepting all of them may be her work. Intellectually she was powerful, able to match her opponent in argument according to the rules of verbal engagement – rules dominated by men. Emotionally, however, Heloise appears more fragile, pining for the man who had possessed her, obsessed with the memories of their time together. Abelard had moved briskly on; Heloise had not. Despite his sexual infatuation – Heloise accused him of having lust rather than love for her and he agreed – he had sloughed it off. She had not, and was even more tormented by awareness that in her subsequent religious life she was a hypocrite in letting longing for him wash over her while going through the motions of being a pious nun. It has been argued that the so-called correspondence was the literary construct of one brain, Abelard's, but it would have been extraordinary for any one twelfth-century writer to characterize the reactions of a man and a woman to the break-up of an infatuation, and to maintain their different stances throughout the exercise, having experienced the one but only imagining the other. We are left with a life of experiences beyond expectation and stranger than fiction.

Marie de France (fl. 1160–90)

Fiction, however, is how our last writer did make her mark. Twelve short poems in Old French in British Library Harley 978, a thirteenth-century manuscript, are now generally known as *The Lais of Marie de France*. The first of them, 'Guigemar' has at the start of the second sentence 'hear my lords the words of Marie'. There is no proof that all twelve are the work of the same author, it could be that the name Marie was a scribal addition, and it is possible there was not a woman author at all. The same manuscript also contains a collection of fables. In this set, the epilogue offers the information 'at the close of this text, which I have written and composed in French, I shall name myself for posterity: my name is Marie and I come from France'. A rather different text, *Espurgatoire Seint Patriz* (St Patrick's Purgatory) contains the lines 'I Marie have recorded for posterity the book dealing with the purgatory'. These three Maries are commonly identified as one person, believed to be a noblewoman of French descent and ecclesiastical education, living in England in the later twelfth century. Many particular identifications have been suggested – Eleanor of Aquitaine's daughter Marie of Champagne, the patron of Chrétien de Troyes, King Stephen's daughter Marie, Countess of Boulogne, sometime abbess of Romsey, an illegitimate daughter of Geoffrey Plantagenet who became abbess of Shaftesbury, another abbess, Mary, of Reading, and another Marie, daughter of Waleran de Beaumont (alias de Meulan), a lord of the Vexin. The actual form 'Marie de France' is found only from the sixteenth century. Alongside the references to an authorial Marie within the works, there is supporting evidence from another writer: in Denis Piramus's poem on the life of St Edmund the king dating from c.1180 he mentions that 'Dame Marie' wrote lays in verse, which were very popular especially with the ladies. Two other internal clues prove too vague to be helpful: the lays' prologue dedication to 'a noble king' and the fables' declared commission by a count William: there are several identifications possible for each of these.

'Marie de France' therefore represents, at present state of knowledge, a sort of identikit noblewoman author of the later twelfth century, who produced dainty entertainment in palatable sized gobbets for the Anglo-Norman aristocracy. Certain characteristics of the lays have been thought to suggest a feminine touch – a lack of interest in details of weaponry or warlords (though not a disregard for chivalry), a tendency to make the heroines the resourceful partner, and some concern for the treatment of infants in the stories. 'Marie' translated the *Espurgatoire* from Latin into French, and the fables from English into French, so if these are the work of the same 'Marie' she had a good command of the three languages. The tales rove over England and Wales, Brittany and Normandy, suggesting an Anglo-Norman milieu for both audience and author, though the stories appealed more widely and were translated into Italian, German, Old Norse, English and Latin in the medieval period. In their introduction to *The Lais of Marie de France* Burgess and Busby suggest the prominence of adultery as a motif, and some cavalier dissolutions of marriage and interest in chivalry all indicate the author was not 'steeped in ecclesiastical ideology', even though several abbesses are among the suggested identifications, and the same editors consider her education 'almost certainly religious'.[6] Hrotsvit and Heloise have already shown us, however, that an abbess and her flock were not always exclusively steeped in ecclesiastical ideology.

As an unidentified person, 'Marie de France' incorporates many features of the aristocratic culture of her time. To call her 'the earliest known French woman poet', as claimed on the cover of the Burgess and Busby edition, is going too far, however, without qualifying 'earliest', 'French' and 'poet'. Two of the Provençal *trobairitz*, the Countess of Dia and Castelloza, cannot be ignored. Dates are uncertain for any of the three, but the countess could be as early as the third quarter of the twelfth century. Even if Marie is indeed the earliest it needs to be remembered that other women were writing French poetry of high quality around the time, though the 'French' of the north and south is different. As the Provençal lyrics were not narrative, Joan Ferrante's phrasing of Marie's claim to fame as 'the first known woman to write narrative poetry in the vernacular in western Europe' is sounder.[7] In her primacy, 'Marie' has to be seen as exceeding expectation; in other respects she represents the top line of the possible. The attribution of the corpus of works described above to her is buttressed by a series of assumptions: that a well-born woman (as indicated by her 'courtly' interests) could be so well educated (as to translate between three languages) and could be so successful (attested by Denis Piramus) that work was commissioned (internal evidence in the Fables) from her. Three times at least this 'Marie' inserted her name into her poetry; this was still an age when much composition remained anonymous, therefore in attaching her name to her work Marie was in the forefront of changing literary fashion (anonymity diminishes with the thirteenth century). If she put her name in other works, copyists did not pass it on. What we can hold on to is the fact that even when it was not necessary to attach an author's name to a piece of work, this woman's name was attached to three particular pieces, two of which potentially open up the authorship to other lays and fables of similar style found in the same manuscript (in the Harley 978) and found in other manuscripts singly and in various groupings not always in the same order. To have the author's name in the first lay and at the end of the fables makes more sense of this being a claim to authorship of the group in question than if the name was found in one of the lays or one of the fables embedded in the middle of the sets.

Admittedly, however, it was also easy for an attributed work to attract accretions and end up with more than one author's contributions all imagined to be of one origin. Including 'Marie de France' in this chapter might seem a step too far, claiming a woman writer when it is not known who she was, if there was only one of her, if there was ever for certain such a woman at all. Regarding 'Dame Trota/Trotula' of Salerno, claimed by some as the first female medical professor, and author of a book on the diseases of women, there is even more obscurity. Monica Green's introduction to her English edition of *The Trotula* published in 2001 establishes that the so-called text 'Trotula' was originally three separate works, two being anonymous and the middle one (using the ordering in the 'standard' ensemble) being attributed to a woman healer, Trota of Salerno, author also of the larger *Practical Medicine According to Trota* discovered in the early 1980s but exerpted in the late twelfth-century compilation *On the Treatment of Illnesses*. The name Trocta/Trotta was common in south Italy between the late eleventh and thirteenth centuries and there is no closer identification of this particular one although in Green's opinion 'no doubt that such a healer existed'.[8] Trotula, a diminutive form, applied to the 'little' work of Trota to distinguish it from the bigger work, was mistakenly extended to cover two other anonymous treatises also on aspects of women's health and cosmetics, and then assumed to be the name of the original compiler. Trota is therefore even more obscure than Marie de France, and seems just too nebulous to be given her own section here. Furthermore, there seems to be another peculiarity about her in the context of this chapter. Women practising medicine above the local midwife/family nurse level were 'beyond expectation' generally in Europe, but twelfth-century Salerno was a uniquely advanced medical centre, and 'women of Salerno' are mentioned, in the plural, in twelfth- and thirteenth-century medical texts, indicating that their practices were orthodox and respected, particularly in women's medicine, where it was fully appreciated that female patients might feel it immodest to offer themselves to a male physician.

The women treated in this chapter have been chosen for their exceptional activities. In no way are they presented as typical. But they might have been less extraordinary than we think them, because our knowledge of them derives from their own writings; women's writings from this period are rare survivals, and may well indeed have been rare creations, but it is easy to think that some other women's writings might have been lost, particularly if they were more amateurish than these and the women more obscure. Where a text was tightly associated with a renowned writer, such as Hildegard, it was handed down with its provenance repeatedly recorded. This shows us that an outstanding woman could make her voice heard at the time without resorting to male pseudonym or anonymity. It also shows us that the next generations were willing to carry on taking seriously work originating with a woman. But for women writers the textual thread is often tenuous, as Dhuoda's case illustrates perfectly, the *Handbook* being known from one late tenth–early eleventh-century text consisting of nine fragments, a seventeenth-century copy (with errors) of a different earlier text, and a fourteenth-century text (corrected against another lost early copy) itself only discovered in the 1950s. It will be disappointing if some as yet unnoticed clues in manuscripts somewhere do not bring further medieval women and their achievements to light, or supply more information about the ones we recognize but know still comparatively little about at the moment.

8

CONCLUSIONS

Continuity and Change

Throughout the period, many conditioning factors in European women's lives changed little. Social class at birth very much dictated their future potential. Where laws made any gender distinction it was mainly to the woman's disadvantage: first her father, then her husband, overshadowed her, although this was widely seen as protective and for the woman's good, as it often was. The Christian church acknowledged women's souls as equal, but retained distaste for their physical bodies, seen as polluting, and tempting men to sin. Women were not to be countenanced as priests, and from this developed an imbalance in training opportunities, so that they did not enter other professions such as law and medicine either. As far as the administration of justice was concerned they were the less preferred sex even as witnesses, so obviously were not going to take more official roles. In the home they did the housekeeping; on the farm they did the 'lighter' work rearing smaller animals and hens, dairying and weeding and vine tending and helping with the harvest; in trade they were mainly active in the less prestigious local distribution end of the market.

'And yet . . .' we may say. Several Merovingian kings elevated slaves to wives and queens. One of these, Balthild, was recognized as clever, and remembering her own background actually took action to benefit slaves by banning the sale of Christian ones and buying the freedom of some. A saint, she was also a self-made woman who strove to improve conditions for those as low as she once was. This is an extreme example, but most class systems allow some movement and for women in the middle ages this was often by the mechanism of marriage. In *Women in Frankish Society: Marriage and the Cloister 500–900* Suzanne Wemple drew attention to the importance of the social bridging achieved by women of the Merovingian age: the upper classes in marrying across ethnic divides (Gallo-Roman, Frank, Visigoth, Burgundian) and the lower classes intermarrying free with unfree.

Detailed analysis of charters of individual ecclesiastical houses or several in a district is bringing out women as more active than once thought. Their involvement in transactions with husbands and sons does indeed tie them in with family inheritance and property, but seeing their names we begin to feel more assured that men respected not being able to alienate their wives' property without their consent, and, more significantly, we find wives consenting to the alienation of property legally their husband's, indicating a more conjugal sharing attitude in practice than the letter of the law demanded.

In the church, women were certainly kept from priestly ordination and the opportunity for their highest penetration of ministerial activity, the role of deaconess, was cut back, but then we find Hildegard of Bingen on preaching tours and men requesting texts of her sermons. If there was little revolution in women's home management and farm tasks over the period, there was some advance towards the more prestigious capitalizing of trade with women financing *società* and owning parts of mills.

One characteristic of this mixture of continuity and change is that developments were not steadily in one direction. Periods of comparative repression such as the Carolingian disciplining of women in the church came to an end, not as a matter of policy but as a consequence of imperial disintegration and decentralization, causing control by church and state to wither. Periods of openness and innovation, as in the twelfth-century flowering of Fontevrault and the Gilbertines, ran into repression by the end of the century.

How women fared, then, was often a knock-on effect of greater movements in church or society. These too were often less planned than forced by circumstances. Invasions of different peoples with different religions affected both secular and religious society. Invading groups had to fight initially in order to establish themselves, and then had either to carry on fighting until dominant, or compromise, settling for assimilation. The invaded had either to rally to repel the newcomers, or to cope with absorbing them. The former option elevated military priorities among both invaders and invaded, and women tended to become something to protect, or fight over. The latter brought them a more active participation in binding the two groups. But at the end of the period the rallying to repel Arabs from Spain was giving the women needed to establish the advancing frontier settlements new opportunities for an adventurous life and enhanced status.

Another more general changing circumstance was the population expansion clearly visible in the last centuries under review. Whether this sprang from improved climate (benefiting crop yield) or political circumstances (some reduction of war and the deaths and damage it caused, with improvement in trade) or moral pressure (the church's action against infanticide, abortion and contraception) it clearly happened. Once begun, it snowballed as more hands expanded the area under cultivation in 'old Europe' and opened up colonization on the eastern front. Grains and wines were shipped in greater quantity, supporting agricultural specialization and allowing places to rely on food imports, and consequently to do other things than subsistence farming, and landlords strove to attract labour. In the booming twelfth century there was capital to spare to found churches and monasteries and enjoy luxury goods and time-killing literature. However, the expansionist era was heading for trouble by the end of the period, outrunning natural resources.

Expectation and Achievements

The generality of women conformed to society's expectations and passed uncommented as a result. Fortunately for historians, the urge to record, as distinct from comment, has left evidence of a satisfactorily solid kind. The church, in its capacity as the most literate and undying of landowners, saw early value in setting in writing the working resources of its estate units in terms of human stock and peasants' obligations in kind and labour. From the ninth-century ecclesiastical polyptyches to England's Domesday Book of 1086 and manorial surveys of the same and the next century, we can deduce the areas of agricultural economy in which women were most active by specialization (such as milking) or within the allocation of the work the family as a team had to do. In terms of title to estates, the church similarly led the way in recording land transactions to prove its entitlement to properties gifted by the faithful. Here the involvement of women, acting alone, with other women, and with men (mainly husbands and sons) reveals the variations of women's participation in transactions among the property-owning classes. All this can be set against the edited laws of different areas from different times, the practical set against the theoretical.

Modern educational and management psychology stresses the stultifying consequences of expecting too little of pupils or workforces, and it could be that medieval men's most repressive treatment of women actually lay in demanding too little of them as individuals (and certainly as intellects). Women were brought up to give birth to others (as the higher wergild for childbearing age groups makes clear). Therefore, binding in some sort of societally acceptable union for procreation was their normal destiny. In this period in the west (among Christians) lifelong monogamy triumphed over less formal and more temporary arrangements. Marriage was the normal expectation for women, and apart from virginal entry into women's convents, there was not much else for a woman to do, honourably, except toil as an inferior substitute for a man, a weaker worker on land or in manufacture. Any woman who was not willing to marry, or who failed to secure a husband, was faced with only the choice between entering religion, effectively only an upper-class option, or embarking on the financially and physically risky path of 'going it alone' in whatever way she could make ends meet. Women were just not brought up to be independent of men. There were some fortunate enough to inherit land, by locally permitted inheritance sharing with brothers, or by default of male heirs, or by testamentary provision, but mostly they only fell back on these resources after widowhood, not by staying single but in the world. If a widow had supportive children, who did not fight her dower claims, she was better placed than the spinster heiress of equal wealth – less lonely and with support against would be advantage takers. But widows had plenty of problems with both families trying to offload them as liabilities or retain their assets. Women on their own were always liable to be seen as soft pushovers by men scheming for their land, wealth or sexual favour. A fully powered widow might benefit from the experience of running her husband's estate vicariously in time past. It was some protection for virgins or widows to be of saintly reputation and have reliable friends among influential clergy who could offer sanctuary. The weakness of their isolated position is surely reflected in the entry of widows to convents in perhaps surprising proportions – convents were by no means the monopoly of virginal nuns, and widows were valued for their worldly experience, not despised as only next best to virgins.

This said, the religious life, freeing a woman from domestic surroundings and responsibilities, was probably the most developmental environment for a woman in the early middle ages. Three of the five women discussed in Chapter 7 were from this background – Hrotsvit, Hildegard and Heloise. The fourth, the writer known as 'Marie de France' is claimed to be of church education and several of the possible identifications for her are with abbesses. Significantly, exceptional women writers sometimes indicate their 'descent' from learned men. Gandersheim provided Hrotsvit with a magnificently broad library, but in naming her principal

teachers as Riccardis and abbess Gerberga II, Hrotsvit refers to the latter
studying with learned men. Fulbert evidently thought he had secured the
best teacher of the day for Heloise, though the outcome was not what he
expected and underlined the risks of putting girls into male supervision.
Nevertheless, since women's education had fallen behind men's, how else
were women to gain access to the full challenges of education?

If we do not expect religious women to be educated much, or laywomen
at all, we get pleasant surprises in the literary Dhuoda, the capably com-
municative Adela of Blois and Matilda of Tuscany, and the Lincolnshire
landowner's wife Constance Fitz Gilbert who persuaded Gaimar to translate the *Estoire des Engles*, borrowing books to help him. If we expect little
more than liturgical literacy from the nuns and canonesses we find Hrotsvit
and Heloise and Hildegard startling. Beavering away less spectacularly, but
contributing to our favourable perspective, were Leoba and Baudonivia
and the anonymous nun of Chelles as authors, and there were capable copyists in such houses as Wimborne and Chelles. In this area too, events moved
unevenly. The seventh and eighth centuries were a good time for nuns'
educational achievements in the west, but their learning fell away and
they were not participants in the Carolingian renaissance. The Ottonian
renaissance, by contrast, glowed at Gandersheim, under particular royal
favour. The twelfth-century renaissance must have been a mixed blessing
for women. It opened up the study of Roman civil law and canon law and
ancient medicine passed through the Arabs, and Arab mathematical skills.
These were not fields where women were encouraged to participate.
Perhaps some of the medical learning percolated to Hildegard, and Herrad
had access to the infiltration of Arabic knowledge. But, on the other side of
the coin, the respect for the practical women of Salerno gave way to closed
entry to professional medical training as the cathedral schools and nascent
universities, all-male institutions, took increasing control of qualification.

If by looking at twelfth-century women we concluded that women had come
a long way by 1200, we would need to qualify this by acknowledging that we
have less evidence about women from the earlier times. It is not that later
evidence is suddenly showing women more fully because they were being
more noticed, it is simply that there is quantitatively greater evidence. In fact
there may be more of significance to be found for earlier times as further
analysis is made of substantial early charter evidence. Any changes in the
position of women argued from information from one time and place compared with another set has to be contextualized but is well worth the effort.
We cannot say that any 'progress' towards greater equality or self-fulfilment

was the product of conscious policy in the minds of men or women. These very ideas are anachronistic, and many influences were at work. Most women just got on with what was expected of them. A few show us that some were capable of more and achieved it. These high achievers will remain the exception, even if a few others are found through manuscript identification. While we are unlikely to discover parallels to Domesday Book disclosing population data elsewhere, we can hope to learn more of the physical condition of our ancestors of both sexes through biological/medical analysis of organic remains.

NOTES

Introduction

1. H. M. Jewell, *Women in Late Medieval and Reformation Europe 1200–1550* (Basingstoke, 2007).
2. C. Clover, 'The Politics of Scarcity: Notes on the Sex Ratio in early Scandinavia', in H. Damico and A. Hennessey Olsen (eds), *New Readings on Women in Old English Literature* (Bloomington and Indianapolis, 1990), pp. 100–34.
3. S. F. Wemple, *Women in Frankish Society: Marriage and the Cloister 500–900* (Philadelphia, 1981), p. 52 (citing the work of Edouard Salin).
4. R. Collins, *Early Medieval Europe 300–1000*, 2nd edn (Basingstoke and New York, 1999), p. 110.
5. L. M. Bitel, *Land of Women: Tales of Sex and Gender from early Ireland* (Ithaca, NY and London, 1996), p. 7.
6. M. N. Cohen and S. Bennett, 'Skeletal evidence for Sex Roles and Gender Hierarchies in Prehistory', in K. Hays-Gilpin and D. S. Whitley (eds), *Reader in Gender Archaeology* (London and New York, 1998), p. 298, citing the work of Buikstra and Mielke.
7. J. Jesch, *Women in the Viking Age* (Woodbridge, 1994) provides the Scandinavian examples discussed in the next paragraphs.
8. P. Skinner, *Women in Medieval Italian Society 500–1200* (Harlow, 2001), pp. 59–61, 102.
9. L. Schiaparelli (ed.), *Codice Diplomatico Longobardo* (Rome, 1929,1933) cited in Skinner, note 8 above, p. 44; Wemple, *Women in Frankish Society*, pp. 108–20; P. S. Gold, *The Lady and the Virgin: Image, Attitude and Experience in Twelfth-Century France* (Chicago, IL and London, 1994), ch. 4.
10. K. M. Wilson and G. McLeod, 'Sounding Trumpets, Chords of Light and Little Knives: Medieval Women Writers', in L. Mitchell (ed.), *Women in Medieval Western European Culture* (New York and London, 1999), p. 338.

Contemporary Gender Theory and Society's Expectations of Women

1. Quoted in A. Blamires, *The Case for Women in Medieval Culture* (Oxford, 1997), p. 75. The Nyssa and Chrysostom views are ibid., pp. 77–8, and Chrysostom's criticism of Adam (cited below), p. 114.
2. Ibid., p. 187.
3. M. M. Sheehan, *Marriage, Family and Law in Medieval Europe*, ed. J. K. Farge (Toronto, 1996), pp. 278–91. The text of the letter, with omissions, is printed

in translation in *Love, Marriage and Family in the Middle Ages*, ed. J. Murray (Peterborough, Ont., 2001), pp. 234–41.

4. J. Goody, *The Development of the Family and Marriage in Europe* (Cambridge, 1983), p. 67.

5. P. Guichard and J.-P. Cuvillier, 'Barbarian Europe', in *A History of the Family*, ed. A. Burguiére, C. Klapisch-Zuber, M. Segalen and F. Zonabend, vol. I (Cambridge MA, 1996), p. 346.

6. J. Riddle, 'Contraception and Early Abortion in the Middle Ages', in *Handbook of Medieval Sexuality*, ed. V. L. Bullough and J. A. Brundage (New York and London, 1996), pp. 261–77.

7. G. Clark, *Women in late Antiquity: Pagan and Christian Life-styles* (Oxford, 1993), p. 87.

8. Ibid., p. 23.

9. Quoted from Sean O Faoláin's translation in P. B. Ellis, *Celtic Women: Women in Celtic Society and Literature* (London, 1995), p. 46.

10. J. Jesch, *Women in the Viking Age* (Woodbridge, 1991), p. 172.

The Practical Situation: Women's Function in Rural Communities

1. *Colonus* was the original Roman term for a free tenant cultivating another person's land, but after 322 the *colonus* had been less free, being tied to the soil and his descendants after him. The *lidus* had been a barbarian settled by Romans on abandoned lands to keep them cultivated. Souter's *Glossary of Later Latin to 600 AD* (Oxford, 1949) defines *colona* as a woman cultivator of a rented farm, a farmer's wife, and a hired woman servant, which shows how imprecise it had become.

2. The Neuillay entry is printed in *Love, Marriage and Family in the Middle Ages: A Reader*, ed. J. Murray (Peterborough, Ont., 2001), pp. 336–8; Murray also prints the entry for Coudray-sur-Seine, pp. 338–40.

3. D. Herlihy, *Medieval Households* (Cambridge, MA and London, 1985), pp. 70–1.

4. *English Historical Documents*, vol. 2, ed. D. C. Douglas and G. W. Greenaway (London, 1968), pp. 816–18; 822–3; 832; 835.

5. J. Jochens, *Women in Old Norse Society* (Ithaca, NY and London, 1995), chs 5 and 6.

6. G. Duby, *L'Economie rurale et la Vie des Campagnes dans l'Occident médiéval* (Paris, 1962), translated by C. S. Postan as *Rural Economy and Country Life in the Medieval West* (London, 1968), pp. 33, 383–4.

7. Ibid., from the English edition, pp. 375, 458, 369–70, 471–2, 439, 444, 446, 476, 468–9.

8. L. Bitel, *Land of Women: Tales of Sex and Gender from early Ireland* (Ithaca, NY and London, 1996), pp. 5–7, 117, 123–31.

9. A. King, 'Gauber High Pasture, Ribblehead – an Interim Report', in *Viking Age York and the North*, ed. R. A. Hall (Council for British Archaeology Research Report 27, 1978, reprinted 1982), pp. 21–5.

10. E. Coleman, 'L'infanticide dans le haut Moyen Age', *Annales-Economies-Sociétés-Civilisations*, 29 (1974), 315–35, translated as 'Infanticide in the early Middle Ages', in S. M. Stuard (ed.), *Women in Medieval Society* (Philadelphia, 1976), pp. 47–70; Herlihy, *Medieval Households*, pp. 64–8.

The Practical Situation: Women's Function in Urban Communities

1. P. Skinner, *Family Power in Southern Italy: the Duchy of Gaeta and its Neighbours, 850–1139* (Cambridge, 1995), pp. 60–1, 73–4. Further references to Skinner and/or Gaeta in this chapter are to this work except where otherwise stated.
2. H. M. Jewell, *Women in Late Medieval and Reformation Europe 1200–1550* (Basingstoke, 2007).
3. H. Dillard, *Daughters of the Reconquest: Women in Castilian Town Society 1100–1300* (Cambridge, 1984). All citations of Castilian towns in this chapter refer to this highly informative study.
4. S. A. Epstein, *Genoa and the Genoese, 958–1528* (Chapel Hill, NC and London, 1996). References to Epstein are all to this work.
5. The *commenda* was a commercial contract whereby the travelling partner used an investor's capital for a venture, usually taking a quarter of the profit. In the *società* both partners contributed capital; the travelling one put in less but had an even share of the net profit to compensate for doing the work. The sea-loan was a more straightforward borrowing of money for a venture, to be repaid at a fixed sum on safe return from the voyage.
6. P. Skinner, *Women in Medieval Italian Society 500–1200* (Harlow, 2001), p. 173.
7. P. F. Wallace, 'Archaeology and the Emergence of Dublin as the Principal Town of Ireland', in J. Bradley (ed.), *Settlement and Society in Medieval Ireland* (Kilkenny, 1988), pp. 139–40.
8. H. K. Kenward et al., 'The Environment of Anglo-Scandinavian York', in *Viking Age York and the North*, ed. R. A. Hall, CBA Research Report 27 (1978, reprinted 1982), p. 67.
9. Skinner, *Women in Medieval Society*, p. 164.
10. Ibid., p. 174.

Women and Power: Royal and Landholding Women

1. J. T. Nelson, 'Women at the court of Charlemagne: A Case of Monstrous Regiment?', in J. C. Parsons (ed.), *Medieval Queenship* (Stroud, 1998), p. 54.
2. Cited in K. S. Nicholas, 'Countesses as rulers in Flanders', in T. Evergates (ed.), *Aristocratic Women in Medieval France* (Philadelphia, 1999), p. 123.
3. P. Stafford, *Queens, Concubines and Dowagers* (London, 1998), p. 38.
4. Ibid., p. 116.
5. J. Nelson, 'Brunhild and Balthild in Merovingian history', in D. Baker (ed.), *Medieval Women* (Oxford, 1978), pp. 31–77.
6. P. Skinner, *Women in Medieval Italian Society 500–1200* (Harlow, 2001), p. 140.
7. M. Hivergneaux, 'Queen Eleanor and Aquitaine 1137–89', in *Eleanor of Aquitaine Lord and Lady*, ed. B. Wheeler and J. C. Parsons (New York and Basingstoke, 2002), pp. 55–76.
8. G. Duby, *Rural Economy and Country Life in the Medieval West*, trans. C. Postan (London, 1968), p. 442.
9. S. F. Wemple, *Women in Frankish Society: Marriage and the Cloister 500–900* (Philadelphia, 1981), p. 101.
10. J. M. Bak, 'Roles and Functions of Queens in Árpádian and Angevin Hungary', in *Medieval Queenship*, pp. 14, 16–17.

Women and Religion

1. B. L. Venarde, *Women's Monasticism and Medieval Society: Nunneries in France and England, 890–1215* (Ithaca, NY and London, 1997), p. 156; J. van Egen, 'Abbess: Mother and Teacher' in *Voice of the Living Light: Hildegard of Bingen and her World*, ed. B. Newman (Berkeley, Los Angeles and London, 1998), p. 30.
2. Ibid., p. 31.
3. J. T. Schulenburg, *Forgetful of their Sex: Female Sanctity and Society, ca. 500–1100* (Chicago, IL and London, 1998), pp. 63–5.
4. *Sainted Women of the Dark Ages*, ed. and trans. J. A. McNamara and J. E. Halborg with E. G. Whatley (Durham, NC and London, 3rd printing 1996), p. 94.
5. Ibid., p. 203.

Women who Exceeded Society's Expectations

1. B. Wheeler, 'Introduction', in B. Wheeler (ed.), *Listening to Heloise: the Voice of a Twelfth-Century Woman* (Basingstoke, 2000), p. xvii.
2. E. Amt (ed.), *Women's Lives in Medieval Europe: A Sourcebook* (New York and London, 1993), pp. 149, 146.
3. P. Dronke, *Women Writers of the Middle Ages* (Cambridge, 1984), pp. 69–70, quoted in K. Wilson, *Hrotsvit of Gandersheim: a Florilegium of her Works* (Woodbridge, 1998), p. 41 n. 1. (Dronke gives a good account of Gandersheim's unusual characteristics.)
4. *The Letters of Abelard and Heloise*, ed. and trans. B. Radice (Harmondsworth, 1974), p. 46. This edition is the most accessible English translation, from which the quotations here are taken (including the letter of Peter the Venerable).
5. C. J. Mews, 'Philosophical Themes in the *Epistolae Duorum Amantium*: The First Letters of Heloise and Abelard', in Wheeler, *Listening to Heloise*, pp. 35–52; Mews and N. Chiavaroli (ed. and trans.), *The Lost Love Letters of Heloise and Abelard: Perceptions of Dialogue in Twelfth-Century France* (New York and Basingstoke, 1999).
6. *The Lais of Marie de France*, trans. with an Introduction by G. S. Burgess and K. Busby (Harmondsworth, 2nd edn., 1999), p. 18. This edition offers the most accessible version for English readers and has been used here.
7. J. Ferrante, 'The French Courtly Poet Marie de France', in K. Wilson (ed.), *Medieval Women Writers* (Manchester, 1984), p. 64.
8. *The Trotula: A Medieval Compendium of Women's Medicine*, ed. and trans. M. H. Green (Philadelphia, 2001), p. 49.

FURTHER READING

Introduction

Amt, E. (ed.), *Women's Lives in Medieval Europe: A Sourcebook* (New York and London, 1993).

Bitel, L. M., *Women in Early Medieval Europe 400–1100* (Cambridge, 2002).

Dronke, P., *Women Writers of the Middle Ages: a Critical Study of Texts from Perpetua †203 to Marguerite Porete †1310* (Cambridge, 1984).

Ennen, E., trans. E. Jephcott, *The Medieval Woman* (Oxford, 1989).

Herlihy, D., *Medieval Households* (Cambridge, MA and London, 1985).

Herlihy, D., 'Life Expectancies for Women in Medieval Society', in *The Role of Women in the Middle Ages*, ed. R. T. Morewedge (Albany, NY, 1975), pp. 1–22.

Jesch, J., *Women in the Viking Age* (Woodbridge, 1991).

Stuard, S. M. (ed.), *Women in Medieval Society* (Philadelphia, 1976).

Wilson, K. M. (ed.), *Medieval Women Writers* (Manchester, 1984).

Wilson, K. M. and Margolis, N. (eds), *Women in the Middle Ages: An Encyclopedia* (Westport, CT and London, 2 vols, 2004).

Contemporary Gender Theory and Society's Expectations of Women

Blamires, A., *The Case for Women in Medieval Culture* (Oxford, 1997).

Blamires, A., with Pratt, K. and Marx, C. W. (eds), *Women Defamed and Women Defended* (Oxford, 1992).

Brundage, J. A., 'The Merry Widow's Serious Sister: Remarriage in Classical Canon Law', in *Matrons and Marginal Women in Medieval Society*, ed. R. R. Edwards and V. Ziegler (Woodbridge, 1995), pp. 33–48.

Bullough, V. L. and Brundage, J. A. (eds), *Handbook of Medieval Sexuality* (New York and London, 1996).

Burguière, A., Klapisch-Zuber, C., Segalen, M. and Zonabend, F. (eds), *A History of the Family*, vol. 1 *Distant Worlds, Ancient Worlds*, trans. S. H. Tenison, R. Morris and A. Wilson (Cambridge, MA, 1996).

Cadden, J., *Meanings of Sex Difference in the Middle Ages: Medicine, Science and Culture* (Cambridge, 1993).

Clover, C. J., 'The Politics of Scarcity: Notes on the Sex Ratio in Early Scandinavia', in *New Readings on Women in Old English Literature*, ed. H. Damico and A. H. Olsen (Bloomington and Indianapolis, IN, 1990), pp. 100–34.

Dixon, L. S., 'The Curse of Chastity: the Marginalization of Women in Medieval Art and Medicine', in Edwards and Ziegler (eds), *Matrons and Marginal Women*, pp. 49–74.

Ferrante, J. M., *To the Glory of her Sex: Women's Roles in the Composition of Medieval Texts* (Bloomington and Indianapolis, IN, 1997).

Frakes, J. C., *Brides and Doom: Gender, Property and Power in Medieval German Women's Epic* (Philadelphia, 1994).

Gold, P. S., *The Lady and the Virgin: Image, Attitude and Experience in Twelfth-Century France* (Chicago, IL and London, 1985).

McCracken, P., *The Romance of Adultery: Queenship and Sexual Transgression in Old French Literature* (Philadelphia, 1998).

MacNamara, J. A. and Wemple, S. F., 'Marriage and Divorce in the Frankish Kingdom', in Stuard, S. M. (ed.), *Women in Medieval Society* (Philadelphia, 1976), pp. 95–124.

McNeill, J. T. and Gamer, H. M. (eds and trans), *Medieval Handbooks of Penance: a Translation of the Principal Libri Poenitentiales and Selections from Related Documents* (New York, 1938, 1990).

Sheehan, M. M., *Marriage, Family and Law in Medieval Europe, Collected Studies*, ed. J. K. Farge (Toronto, 1996).

Stafford, P. and Mulder-Bakker, A. B. (eds), *Gendering the Middle Ages* (Oxford, 2001).

Stuard, S., 'The Dominion of Gender: Women's Fortunes in the High Middle Ages', in *Becoming Visible: Women in European History*, ed. R. Bridenthal, C. Koonz and S. Stuard, 2nd edn (Boston, MA, 1987), pp. 153–72.

Van Houts, E., *Memory and Gender in Medieval Europe 900–1200* (Basingstoke, 1999).

Wemple, S. F., *Women in Frankish Society: Marriage and the Cloister 500–900* (Philadelphia, 1981).

The Practical Situation: Women's Function in Rural Communities

Bitel, L., *Land of Women: Tales of Sex and Gender from Early Ireland* (Ithaca, NY and London, 1995).

Coleman, E., 'Infanticide in the early Middle Ages', in Stuard, S. M. (ed.), *Women in Medieval Society* (Philadelphia, 1976), pp. 47–70.

Duby, G., *Rural Economy and Country Life in the Medieval West*, trans. C. Postan (London, 1968).

Herlihy, D., *Medieval Households* (Cambridge, MA and London, 1985).

Jochens, J., *Women in Old Norse Society* (Ithaca, NY and London, 1995).

King, A., 'Gauber High Pasture Ribblehead – an Interim Report', in *Viking Age York and the North*, ed. R. A. Hall (CBA Research Report no. 27, 1978, reprinted 1982), pp. 21–5.

Murray, J. (ed.), *Love, Marriage and Family in the Middle Ages: A Reader* (Peterborough, Ont, 2001).

The Practical Situation: Women's Function in Urban Communities

Dillard, H., *Daughters of the Reconquest: Women in Castilian Town Society 1100–1300* (Cambridge, 1984).

Epstein, S. A., *Genoa and the Genoese 958–1528* (Chapel Hill, NC and London, 1996).

Jesch, J., *Women in the Viking Age* (Woodbridge, 1991).

Nicholas, D., *Urban Europe 1100–1700* (Basingstoke and New York, 2003).

Skinner, P., *Family Power in Southern Italy: the Duchy of Gaeta and its Neighbours 850–1139* (Cambridge, 1995).

Wallace, P. F., 'Archaeology and the Emergence of Dublin as the Principal Town of Ireland', in *Settlement and Society in Medieval Ireland: Studies presented to F. X. Martin O.S.A.*, ed. J. Bradley (Kilkenny, 1988) pp. 123–60.

Women and Power: Royal and Landholding Women

Baker, D., 'A Nursery of Saints': St Margaret of Scotland reconsidered', in *Medieval Women*, ed. D. Baker (Studies in Church History, Subsidia 1; 1978), pp. 119–41.

Erler, M. and Kowaleski, M. (eds), *Women and Power in the Middle Ages* (Athens, GA and London, 1988).

Evergates, T. (ed.), *Aristocratic Women in Medieval France* (Philadelphia, 1999).

Nelson, J. T., 'Queens as Jezebels: the Careers of Brunhild and Balthild in Merovingian History', in Baker, *Medieval Women*, pp. 31–77.

Parsons, J. C. (ed.), *Medieval Queenship* (Stroud, 1994).

Skinner, P., *Women in Medieval Italian Society 500–1200* (Harlow, 2001).

Stafford, P., *Queen Emma and Queen Edith: Queenship and Women's Power in Eleventh-Century England* (Oxford, 1997).

Stafford, P., *Queens, Concubines and Dowagers: the King's Wife in the Early Middle Ages* (London, 1983, 1998).

Wall, V., 'Queen Margaret of Scotland (1070–1093): Burying the Past, Enshrining the Future', in *Queens and Queenship in Medieval Europe*, ed. A. Duggan (Woodbridge, 1997), pp. 27–38.

Wheeler, B. and Parsons, J. C. (eds), *Eleanor of Aquitaine: Lord and Lady* (Basingstoke and New York, 2002).

Women and Religion

Baroja, J. C., *The World of the Witches*, trans. O. N. V. Glendinning (Chicago, 1965).

Baumgarten, E., *Mothers and Children: Jewish Family Life in Medieval Europe* (Princeton, NJ and Oxford, 2004).

Clark, A. L., 'Holy Woman or Unworthy Vessel? The Representations of Elisabeth of Schönau', in *Gendered Voices: Medieval Saints and their Interpreters*, ed. C. M. Mooney (Philadelphia, 1999), pp. 35–51.

Duby, G., *Women of the Twelfth Century*, vol. 3, *Eve and the Church*, trans. J. Birrell (Cambridge, 1998).

Edgington, S. B. and Lambert, S. (eds), *Gendering the Crusades* (Cardiff, 2001).

McNamara, J. A. and Halborg, J. E. with Whatley, E. G. (eds and trans), *Sainted Women of the Dark Ages* (Durham, NC and London, 1992).

McNeill, J. T. and Gamer, H. M. (eds and trans), *Handbooks of Penance: a Translation of the Principal Libri Poenitentiales and Selections from Related Documents* (New York, 1938, 1990).

Ranft, P., *Women and the Religious Life in Premodern Europe* (Basingstoke, 1996).

Schulenburg, J. T., *Forgetful of their Sex: Female Sanctity and Society ca500–1100* (Chicago, IL and London, 1998).

Schulenburg, J. T., 'The Heroics of Virginity: Brides of Christ and Sacrificial Mutilation', in *Women in the Middle Ages and Renaissance*, ed. M. B. Rose (Syracuse, NY, 1986), pp. 29–72.

Schulenburg, J. T., 'Women's Monastic Communities 500–1100: Patterns of Expansion and Decline', *Signs* (Winter 1989), 14, no. 2, 261–92.

Spearing, E. (ed.), *Medieval Writings on Female Spirituality* (Harmondsworth, 2002).

Talbot, C. H. (ed. and trans.), *The Life of Christina of Markyate: a Twelfth-Century Recluse* (Oxford, 1959).

Venarde, B. L., *Women's Monasticism and Medieval Society: Nunneries in France and England 890–1215* (Ithaca, NY and London, 1997).

Women who Exceeded Society's Expectations

Berger, M. (ed.), *Hildegard of Bingen on Natural Philosophy and Medicine* (Woodbridge, 1999).

Burgess, G. S. and Busby, K. (eds and trans), *The Lais of Marie de France* (Harmondsworth, 2nd edn, 1999).

Dhuoda: Handbook for William: a Carolingian Woman's Counsel for her Son, ed. C. Neel (Washington, DC, 1991/1999).

Dhuoda: *Liber Manualis: Handbook for her Warrior Son*, ed. M. Thiébaux (Cambridge, 1998).

Dronke, P., *Women Writers of the Middle Ages: a Critical Study of Texts from Perpetua †203 to Marguerite Porete †1310* (Cambridge, 1984).

Flanagan, S., *Hildegard of Bingen 1098–1179: A Visionary Life* (London and New York, 1989).

Green, M. H. (ed. and trans.), *The Trotula: a Medieval Compendium of Women's Medicine* (Philadelphia, 2001).

The Letters of Hildegard of Bingen, ed. and trans J. L. Baird and R. K. Ehrman, 3 vols (Oxford, 1994, 1998, 2004).

Mews, C. J., *Abelard and Heloise* (Oxford, 2005).

Mews, C. J. (ed. and trans.) and Chiavaroli, N. (trans.), *The Lost Love Letters of Heloise and Abelard: Perceptions of a Dialogue in Twelfth-Century France* (New York and Basingstoke, 1999).

Newman, B., *Sister of Wisdom: St Hildegard's Theology of the Feminine* (Berkeley and Los Angeles, 1987).

Newman, B. (ed.), *Voice of the Living Light: Hildegard of Bingen and her World* (Berkeley and Los Angeles and London, 1998).

Newman, B., 'Hildegard and her Hagiographers: the Remaking of Female Sainthood', in Mooney, C. (ed.), *Gendered Voices: Medieval Saints and their Interpreters* (Philadelphia, 1999), pp. 16–34.

Radice, B. (ed. and trans.), *The Letters of Abelard and Heloise* (Harmondsworth, 1974).

Wheeler, B., *Listening to Heloise: the Voice of a Twelfth-Century Woman* (Basingstoke, 2000).

Wilson, K. M. (ed.), *Medieval Women Writers* (Manchester, 1984).

Wilson, K. M. (ed.), *Hrotsvit of Gandersheim: a Florilegium of her Works* (Woodbridge, 1998).

INDEX

NB Persons, places, sources and concepts handled in the text would swell this index unmanageably if all were individually entered into it and on each occurrence. Therefore the index is pruned to guide the reader to pages where the reference has particular importance as information, illustration, comment or for cross-reference purposes.

Printed in Great Britain
by Amazon